The Other Missouri History

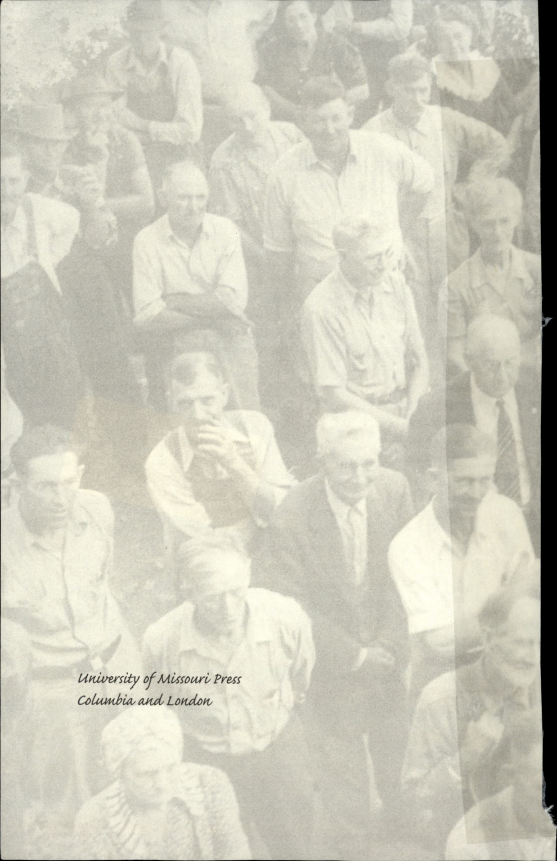

University of Missouri Press
Columbia and London

The ^Other Missouri History

Other

Populists,
Prostitutes,
and
Regular
Folk

Edited with an Introduction by **Thomas M. Spencer**

Library of Congress Cataloging-in-Publication Data

The other Missouri history : populists, prostitutes, and regular folk / edited with an
introduction by Thomas M. Spencer.

    p.   cm.
  Includes index.
  ISBN 0-8262-1565-3   (alk. paper)
1. Missouri—History.   2. Missouri—Social conditions.   I. Spencer, Thomas M.
(Thomas Morris), 1967–
  F466.5.o86   2004
  977.8—dc22

2004021276

∞ This paper meets the requirements of the
American National Standard for Permanence of Paper
for Printed Library Materials, Z39.48, 1984.

Text design: Stephanie Foley
Cover design: Kristie Lee
Typesetter: Crane Composition, Inc.
Printer and binder: The Maple-Vail Book Manufacturing Group
Typefaces: Brighton Light, Minion, and Myriad

Contents

Acknowledgments

Like many products of the academic world, this book had its genesis in a conversation with a colleague—in this case, with Stephen McIntyre of Southwest Missouri State University. In April 1999, Steve and I talked about how we would enjoy putting together an anthology of essays in Missouri social history. We knew many people doing excellent work in this field and decided to pursue our idea. The volume would certainly be useful for classes in Missouri history. After speaking with Beverly Jarrett at the University of Missouri Press, the two of us put out a call for papers, and the project officially started.

Now, five years later, I am delighted to see the project through to its conclusion. Although Steve grew too busy with other pursuits to remain with this project, he did a great deal of work during the first several years and deserves to be acknowledged and thanked here.

I must also acknowledge the professionalism, perseverance, and patience of the staff at the University of Missouri Press. Bev Jarrett "kept the faith" even when mine was flagging. I also must acknowledge the fine efforts of the editorial and production staff—particularly Jane Lago—and the marketing staff as well.

However, the greatest thanks must go to my fellow contributors. These eight hardy souls remained on board with this project through months of shaping, revising, and editing. I have enjoyed getting to know them, and it is my pleasure to present their excellent scholarship to the world via this book. Together, we are making a substantial contribution to the understanding of our state's history.

The Other Missouri History

The Many Acts of the Small

An Introduction to the Other Missouri History

THOMAS M. SPENCER

Mark Twain once wrote, "History, although sometimes made up of the few acts of the great, is more often shaped by the many acts of the small." This volume of essays offers ample evidence to support Twain's declaration, reflecting the approach of a generation of historians who practice what Eric Foner has labeled the "new American history," which emphasizes the lives of ordinary Americans rather than the machinations of political and economic elites. Foner contends that history is an exercise in "collective self-discovery about the nature of our society."[1] This new approach has transformed scholarship in American history in the last three decades.

Correspondingly, the "new" Missouri history began to appear around the same time. In the early 1970s, Gary Fink examined the political activity of the Missouri labor movement in a book that is still widely cited by labor historians. In the 1980s, David Thelen authored a major reinterpretation of Missouri in the Gilded Age and Progressive Era, a study that was inspired by the new historical approaches emerging at the time. A few years later, Thelen's student Michael Cassity published a monograph examining the impact of the nineteenth-century market revolution on workers and farmers in Pettis County. At about the same time, Gary Kremer and many others began intensive production of what has grown to be a large number of works on the African American experience in Missouri. During the 1980s and

---

1. Eric Foner, *The New American History* (Philadelphia: Temple University Press, 1997), xiii.

early 1990s, *Gateway Heritage,* under the editorship first of Kenneth Winn and later Martha Kohl, published important articles on varied topics in Missouri social history. In the 1990s, Gregg Andrews published two works addressing issues of class and gender in small-town Missouri. More recently, the University of Missouri Press published a long-awaited anthology of essays on Missouri women's history.[2]

The essays in this volume reflect continuing scholarship in Missouri history using the "new-history" approach. All of the essays examine how ordinary Missourians dealt with problems that arose as significant social and economic change took place. The problems they faced are now quite familiar to us: the aftermath of war, racial and class discrimination, crime and violence, and economic, social, and cultural changes brought about by industrialization. As practitioners of this "new" approach to history have discovered, the social location of Americans (and Missourians) impacted their view of problems and the various proposed solutions. In our collective effort to include various subsets of the nonelite population, the essayists in this volume focus on a rather diverse group of Missourians—hence the populists, prostitutes, and "regular" or "ordinary" folks in this book's title.

Along with the rest of the nation (and the South in particular), Missourians faced tremendous challenges in the aftermath of the Civil War. How did Missourians deal with the issue of race after the abolition of slavery? In what ways did race remain an important social and political marker in Missouri? After the dislocations and violence of

---

2. Gary M. Fink, *Labor's Search for Political Order: The Political Behavior of the Missouri Labor Movement* (Columbia: University of Missouri Press, 1974); David P. Thelen, *Paths of Resistance: Tradition and Democracy in Industrializing Missouri* (London: Oxford University Press, 1986); Michael Cassity, *Defending a Way of Life: An American Community in the Nineteenth Century* (New York: State University of New York Press, 1989); Lorenzo J. Greene, Gary R. Kremer, and Antonio F. Holland, *Missouri's Black Heritage,* rev. ed. (Columbia: University of Missouri Press, 1993); Gary R. Kremer, *James Milton Turner and the Promise of America: The Public Life of a Post–Civil War Black Leader* (Columbia: University of Missouri Press, 1991); Gregg Andrews, *City of Dust: A Cement Company Town in the Land of Tom Sawyer* (Columbia: University of Missouri Press, 1996); and Gregg Andrews, *Insane Sisters: Or, the Price Paid for Challenging a Company Town* (Columbia: University of Missouri Press, 1999); LeeAnn Whites, Mary C. Neth, and Gary R. Kremer, eds., *Women in Missouri History: In Search of Power and Influence* (Columbia: University of Missouri Press, 2004).

the war, did Missourians on both sides continue to find themselves fighting the Civil War? Did it change their approach to politics and economic development?

Gregg Andrews explores how ordinary people dealt with these problems in his essay, "The Racial Politics of Reconstruction in Ralls County, 1865–1870." After emancipation, race remained an important part of life and an important weapon in Missouri politics. Andrews examines how race shaped the political culture in Ralls County during the Reconstruction Era, arguing that it was not the "vindictiveness" of the controversial "test oath" that doomed the Radicals in the county. Instead, it was the Radicals' attempts to forge a political alliance with blacks that frightened whites away from their party in the 1860s. Andrews finds that race-baiting was prominently used by editors of the *Ralls County Record* to discredit Radicals in the county and was perhaps the most powerful political weapon that conservatives and Democrats could use to gain the allegiance of voters. Andrews demonstrates how these groups used such racial appeals relentlessly during the era to regain control over county governments. Following emancipation, race became an effective political tool that conservative politicians used to weaken and ultimately destroy the Radical party in Ralls County.

My own contribution to the volume, "The Bald Knobbers, the Anti–Bald Knobbers, Politics, and the Culture of Violence in the Ozarks, 1860–1890," examines the widespread violence in rural Missouri that developed as a result of the Civil War. Focusing on one of the more famous episodes in the history of the Ozarks, the essay traces the rise of the "Bald Knobbers" vigilante band in Taney and Christian counties in the 1880s. Historians have often described these vigilante groups as an attempt to "restore order" and thus encourage economic development in the region. Continuing with this reasoning, some historians have contended that these groups represented either a resistance to modernization or an attempt to advocate modernization. A careful analysis of the membership of the groups in question reveals, however, that regional loyalties and the desire for political control were the most important reasons for Ozarks vigilantism. Furthermore, the vigilantism and politically motivated violence of the 1880s and 1890s in southwest Missouri were legacies of a "culture of violence" perpetuated by the experiences of the Civil War in the region.

Both of these essays demonstrate that Missourians found themselves facing a changed social and political system in the aftermath of the war. Race was used to unite whites and to mount a political counter-revolution during the 1870s. Andrews shows how this was certainly the case in Ralls County. While the same political counterrevolution had taken place in Taney County during the 1870s, Unionists later used the violent means they had learned during the war to return themselves to power in the 1880s and 1890s. Both of these essays also demonstrate that fear—whether of racial mixing or violence—was still a very effective political weapon.

Not surprisingly, race continues to be an important social marker in Missouri, particularly in St. Louis, one of the state's largest cities. While the city has always been home to a plurality of Missouri's African Americans, white working-class St. Louisans have always been fearful of the integration of black workers into the labor market. In "Race, Citizenship, and the Origins of Organized Labor in Antebellum St. Louis," Daniel A. Graff shows that race was an important issue long before the Civil War. Graff examines the journeymen tailors' strike of 1835 and contends that it was fought and won largely "on the terrain of race." Master tailors tried to mobilize St. Louisans against the strike by raising the specter of the strike leading to an influx of free blacks and disorder into the city. Graff maintains, however, that the tactic failed because white racial consciousness was so pervasive by the 1830s that it was difficult to mobilize the white community against itself. Graff contends that in St. Louis a white racial consciousness was fully formed by the middle 1830s.

In "Race, Power, and the Building Trades Industry in Postwar St. Louis," Deborah J. Henry discovers that more than a century after the Civil War, not that much had changed with regard to white working-class St. Louisans' attitudes towards African American workers. Henry's essay examines the role race played in the building trades during the period after World War II. Henry finds that, despite the inclusive rhetoric of urban renewal advocates, during the 1940s and 1950s, skilled black construction workers were blocked from access to jobs by the city's lily-white building trades unions. Worried that rocking the boat would slow the progress of construction, city leaders in St. Louis toned down their rhetoric about equal opportunity and looked the other way. Henry points out that this has had major consequences for African Americans in the building trades ever since, as this segment of the workforce in St. Louis remains largely white to the present day. While many in St. Louis insist that racism and discrimination are a thing of the past, Henry's article tells a very different—and important—story. Henry's essay provides ample evidence that beneath the city's veneer of racial progress, racial discrimination is alive and well in St. Louis today.

Farmers are another popular topic of study for those practicing the "new American history." While the earlier essays in the anthology demonstrate that race and violence were often used as political tools in the state during the late nineteenth century, there were other major obstacles to political radicalism as well—particularly among the state's farmers. Michael J. Steiner's essay, "The Failure of Alliance/Populism in Northern Missouri," provides insight into the economic and rhetorical reasons for the failure of populism in Missouri. Steiner contends that white farmers in northern Missouri were happy with the status quo and rejected calls for radical reform and major change in the agricultural economy. Appeals to farmers as a distinct and aggrieved class in northern Missouri were therefore doomed to fail among those who were relatively prosperous economically and therefore "comfortably settled" in their political outlook.

Unlike their white farming brethren, blacks faced a much more difficult existence during the late nineteenth and early twentieth centuries. Correspondingly, black farmers, most of whom were employed as sharecroppers, eventually staged protests against their deplorable working and living conditions. Bonnie Stepenoff chronicles the life of African American sharecroppers in southeast Missouri in "Survival Strategies of Farm Laborers in the Missouri Bootheel, 1900–1958." She discovers that black sharecroppers were treated more poorly than white sharecroppers and contends that African American sharecroppers had to employ various strategies to survive, especially during the lean years of the Great Depression.

The poverty of sharecroppers in the bootheel region became public knowledge during the New Deal when the press began to report that the public assistance programs were appallingly inadequate. In 1938, faced with eviction by landowners, black sharecroppers staged a mass protest along the highways in southeast Missouri. Stepenoff tells the story of several prominent African American union organizers in southeast Missouri and discusses the end of the tenant farm system in the 1940s and 1950s. Clearly, farmers did not vote as a monolithic block; a farmer's political views differed greatly depending upon his social location—in this case, race and class.

Women began to become active in public life during the late nineteenth and early twentieth centuries. Janice Brandon-Falcone's essay, "Constance Runcie and the Runcie Club of St. Joseph," examines the first two decades of an important women's club that still exists in St. Joseph, Missouri. Brandon-Falcone examines the fascinating life of Constance Runcie, granddaughter of the famous utopian socialist Robert Owen. The Runcie Club, in addition to providing an important place for cultural and spiritual uplift for its members, also provided Constance Runcie with a safe and socially sanctioned way to make a comfortable living. Falcone contends that the club, while never radical in its political outlook, nevertheless prepared women in St. Joseph for later political activity.

Robert Faust's "Women, Identity, and Reform in Missouri's Lead Belt, 1900–1923" also takes women's club work as its topic, examining the Mothers' and Patrons' Club in what was then a mining town, Flat River, Missouri. Unlike the Runcie Club, the Mothers' and Patrons' Club was fairly radical in its critique of the mining companies in the area—despite the fact that most of the women's husbands were employees (and usually managers) of the companies. The Mothers' and Patrons' Club (which later became the Lead Belt Woman's Club and subsequently the Flat River Woman's Club) helped create many important local agencies and encouraged needed reforms for the people of Flat River.

In turn-of-the-century Missouri, women were not only instigators of reform but also the subjects of it. In "Prostitution and Reform in Kansas City, 1880–1930," Amber R. Clifford sees Kansas City's reformers as part of a national movement. Clifford insists that the struggle over prostitution was one of class, in which reformers tried to make sure that middle-class Victorian moral sensibilities about gender conventions and sexuality prevailed over more permissive working-class attitudes. She also profiles Kansas City's most famous madam, Annie Chambers. Clifford notes, ironically, that the stained-glass window of Chambers's bawdy house eventually became a central feature of a restaurant in the Country Club Plaza in Kansas City in the 1920s.

Together, these nine essays demonstrate that the social categories of race, class, and gender have greatly impacted the lives of "ordinary" or "regular" Missourians for the last two centuries and continue to do so today. The authors whose articles appear in this anthology contend that the "many acts of the small" in Missouri history tell much about the people and the society of this state and provide important lessons about the mistakes of the past and guidance for the future.

The Racial Politics of Reconstruction in Ralls County, Missouri, 1865–1870

GREGG ANDREWS

With modifications, the dominant interpretation of Radical Reconstruction in Missouri (1865–1870) as an era of Radical "vindictiveness" has had amazing staying power in the literature on this era in Missouri politics. William E. Parrish's excellent state-level studies of the period—*Missouri under Radical Rule, 1865–1870* (1965) and *A History of Missouri: Volume III, 1860 to 1875* (1973)—provided an important corrective to the long-standing demonization of the state's Radicals but nonetheless reinforced the "vindictive" interpretation of their legacy. These studies were written at a time when "revisionist" scholars were in the early stages of a systematic assault on the Dunning school's portrayal of Reconstruction in the South as a tragic episode in which northern Republicans and carpetbaggers, white "scalawags," and former slaves tyrannized over democracy-loving white Southern Democrats. Although Parrish recognizes many of the Radicals' important achievements and treats the political history of Reconstruction with considerable balance, he concludes that Radicals might have been more successful were it not for their unnecessary, extreme vindictiveness.[1]

1. William E. Parrish, *Missouri under Radical Rule, 1865–1870* (Columbia: University of Missouri Press, 1965); William E. Parrish, *A History of Missouri: Volume III, 1860 to 1875* (Columbia: University of Missouri Press, 1973). On the Dunning school and Reconstruction, see especially William A. Dunning, *Reconstruction: Political and Economic* (New York: Harper and Brothers, 1907), and Claude G. Bowers, *The Tragic Era: The Revolution after Lincoln* (Cambridge: Houghton Mifflin Company, 1929). For a defense of Republican motives and policies by a Kansas City judge who was a

Soon after the publication of *Missouri under Radical Rule,* Fred De-Armond wrote an article in which he praised the overall record of Radicals and put some of their most controversial policies into perspective. Emphasizing the prevailing lawlessness and terror at the end of the Civil War, DeArmond defended unpopular Radical initiatives as temporary measures necessary to guide the state from war to peace and to minimize racial violence. Besides, he argued, such measures were consistent with policies at the national level.[2]

In the thirty-five years since DeArmond's forthright call for a revisionist treatment of Reconstruction in Missouri, however, Missouri scholars have tended to shy away from a frontal assault on the "vindictive" interpretation. The historiography of Reconstruction in Missouri still awaits a revisionist synthesis that explores how the important variables of race, class, and gender intersected to shape Reconstruction. In the meantime, however, we need more local studies conducted within this overarching framework, along with similar studies of the transition from slavery to freedom in the state. Such studies require, above all, a much more thorough examination of the pernicious role of racism on the local level.[3]

In a recent article, Martha Kohl provides a much more favorable view of the controversial test oath, one of the Radicals' main instruments for holding on to power in postbellum Missouri. In her view, the test oath was more than a mere grab for power by Radicals obsessed with punishing Confederate sympathizers. Some Radicals were

---

former Union soldier, see H. C. McDougal, "A Decade of Missouri Politics—1860 to 1870, from a Republican Viewpoint," *Missouri Historical Review* 3 (January 1909): 126–53.

2. Fred DeArmond, "Reconstruction in Missouri," *Missouri Historical Review* 61 (April 1967): 364–77.

3. For a sample of such studies on other Southern states, see, for example, Victoria E. Bynum, *The Free State of Jones: Mississippi's Longest Civil War* (Chapel Hill: University of North Carolina Press, 2001), chapter 7; Jane Dailey, *Before Jim Crow: The Politics of Race in Postemancipation Virginia* (Chapel Hill: University of North Carolina Press, 2000); Laura F. Edwards, *Gendered Strife and Confusion: The Political Culture of Reconstruction* (Urbana: University of Illinois Press, 1997); Stephen Kantrowitz, *Ben Tillman and the Reconstruction of White Supremacy* (Chapel Hill: University of North Carolina Press, 2000); and LeeAnn Whites, *The Civil War as a Crisis in Gender: Augusta, Georgia, 1860–1890* (Athens: University of Georgia Press, 1995).

clearly itching for revenge because of the death and destruction produced by the state's vicious guerrilla war, but more importantly, the
test oath was an important tool with which to enforce the Radicals'
"vision of community" and blueprint for social and economic progress in Missouri. This blueprint included encouraging Confederate
sympathizers to leave the state, and it included attracting northern
capital and hardworking immigrants to convert Missouri into a land
of dynamic industrial and agricultural enterprises. An important part
of the Radical vision was also to grant full citizenship and voting
rights to African Americans. This would ensure their full participation
in a reconstructed society in which greater racial justice and harmony
would prevail.[4]

If the test oath represented a vision of community on the part of its
proponents, it is equally true that opponents of the test oath embraced a vision of community that excluded African Americans. In
this essay, I will explore the important role of race in shaping the political culture of Reconstruction in the northeastern Missouri county
of Ralls. Paying special attention to the test oath and the language of
racism in the county's main (and only surviving) newspaper from
that era, I argue that it was not vindictiveness that limited the popu-
larity of Radicals, but rather, their attempt to forge even a limited political alliance with the county's black residents.

Ralls County, where slaves had represented 20.8 percent of the population in 1860, has been virtually ignored by scholars. Ralls, along
with the other nearby Salt River counties of Lincoln, Marion, Monroe,
and Pike, comprised an area that contained one-eighth of Missouri's
slave population before the war. This was the area, located on the edge
of Missouri's "Little Dixie" region, that produced Mark Twain, whose
brief experience as a pro-Confederate ranger centered around Marion
and Ralls counties.[5]

The partisan divisions that had wracked Ralls during the war con-

---

4. Martha Kohl, "Enforcing a Vision of Community: The Role of the Test Oath in
Missouri's Reconstruction," *Civil War History* 40, no. 4 (1994): 292–307. See also
Parrish, *Missouri under Radical Rule*, 268–69.

5. *Ninth Census—Volume I: The Statistics of the Population of the United States,
1870* (Washington, D.C.: Government Printing Office, 1872), 43, 45; David D.
March, *The History of Missouri* (New York: Lewis Historical Publishing, 1967), 1:810;
Charles Neider, ed., *The Autobiography of Mark Twain* (New York: Harper and Row,
1975), 111. On the history of slavery in Missouri's Little Dixie, see R. Douglas Hurt,

tinued to plague the county in the war's aftermath. In the first issue of the *Ralls County Record* on June 29, 1865, editor Thomas R. Dodge denounced the Confederacy for instigating the Civil War, and he celebrated the defeat of states' rights philosophy. He also rejoiced that the nation was now free of the "curse of slavery." Dodge, a Kentucky-born Conservative Unionist, urged reconciliation and leniency toward ex-Confederates. He knew, of course, that Ralls had been bitterly divided during the war. He was well aware, too, that the war had left a legacy of bushwhacking, personal and partisan feuding, racial hatreds, and indiscriminate violence. Nevertheless, the opening issue of his newspaper featured a message of optimism, forgiveness, and reconciliation.[6]

Within just a few weeks, however, as Radical Unionists and former slaves mobilized to implement Missouri's Radical Constitution of 1865 and push for black voting and citizenship rights, nasty attacks on white Radicals and African Americans filled Dodge's columns. As Ralls County underwent "reconstruction," the county seat newspaper assumed a leading role in blocking enforcement of the state's new constitution. With highly personal attacks and naked appeals to "white supremacy," Dodge blasted Radicals, particularly those in the Unionist community of Madisonville in Jasper township. He attacked the stringent test oath, disfranchisement of Confederate sympathizers, and efforts to empower the county's black population. By 1870, when Missouri repealed the test oath, even though the Fifteenth Amendment to the U.S. Constitution guaranteed black voting rights—at least on paper—his newspaper's steady drumbeat of racist articles and editorials had contributed to the defeat of Radical Republican efforts to forge an interracial political coalition and take command of the Ralls courthouse.[7]

———

Agriculture and Slavery in Missouri's "Little Dixie" (Columbia: University of Missouri Press, 1992). On Ralls County, see Goldena Howard, *Ralls County Missouri* (Marceline, Mo.: Walsworth, 1980); and Gregg Andrews, *City of Dust: A Cement Company Town in the Land of Tom Sawyer* (Columbia: University of Missouri Press, 1996).

6. *Ralls County Record*, June 29, 1865; *History of Audrain County, Missouri* (St. Louis: National Historical Company, 1884), 461–63; John P. Fisher, "A History of the *Ralls County Record*: 100 Years of Public Service, 1865–1965," 3. For an excellent study of the guerrilla war in Missouri, see Michael Fellman, *Inside War: The Guerrilla Conflict in Missouri during the American Civil War* (New York: Oxford University Press, 1989).

7. On the debate over granting voting rights to African Americans in Missouri, see Martha Kohl, "From Freedom to Franchise: The Debate over African American

The test oath, required by Missouri's newly ratified constitution, re-placed an earlier wartime test oath that was generally weak and inef-fective. The new one, given added teeth by a strict voter registration apparatus, banned from voting anyone who had taken up arms against the federal government or who had provided any kind of support to those who had done so. In addition, the Constitution of 1865 gave the governor power to dismiss state and local attorneys and judges whom he deemed hostile to it. It also required a similar test oath (declared unconstitutional by the U.S. Supreme Court in early 1867) for all preachers, lawyers, teachers, corporation officers, and jurors. These draconian restrictions put Missouri in the national vanguard of Rad-icalism, threatening a genuine restructuring of power from the county level to the statehouse.[8]

The Radicals' blueprint for change, particularly in regard to black civil rights and disfranchisement of Confederate sympathizers, came under attack in Ralls County immediately after the war. Dodge and his coeditor (and brother-in-law) Clay Crittenden Menefee Mayhall, a fellow Conservative Unionist, blasted Radicals for allegedly driving ex-Confederates from their homes. The *Ralls County Record*, accusing Radicals of political opportunism, criticized them for agitating on the issue of black suffrage, which, although not granted by the state's new constitution, was the subject of intense debate around the state and nation. Condemning black suffrage, the newspaper launched a blister-ing attack that invoked racist animal imagery to taunt white Radicals: "Surely the Radical party of Missouri is not so low down that it cannot be saved only through the influence of the 'sweet-scented African!'"[9]

Enfranchisement, 1865–1870," *Gateway Heritage* 16 (spring 1996): 22–35. For an overview of the impact of Reconstruction on African Americans in Missouri, see Lorenzo J. Greene, Gary R. Kremer, and Antonio F. Holland, *Missouri's Black Heri-tage*, rev. ed. (Columbia: University of Missouri Press, 1993), 88–103, and Parrish, *History of Missouri: Volume III*, chapter 6.

8. Eric Foner, *Reconstruction: America's Unfinished Revolution, 1863–1877* (New York: Harper and Row, 1988), 42; Parrish, *History of Missouri*, 3:134. On Missouri's Constitutional Convention of 1865 and ratification, see especially David D. March's articles, "Charles D. Drake and the Constitutional Convention of 1865," *Missouri Historical Review* 47 (October 1952): 110–23, and "The Campaign for the Ratifi-cation of the Constitution of 1865," *Missouri Historical Review* 47 (April 1953): 223–32.

9. *Ralls County Record*, August 31, 1865; *Portrait and Biographical Record of Marion, Ralls, Pike Counties, Missouri, 1895*, rev. ed. (New London, Mo.: Ralls County Book Company, 1982), 272–73.

Such racist appeals became even uglier as the newspaper engaged in a running battle with the Radical newspaper in nearby Hannibal, Marion County. Dodge, in an attack on J. R. Winchell, the editor of the *North Missouri Courier,* complained that "he has 'nigger on the brain' to such an alarming extent that he cannot see anything beyond a wooly head. He wishes to see the negro placed upon social and political equality with the white man."[10]

This racialized discourse was common in the newspaper's scathing denunciation of Radical politicians who stood for "negro suffrage, negro equality, and everything else pertaining to the elevation of the negro and the degradation of the white man." Conjuring up images of male ex-slaves as animals and sexual predators who would naturally feast on white women, the editors asked rhetorically, "Can our Ralls Radicals . . . take to their bosoms the 'sweet-scented' African? Give him the ballot, invite him to their tables, hand over to their *tender* embraces their lovely daughters?"[11]

The *Ralls County Record* aimed much of its fire at Jasper township's Madisonville, a community stronghold of Radicalism, where bushwhackers had burned a few public buildings during the war. In February 1865, Madisonville's Union League No. 188 had petitioned the governor to remove disloyal officials in Ralls County on grounds that their commitment to the Union was only superficial. Led by officers John Wasson, Ignatius Murphy, James Webb, and Charles Laylin, the Union League in Madisonville insisted that county officials were shielding rebels, either because they were outright Confederate sympathizers or because they were too weak to challenge the rebels. League members pointed out, for example, that incumbent sheriff William Newland, a former large slaveholder and a former state senator and Speaker of the House in the state legislature, had consistently summoned fewer than one-eighth of jurors from the ranks of Unionists in the county. This, they complained, meant that "it was impossible to convict a rebel for any crime whatever."[12]

10. *Ralls County Record,* March 1, 1866.

11. Ibid., June 28, 1866. For a concise discussion of such racialized, gendered images, see Jacquelyn Dowd Hall, "'The Mind That Burns in Each Body': Women, Rape, and Racial Violence," *Southern Exposure* 12 (November/December 1984): 61–71.

12. Madisonville Council No. 188, Petition to Gov. Thomas C. Fletcher, February 22, 1865, and Petition of Members of the loyal league No. 188 at Madisonville, to Gov. Thomas C. Fletcher, February 1, 1865; both in box 16, file 10, Governors Papers,

Tensions mounted in Ralls County as Samuel Megown, the supervisor of voter registration, began his work in preparation for the elections of 1866. Megown, who in 1836 had migrated to the county from Pittsburgh, Pennsylvania, was a Democrat who converted to Radical Unionism and faced death threats during the war. With the aid of appointed officers, he took testimony, heard appeals, and compiled lists of eligible and ineligible voters for the election that fall.[13]

Among those disfranchised were newspaper editor Dodge and Abraham McPike, even though both were Conservative Unionists who had taken the test oath. McPike, who had owned fifty-one slaves and thus had been Ralls's largest slaveholder before the war, had nevertheless been an officer in the Sixty-ninth Regiment of the Missouri Militia, and he sued Megown and the Board of Registrars for civil damages in the amount of ten thousand dollars. The Missouri Supreme Court ruled that the board's action may have been driven by malice and personal spite, thus remanding the case and determining that Megown and his registrars were not immune from civil proceedings.[14]

Thomas C. Fletcher, 1865–1869, RG 3, Missouri State Archives (hereinafter cited as MSA), Jefferson City, Mo.; Missouri General Assembly 18th Roster, 1854–1855, Western Historical Manuscripts Collection–Columbia (hereinafter cited as WHMC-C); 1860 Census Population Schedules, Missouri: Slave Schedules, Ralls County, microfilm roll 146; Roy D. Blunt, Secretary of State, comp., *Historical Listing of the Missouri Legislature* (Jefferson City, Mo., 1988), 90.

Unionists in Ralls County had endured wartime harassment by rangers under the command of Captain Washington MacDonald. Three of the ten rebel prisoners— Herbert Hudson, Marion Lair, and John M. Wade—who were executed in 1862 in nearby Palmyra, Marion County, by Union general John McNeil, were from Ralls County. Federal forces and Union militia were stationed at the courthouse in New London. Howard, *Ralls County,* 104–5; *The War of the Rebellion: A Compilation of the Official Records of the Union and Confederate Armies* (Washington, D.C: Government Printing Office, 1888), 22:817.

13. *Portrait and Biographical Record of Marion, Ralls, Pike Counties,* 549–50; Gregg Andrews, *Insane Sisters: Or, the Price Paid for Challenging a Company Town* (Columbia: University of Missouri Press, 1999), 19–20; Howard, *Ralls County,* 106, 111.

14. Howard, *Ralls County,* 65, 117; *Ralls County Record,* July 1, 1865; 1860 Census Population Schedules, Missouri: Slave Schedules, Ralls County, microfilm roll 146; *Abraham McPike, Plaintiff Error, v. Samuel Megoun* [sic] *et al., Defendants in Error,* October term, 1869, case no. 5, box 681, Missouri Supreme Court files, MSA. For the published ruling in this case, see *Missouri Reports,* 44:491–500. McPike continued to press his damages suit but finally dropped it on February 29, 1872. See *Abraham McPike vs. Samuel M. Megown et al.,* case no. 1311, Marion County Circuit Court Records, vol. 17, box 74, pp. 177, 242, 246, 316, MSA.

These cases, along with increasing partisan strife, set the tone for a volatile election campaign. To prepare for the fall elections, Conservative Unionists and Confederate sympathizers formed Andrew Johnson Clubs to oppose Radicals in the U.S. Congress who were challenging the president's lenient Reconstruction policies and his opposition to federal support for black education and citizenship rights. At the same time, James Milton Turner and other black leaders in the Missouri Equal Rights League, joined by many white Radicals, worked hard for a greater federal role to ensure African Americans access to the full fruits of citizenship, including voting rights.[15]

The *Ralls County Record* bitterly attacked black participation in Union League meetings conducted by white Radicals in the county. Resorting to race-baiting, the newspaper regularly singled out Captain Eli Southworth, a white New York–born Radical lawyer elected to the state legislature in 1864 who had lived in the county long before the war. He also served as legal counsel for Samuel Megown and his voter registration officers. In his editorials, Thomas Dodge blasted him hard and often, routinely referring to him as "Southworthless." When Southworth criticized the newspaper's unrelenting attacks on Unionists, as well as President Johnson's Reconstruction policies, at a meeting of 350 black and white Radicals in Madisonville on July 28, 1866, Dodge responded by using demeaning language and animal imagery to stir racist animosities and denounce Radicals. Insulting both Southworth and the black members of the audience, Dodge applied his racist stereotypes to Southworth: "He perspired freely," Dodge wrote contemptuously, "and smelled something like one of his sable hearers."[16]

This meeting had infuriated Dodge. He attacked John A. Lennon, who, as colonel of the Sixth-ninth Regiment of the Missouri Militia, was in charge of protecting public safety in Ralls County, for a speech that he, too, gave at the meeting. According to Dodge, Lennon supported

15. For a biography of Turner, see Gary R. Kremer, *James Milton Turner and the Promise of America: The Public Life of a Post–Civil War Black Leader* (Columbia: University of Missouri Press, 1991).

16. *Ralls County Record,* August 2, 1866; United States Federal Manuscript Census, District No. 73, Ralls County, Missouri, 1850; Samuel Megown, Supervisor of Registration Ledger, Ralls County, 1866, collection no. 2060, WHMC-C; Blunt, *Historical Listing of the Missouri Legislature,* 115. For further discussion of the politics of racial identity in other states during this era, see, for example, Dailey, *Before Jim Crow,* especially chapter 5.

universal suffrage, male and female, black and white. What particularly angered Dodge and Conservative Unionists was the formation of an independent company of militia at that meeting after a speech by Megown. According to Megown, Governor Thomas C. Fletcher had called for the creation of such a militia to protect Ralls civil officers in the discharge of their duties.[17]

Lennon also protested the formation of an independent company. He complained to the adjutant general's office in Jefferson City, insisting that he was perfectly capable of enforcing the law. He stressed that most Ralls citizens had utmost faith in his ability and patriotism.[18]

Despite Lennon's assurances, violence broke out in Madisonville after the meeting on July 28. Although Radicals were overwhelmingly predominant in the community, Conservative Unionists chose to hold a meeting there on the same date as that of the Radical meeting. Johnson Club No. 5, headed by state senatorial candidate William Newland, held a meeting just a mile away. After the meetings ended, fights erupted. Killed were John Dickinson (Dickerson), a Conservative Unionist, and Milo E. Laylin, a Radical. Six men (three Conservatives and three Radicals) were also wounded in the fray.[19]

Both sides blamed the other, and political ferment in Ralls County increased. James Glascock, a former large slaveholder and Conservative Unionist, presided over the formation of Johnson Club No. 7 in Saverton township on August 4. The club appointed a central committee of Hiram Glascock, Neil Cameron, and Sylvester Hickman to meet with the countywide central committee two days later. On August 24, 1866, Governor Fletcher wrote to Southworth and fellow Ralls Radical Reuben St. John, declining because of schedule demands

17. *Ralls County Record,* August 2, 1866; Col. John A. Lennon to Adjutant General's Office, July 29, 1866, collection no. 970, f. 376, Alvord Collection, WHMC-C. Governor Fletcher had requested but was refused help from the U.S. cavalry against bushwhackers in the state. On his wider use of what were often highly partisan militia organizations to ensure law and order, see Parrish, *History of Missouri,* 3:139–40.

18. Lennon to Adjutant General's Office, July 29, 1866, collection no. 970, f. 376, Alvord Collection, WHMC-C.

19. Ibid.; *Ralls County Record,* August 2, 9, 1866. Six men were indicted on murder charges, but those charges were dropped when they pleaded guilty to a less serious charge of rioting and paid a small fine. See Ralls County, Circuit Court Record, vol. F, 290–95, 329–31, MSA. Parrish, *History of Missouri,* 3:138–39, erroneously claims that nine men were killed in this confrontation.

an invitation to join them for a meeting in the area. Fletcher urged them, however, to provide him with additional information about law and order in the county and to provide the names of some trusted men who might replace the militia officers if the latter were not trustworthy.[20]

Although Missouri Radicals significantly increased their control in the legislature in the elections that fall, the results in Ralls County told a different story. Despite the "mean tricks" of Megown's Board of Voter Registration, the entire Radical slate of candidates went down to defeat as Conservative election judges, some of whom had been disqualified as registered voters by Megown, sat at the election tables in Saverton, Clay, and Spencer townships.[21]

Charging fraud, Luzerne Bulkley, the county's Radical candidate for the Missouri House of Representatives, successfully challenged the election's legality. Bulkley was a former captain in Company E, Eleventh Missouri State Cavalry, who once served as provost marshal and as a member of the General Courts-Martial of the Department of the Missouri. The state legislature overturned the election of his opponent, Henry C. Wellman, and granted Bulkley a seat in the House.[22]

Whereas the *Ralls County Record* complained that Bulkley occupied a "stolen seat" in the state legislature, local Radicals charged that Conservative election judges had undercounted Radical votes. The *North Missouri Courier* reprinted a letter signed by twenty-five disgruntled Radical voters from Clay township denouncing the election returns in Ralls County. The Hannibal newspaper likewise accused Ralls Conservatives of fraud and cheered the fact that Bulkley had regained his legislative seat from Wellman.[23]

20. *Ralls County Record,* August 9, 1866; Thos. C. Fletcher to Hons. E. W. Southworth and Reuben St. John, August 24, 1866, reproduced in "Newspaper clipping—'Astounding Revelations,'" William C. Breckenridge Papers, collection no. 1036, vol. 16, roll 2, WHMC-C; Mark Twain, "The Private History of a Campaign That Failed," 1885; Howard, *Ralls County,* 108–9; Andrews, *Insane Sisters,* 17–18. I would like to thank John Graves of St. Louis for generously sharing materials on the Glascock family's history.

21. Parrish, *History of Missouri,* 3:140; *Ralls County Record,* November 15, 22, 1866, and January 3, 1877.

22. *Ralls County Record,* January 3, February 21, 1867; *Portrait and Biographical Record of Marion, Ralls, Pike Counties,* 286–87.

23. *Ralls County Record,* January 9, 1868; *North American Courier,* January 10, February 22, 1867.

The election underscored the precariousness of Radicals in Ralls County. Unless they could gain political allies and votes through black suffrage or tighten application of the test oath to achieve a more stringent disfranchisement of Confederate sympathizers, they held little hope of taking control of the courthouse. Missouri's new Radical-dominated legislature passed a black suffrage amendment shortly after the election, but the amendment would require the approval of voters in the election of 1868.[24]

With Conservatives firmly in control of the county courthouse, Dodge used the *Ralls County Record* to unleash a barrage of editorials to sway public opinion against black suffrage. When W. W. Thayer, a Radical pro–civil rights editor from Boston, took over the editorial department of Hannibal's *North Missouri Courier* in the spring of 1867, Dodge's racial poison spewed forth with yet greater intensity. He denounced Thayer for endorsing national black leader Frederick Douglass for Congress, using gross caricatures to dismiss his editorial opponent. "Well, Mr. Thayer may be for aught we know to the contrary, socially much of a gentleman," wrote Dodge, "but politically, wool sticketh out hugely."[25]

Dodge insisted that his opposition to black suffrage was not based on color, but rather on an alleged lack of intelligence, "either natural or educational," on the part of African Americans. He baited Thayer further by asking if Radicals would go so far as to endorse a black vice presidential candidate. In response, Thayer pointed out that there are "ignorant white men" who vote, and he affirmed unequivocally that he would endorse a black vice president if that candidate had the necessary skills. In fact, he added, "We will go farther. We will advocate the election of a black *woman* for that office, or for the Presidency, if the voters . . . think that she is the only suitable person that can be found to care for national interests."[26]

By the time Megown and his voting registrars began their work for the elections of 1868, the national and local political climate had become even more bitter as the result of President Johnson's impeachment early that year. With Congressional Radicals in control of Reconstruc-

24. Parrish, *History of Missouri*, 3:143, 150.
25. Dodge's editorial as reprinted in *North Missouri Courier*, April 25, 1867.
26. *North Missouri Courier*, July 18, November 14, 1867.

tion, moreover, Southern states wrote new constitutions that granted universal suffrage for men and provided for state support for education regardless of race. Because of the participation of black delegates in state constitutional conventions, opponents heaped scorn on these so-called "Black and Tan" conventions. The *Ralls County Record*, conjuring up images of a nation in which whites now were victims of black tyranny, launched an appeal to "every Democrat and Conservative who desires to see our country again ruled by white men and for white men, who respect and revere the Constitution of our fathers as a sacred instrument."[27]

When the Ku Klux Klan appeared as an instrument of white racial control in Ralls County, Dodge steered the newspaper on a contradictory editorial course in regard to the Klan's activities. Although he expressed disapproval of all secret political organizations, including the "Grand Army of the Republic and other dark lantern Radical societies," he downplayed fears of the Klan's threat. When it came to the issue of vigilante justice, he tried to have it both ways. For example, when the Klan set out east of New London on July 4, 1868, to "administer a dose of 'hickory oil' " to "an impudent negro" who allegedly bragged about the "many outrages he had committed upon defenceless women" while serving in the Union army in the South, Dodge said that the law should punish the Klan if the intended victim (who had successfully evaded them) was not guilty of the charges. If the charges were true, however, then Dodge argued that the black man "deserves death." Dodge went even further, recommending mob actions in other similar cases. "We are no apologists for impudent negroes nor advocates of mob law," he wrote, "but think that if a few more in this neighborhood were dealt with in a similar manner the community would be much better off."[28]

Encouraging fears that white women might be sexually attracted to black men, Dodge especially relished taunting white Radicals about their alleged support for social equality between the races. In a story entitled "A Radical Woman," the newspaper reported on February 6, 1868, that when the wife of a Ralls Radical had recently done "a regular old-fashioned 'hoe-down' with a gentleman of the African persuasion,"

27. Fisher, "History of *The Ralls County Record*," 5.
28. *Ralls County Record*, May 7, July 9, 1868.

her husband was so upset that he packed his bags and intended to leave the household. Her husband then changed his mind and stayed, but Dodge taunted him, emphasizing that as "an uncompromising Radical, he should not object to things of so trivial a nature." Dodge added that "this first step toward negro equality is by the teachings of the Radical leaders, and our advice is, when your wife wishes to indulge in a 'social dance' with your 'cullud brethren' to grin and bear it."[29]

As Missouri voters prepared to determine the fate of black suffrage in the election of 1868, the *Ralls County Record* stepped up its highly personalized attacks on Megown and county Radicals. Dodge, calling Megown "that conglomeration of political and personal dishonesty . . . [who] never engaged in anything of an honest nature," described Ralls Radicals as "hyenas" and "scurvy villains." He accused them of still trying to "work their polluted carcasses into the high places of the county, and to milch from the public Treasury the honest earnings of citizens."[30]

As a resurgent Democratic party became more organized, Dodge urged all opponents of Radicalism to join Democratic township clubs in order to defeat Radicals at the polls. Calling on Democrats, former Whigs, and Conservatives to unite, he used slavery metaphors to describe the plight of white men under a national government that used military occupation of the South to promote "negro supremacy." Democratic township clubs soon formed, and in July 1868, William Newland presided over a meeting of the Ralls County Democratic party to elect delegates to the state and Congressional conventions.[31]

With the approaching election, internal splits further weakened the ranks of Ralls Radicals. In July 1868, Richard Dalton, a prominent Saverton township Radical attorney, severed his ties to Radicals and gave a speech at the Democratic convention. The *Ralls County Record*

29. Ibid., February 6, 1868. On sex across racial lines during the Civil War and Reconstruction era, see, for example, Martha Hodes, *White Women, Black Men: Illicit Sex in the Nineteenth-Century South* (New Haven: Yale University Press, 1997); Martha Hodes, ed., *Sex, Love, Race: Crossing Boundaries in North American History* (New York: New York University Press, 1999), 237–313; and Bynum, *Free State of Jones*.

30. *Ralls County Record*, January 30, 1868. For similar uses of animalistic imagery against white Republicans in Granville County, North Carolina, see Edwards, *Gendered Strife*, 231.

31. *Ralls County Record*, February 6, 13, July 23, 1868; Parrish, *History of Missouri*, 3:239–40.

praised Dalton's decision to join "the white man's party," emphasizing that he had long been fed up with the Radicals' alleged corruption and dishonesty.[32]

The test oath became an even more restrictive instrument in the hands of Radicals in the election of 1868. In Ralls County, there were 522 individuals on the list of rejected voters, compared to 579 on the list of qualified voters. This meant that the test oath disfranchised 47.4 percent of otherwise eligible voters in the county—a significantly higher percentage than the statewide average.[33]

The election of 1868 marked the high point of Missouri Radicalism, even though voters defeated the black suffrage amendment. Joseph W. McClurg, a Radical, won the gubernatorial race, and Radicals easily held onto their control of both houses of the Missouri legislature. Once again, however, in a few counties, Radicals needed the help of Secretary of State Francis Rodman to overturn the official election returns.[34]

Despite Radicalism's statewide electoral successes, the struggle for the Ralls County courthouse became even more contentious with Democrats in control. George Mayhall, the Democratic clerk of the county court, threw out all of the votes from Jasper township because of an alleged technicality. Mayhall's action allowed Democratic candidate Henry C. Wellman, who was on the list of rejected voters for belonging to an "unlawful organization," to defeat his Radical opponent, Wilson B. Elliott, by a margin of only two votes. In Jasper township, Wellman had received only 17 votes, compared to 82 for Elliott. Had Jasper's votes not been rejected, Elliott would have defeated Wellman by a margin of 63.[35]

---

32. *Ralls County Record*, July 23, 1868. On Dalton, see his obituary in ibid., September 4, 1925.

33. Megown, Record of the Supervisor of Registration, WHMC-C. For a discussion of the statewide percentage, see Kohl, "Enforcing a Vision," 292n1. A defiant Dodge remained on the list of rejected voters because he reportedly boasted that he had advocated secession. See also Parrish, *Missouri under Radical Rule*, 282.

34. Parrish, *History of Missouri*, 3:246–47.

35. George H. Shields, attorney at law, Hannibal, to Hon. Thomas C. Fletcher, Governor of Missouri, December 4, 1868, Governors Papers, Thomas C. Fletcher, box 16, file 10, MSA; Megown, Supervisor of Registration Ledger, WHMC-C. Edwards, *Gendered Strife*, 219–21, shows that Democrats used similar tactics, including throwing out the returns from a Republican township, to subvert the election process in Granville County, North Carolina.

Elliott and three other Radical candidates—Thomas C. Rice (assessor), Samuel McCune (sheriff), and Reuben St. John (treasurer)—hired George H. Shields, a Radical Hannibal attorney, to challenge the "sharp practice" of the county clerk. Shields insisted that Mayhall had thrown out the votes illegally and that there was nothing about Jasper's poll book that did not conform to the law. "Anyone half way fair minded could not hesitate to count this book," Shields complained to Governor Fletcher, "& it develops an arbitrary perversion of common sense to accomplish a partisan election."[36]

In Shields's view, Mayhall had implemented a Democratic strategy designed to force Radicals to contest his action before a Democratic judge and Democratic jurors. This would force Radicals to take the case to an appellate court—a very time-consuming process. By the time the appeal was heard, of course, the term of office would have nearly expired, with Democrats holding office all the while. Urging Governor Fletcher to issue commissions to the rightfully elected Radical candidates, Shields noted: "You will see that the whole radical ticket is elected by the vote of Jasper and it shows that the whole matter was a studied plan to give the certificate to the democrats. All this vicinity are looking anxiously to you as the only source through which we can get justice."[37]

After studying a report on the disputed election, the state legislature ejected Wellman from his seat and gave the election to Elliott. This brought a howl of protest from the *Ralls County Record,* which then disputed the "delusion" in Jefferson City that Ralls "was one of the worst rebel counties in the State." Lashing out at voting registrars, Dodge warned Radicals that opponents would no longer submit to the "worthless vagabonds" in charge of disfranchisement. He hinted that personal harm might come to Megown and his registrars if disfranchisement continued: "The people will have their rights next time, or make the county too hot to hold Radical Registering officers."[38]

In the case of the disputed county offices, Radical candidates had to wait much longer for justice. After the Missouri attorney general filed

36. Shields to Fletcher, December 4, 1868, Governors Papers, Thomas C. Fletcher, box 16, file 10, MSA.

37. Ibid.; Shields to Fletcher, December 17, 1868, Governors Papers, Thomas C. Fletcher, box 16, file 10, MSA.

38. *Ralls County Record,* February 4, 11, 1869.

suits on behalf of McCune, St. John, and Rice, the state supreme court issued judgments of ouster against Democrats John H. Steers (sheriff), George C. Hays (treasurer), and William D. Bishop (assessor) in May 1869. In each case, the Radical candidate would have won if the Jasper township ballots had been counted.[39]

In the editorial opinion of Thomas R. Dodge, the court's ruling was an outrage in part because it elevated to power men who lacked sufficient wealth or social status to hold office. Drawing sharp class distinctions between the opposing candidates, he insisted that public offices "should be held by white men of the manor born, and not by imported carpet-baggers and worthless, irresponsible scallawags who have not the least interest in the county except to plunder its people of their money." When numerous Ralls Radicals offered sworn statements of their real and personal wealth in order to qualify as bondsmen for McCune, Dodge ridiculed the "nabobs" as upstarts who had greatly overstated their wealth. Attacking the sworn statements of the bondsmen, Dodge condescendingly pointed out that, according to the Ralls assessor's records, the official assessed value of their wealth ranged from three to six times less than what they claimed in their own statements.[40]

Dodge also praised Mayhall, the county clerk, for having rejected the election returns of Jasper township. Claiming that the Radicals had merely received a dose of their own medicine, Dodge assured Mayhall that an overwhelming number of Ralls citizens appreciated what he had done. He also insisted that the state court's action did not mean that the Radical candidates would automatically gain access to

39. *State of Missouri ex. rel. Attorney General Petitioners v. George C. Hays,* February term, 1869, St. Louis District, box 683, case no. 5, MSCF-MSA; *State ex. rel. Attorney-General Petitioner v. John H. Steers, defendant,* March term, 1869, *Missouri Reports,* 44:223–29.

40. *Ralls County Record,* March 25, May 13, 1869. The June 17, 1869, issue of the newspaper listed the Radical bondsmen, along with their stated assets, liabilities, and wealth, and contrasted these figures with those provided by the assessor's office. The evidence suggests that most of the Radicals, many of whom owned midsized farms of less than 250 acres, came from the ranks of the county's middle class. Of 1,248 farms in Ralls County in 1870, there were none that contained more than 1,000 acres, and only 7 with acreage between 500 and 1,000. There were 322 farms that consisted of between 100 and 500 acres; 340 between 50 and 100 acres; 425 between 20 and 50 acres; 123 between 10 and 20 acres; and 31 between 3 and 10 acres.

the disputed offices. He predicted that the county court would pursue another important option instead.[41]

Dodge's prediction was accurate. McCune received his commission from Governor McClurg, but the county court judges declared that the sheriff's office was vacant, called for a new election, and appointed Steers to fill it in the meantime. The judges rejected McCune's bond, insisting that their appointment of Steers was legal, since they had declared the office vacant. The court pursued a similar tactic to block Rice from assuming the office of assessor.[42]

Not until December 1869 was Steers finally ousted by the Missouri State Supreme Court, but in the meantime McCune had been denied the sheriff's office for a year. McCune and Rice quickly filed a lawsuit against county clerk George E. Mayhall for refusing to certify their election in 1868. The *Ralls County Record* blasted them, observing that every attorney in the county except one [probably "Southworthless"] had volunteered to defend Mayhall free of charge.[43]

A few months later, Governor McClurg intervened against the Ralls County Court, the source of mischief in the above cases. He appointed Samuel Megown and Joseph Buchanan to replace Nathan S. Dimmitt and Nimrod Waters on the court. When the *Ralls County Record* found out about the governor's actions, it complained that "the Democracy of Ralls county are now as completely subjugated as it is possible for them to be, not by a square fight at the ballot box, but by repeated acts of rascality in the shape of Radical legislation."[44]

While Ralls officials battled each other in the courts over the spoils of office, harassment of African American institutions stepped up in New London after Missouri voters defeated the black suffrage amendment in 1868. Especially targeted was the New London Christian Church, led by Reverend William Wilburn ("Willie Hays"), a former

41. *Ralls County Record,* June 17, 1869.

42. *State of Missouri ex. rel. Samuel C. McCune, Relator, v. the Ralls County Court, Respondent,* and *State of Missouri ex. rel. Thomas C. Rice, Relator, v. the Ralls County Court, Respondent;* both in October term, 1869, *Missouri Reports,* 45:58–62. See also *Ralls County Record,* May 13, 1869.

43. *Ralls County Record,* July 1, December 9, 1869, and March 17, 1870. See also *State of Missouri to the Use of Samuel McCune and Thomas C. Rice, plaintiffs, vs. George E. Mayhall, William Newland, John D. Biggs, Walter McFarland, and John R. Helms, defendants,* Ralls County, Circuit Court Record, 344–45, vol. G, MSA.

44. *Ralls County Record,* March 31, 1870.

slave of the prominent Hays family. During services, young white men and adults regularly assembled outside the building and harassed the congregation. When black church members complained to the *Ralls County Record* in January 1869, the newspaper condemned the harassment but did not urge prosecution of the offenders. Instead, the newspaper only threatened to reveal the names of the boys if such disruptions continued.[45]

The black church in town often showcased the achievements of pupils who attended a special school that opened in early May 1869. When the teacher arrived to open the school for ten students, the *Ralls County Record* contemptuously referred to her as "a female chunk of ebony from Chicago."[46]

When the church hosted a special exhibit to celebrate the students' achievement at the end of the school's first year, attendees were subjected to frightening harassment by a group of young white boys and adult men gathered outside. The hoodlums broke windows, screamed and yelled, and especially insulted the black women in attendance. Even the editors of the *Ralls County Record* condemned the mob's actions, but they refused to reveal the names of those responsible: "We would mention their names, but they are so well-known that a mere allusion to the matter will suffice. . . . We are no apologists for negroes, but when they are trying to improve their minds, they should not be disturbed by the white *trash*."[47]

Attacks on the church at times assumed even more serious proportions, making it increasingly difficult for the newspaper not to endorse harsher punishment for the guilty parties. In October 1869, the

45. *Ralls County Record*, January 28, 1869. On Wilburn and the church, see Howard, *Ralls County*, 176.

46. *Ralls County Record*, May 13, 1869. On black education in Missouri during this period, see Antonio F. Holland and Gary R. Kremer, "Some Aspects of Black Education in Reconstruction Missouri: An Address by Richard B. Foster," *Missouri Historical Review* 70 (January 1976): 184–98; Joe M. Richardson, "The American Missionary Association and Black Education in Civil War Missouri," *Missouri Historical Review* 69 (July 1975): 433–48; Lawrence O. Christensen, "Schools for Blacks: J. Milton Turner in Reconstruction Missouri," *Missouri Historical Review* 76 (January 1982): 121–35; and Patrick J. Huber and Gary R. Kremer, "Nathaniel C. Bruce, Black Education, and the 'Tuskegee of the Midwest,'" *Missouri Historical Review* 86 (October 1991): 37–54.

47. *Ralls County Record*, April 14, 1870.

Ralls County Record reported that recently "a thoughtless young man, while passing the colored church in the lower edge of town, fired two shots at the door in the building, each ball passing through." Although the newspaper urged steps to be taken to end such attacks, its use of the adjective "thoughtless" to describe the young man who fired at the church certainly suggests a deeper desire to downplay the racial malevolence that underlay the incident.[48]

A racial double standard clearly existed when it came to application of the law in New London. In early February 1869, for example, when two black men were charged with rowdy conduct during services at the black church, county judge William E. Harris fined each of them twenty-five dollars plus costs. In this case, the newspaper did not hesitate to mention and belittle the names of those accused.[49]

When Radicals passed the Fifteenth Amendment to the U.S. Constitution to guarantee black male suffrage, the *Ralls County Record* complained that the federal government had gone too far. Noting that black citizens were planning widespread celebrations, the newspaper ridiculed these celebrations and stirred white resentments: "Negro holidays are multiplying so rapidly that they will soon have little time for anything else than jubilating and voting. It is a long, long while since Congress has given white people cause for rejoicing."[50]

The newspaper used a number of linguistic devices to dehumanize African Americans and to belittle their aspirations. It now routinely referred to African Americans as "Fifteenth Amendments," and characterized black funerals as "blackburying parties." Reporting on the arrest of a black woman for insulting a white woman, the newspaper described the black woman as "a dingy, mouse-colored saucy African [who was] impudent [and a] 'she devil.'" Dodge acknowledged that he received complaints about the harshness of his racist language, but he proudly editorialized that he refused to soften it.[51]

Because of such attitudes, violence, and a lack of economic opportunities, the bleaching of Ralls County's population was well underway. At the time of the federal census in 1870, there were 1,255 African

48. Ibid., October 28, 1869.
49. Ibid., February 11, 1869.
50. Ibid., February 24, 1870.
51. Ibid., August 4, 1870, May 7, June 4, 1874.

Americans in the county—a sharp decline of 30.4 percent from the combined slave and free black population of 1,804 in 1860. Despite the exodus of African Americans, the total population of the county had increased from 8,592 in 1860 to 10,510. This meant an increase of 36.5 percent in the white population from 6,788 to 9,255. For black residents who chose to stay in the county, the *Ralls County Record* made clear the restricted terms on which they were welcome: "The negroes of this place and vicinity are becoming very rude in their behavior towards the whites, and unless they change very materially in their conduct we would not be surprised to hear of some 15th amendment performing at the end of a rope."[52]

Amid an increasingly contentious public debate over disfranchisement, a wing of the Radical Unionist party began to distance itself from the test oath. There was growing popular support, even among some Radicals, for reenfranchising Confederates and their sympathizers. In early 1870, the U.S. Supreme Court upheld the constitutionality of Missouri's test oath, but a group of Liberal Republicans, led by U.S. senator Carl B. Schurz and former Senator B. Gratz Brown, emerged within the Radical camp to oppose the test oath and some of the national policies of President Ulysses S. Grant. That summer, after the Radical Union party split at the convention, Liberals chose Brown as their gubernatorial candidate to oppose the Radicals, who again nominated McClurg.[53]

Democrats took advantage of this split by pursuing the so-called Possum strategy in the elections that year. Instead of running their own candidates in statewide races, they encouraged constituents to vote for Brown in hopes of getting the test oath repealed. Only in races where Democrats believed their candidates stood a chance of winning did they compete.[54]

Democrats in Ralls County also benefited from a growing internal split among Radicals along lines of race. In 1870, the *Ralls County Record* estimated that because of the Fifteenth Amendment, there were

52. *Ninth Census—Volume I*, 43–45; *Ralls County Record*, June 16, 1870.

53. See Thomas S. Barclay, *The Liberal Republican Movement in Missouri, 1865–1871* (Columbia: State Historical Society of Missouri, 1926); and Parrish, *Missouri under Radical Rule*, 268–99.

54. William E. Parrish, Charles T. Jones Jr., and Lawrence O. Christensen, *Missouri: The Heart of the Nation*, 2d ed. (Arlington Heights, Ill.: Harlan Davidson, 1992), 208.

at least two hundred black voters, who now held the balance of political power in the county. There were signs, however, of deep disagreements within the coalition of white and black radicals in the county. Just a few days after the election of 1868, the newspaper had gleefully reported a fight "at the black and tan corner" in New London between a white Radical and a "sable-colored gentleman." According to the newspaper, such conflicts had become more common recently.[55]

The *Ralls County Record* enjoyed pointing out the political dilemma of the county's white Radicals as they prepared for the 1870 election. To win, white Radicals might have to concede some political offices to black Radicals, who at the time were threatening to run their own slate of candidates. If Ralls Radicals alienated black voters, they might lose the election.[56]

The 1870 election, which put Liberal Republican B. Gratz Brown in the governor's office, restored Democrats to power in Ralls County, thanks to a lack of enforcement of the test oath. There was only spotty enforcement of the oath around the state, and voting registrars, perhaps out of fear, apparently did not compile a list of qualified voters in Ralls County. This enabled Nimrod Waters and Lewis C. Northcutt, a Liberal Republican, to replace Samuel Megown and Joseph W. Buchanan as county judges. John Megown, a Democratic son of Samuel, was elected as judge of the Probate Court, and former sheriff Steers, a Democrat, reclaimed the sheriff's office from McCune. James W. Lear replaced Eli W. Southworth as clerk of the circuit court. Amid rumors that Radical incumbents might protest that the election was illegal, the *Ralls County Record* urged them to accept the results: "The Democracy of Ralls have manifested a desire to bury the past and live on terms of fraternal friendship with our Radical fellow-citizens, and it is to be hoped that their good intentions will be realized."[57]

Southworth at first refused to surrender the circuit clerk's office, to which Governor Fletcher had appointed him in August 1868. In a letter to Governor-elect Brown, Southworth complained that the election was illegal because there was no complete registration of any township in Ralls County. He pointed out that election judges were

55. *Ralls County Record*, July 14, 1870, November 12, 1868.
56. Ibid., July 14, 1870.
57. Ibid., January 12, 1871.

never given a list of registered voters, and that this had been brought to the secretary of state's attention at the time the election returns were sent to Jefferson City. After a stormy meeting with a visiting delegation of seven prominent Ralls citizens, however, Southworth agreed under protest to vacate the office.[58]

The election of 1870 signaled the end of Reconstruction in Missouri. In a referendum on the test oath, Missouri voters that year overwhelmingly expressed a desire to abolish it. Moreover, fewer Republican politicians now had the stomach for continuing the bitter fight over disfranchisement, especially since black men could now vote.

It was not "vindictiveness," but the Democrats' skillful use of the race card, that sank the Radicals. From its very inception after the war, the *Ralls County Record* made clear the racial issues that underlay the strife between Conservatives and Radicals. Editors Dodge and Mayhall opposed the Fourteenth and Fifteenth Amendments, and when African Americans began to assert the rights of citizenship and voting, the newspaper repeatedly demonized them. To suggest that Radicals might have been more successful had they been less bent on revenge is to ignore this fundamental fact. Short of abandoning the very principles for which at least some of them stood (and many ultimately did abandon their racial idealism), there was little else that Radicals could have done to avoid the wrath of Conservatives.

The failure of the Radicals' vision of economic, social, and racial progress meant that Democrats could now implement their own vision of community, one that did not welcome Republicans or African Americans in Ralls County. The flight of African Americans continued after Reconstruction; by 1900, only 927 black residents—7.5 percent of the population—lived there. By then, it had become a common joke among whites that neither blacks nor Republicans had better be caught in New London after sundown. Jefferson Mayhall, a staunch Unionist, Republican, and former provost marshal in New London, whose brother coedited the *Ralls County Record,* opened a Republican newspaper in 1878, but it collapsed almost overnight.

58. E. W. Southworth to B. Gratz Brown, January 2, 1871, box 21, file 9, Governors Papers, Gratz Brown, 1871–1873, RG 03, MSA; *Ralls County Record,* January 12, 19, 26, February 2, 9, 1871.

Democratic merchants refused to advertise in it, and Republican merchants were afraid to do so.[59]

In the coalition of Liberal Republicans and Democrats that prevailed in 1870, the former were clearly the junior partners. They soon returned to the Republican party, leaving Democrats firmly in control as Missouri ratified a new constitution in 1875—one that ensured the further social marginalization of African Americans. The *Ralls County Record* perhaps best expressed what the failure of Radical Reconstruction would mean to African Americans in the county's years ahead when it reported an incident in which a group of black men and women entered U. C. Hays's ice cream parlor in New London to try to utilize the recent Civil Rights Act of 1875. After Hays refused to serve them, the newspaper warned that if similar incidents arise, "some ebony colored gentleman's skin will be perforated with No. 1 buck-shot."[60]

59. Andrews, *City of Dust*, 10; Fisher, "History of *The Ralls County Record*," 6; *Portrait and Biographical Record of Marion, Ralls, Pike Counties*, 301–2.

60. *Ralls County Record*, July 8, 1875. For a discussion of the Constitution of 1875 and patterns of segregation and racial control in Missouri, see David P. Thelen, *Paths of Resistance: Tradition and Democracy in Industrializing Missouri* (Columbia: University of Missouri Press, 1991), 139–46.

The Bald Knobbers, the Anti–Bald Knobbers, Politics, and the Culture of Violence in the Ozarks, 1860–1890

THOMAS M. SPENCER

On a warm April evening in 1885, a group of about one hundred men met on a treeless hill called Snapp's Bald in Taney County about five miles southwest of Forsyth. They met on the "bald" (as these treeless hills are called) to insure secrecy of the proceedings. These men came together, they claimed, to respond to the outbreak of lawlessness in the county. A tall and imposing man named Nat Kinney led the meeting. After reading a long list of crimes that had gone unpunished, Kinney appealed to those in attendance: "What will become of our sons and daughters? Our lives, our property and our liberty are at stake! I appeal to you, as citizens of Taney County, to say what we shall do. Shall we sit down and fold our arms and quietly submit?" "No!" shouted those in attendance. "Shall we organize ourselves into a vigilance committee and see that when crimes are committed the laws are enforced?" "Yes!" shouted the crowd.[1]

---

1. This version of the meeting comes from Mary Hartman and Elmo Ingenthron, *Bald Knobbers: Vigilantes on the Ozarks Frontier* (Gretna, La.: Pelican Publishing Company, 1988), 36–37. Hartman and Ingenthron's book apparently uses oral histories to close many of the gaps in the group's story. At times, due to a lack of other sources, I am forced to use their versions of events because it is the only one available. I have preferred to cite contemporary newspaper accounts but, unfortunately, that is not always possible.

This meeting was the start of two years of night rides by the vigilante group that called themselves the Bald Knobbers in Taney, Christian, and Douglas counties. During this period, the Bald Knobbers received much public criticism, and a group calling itself the "Anti–Bald Knobbers" rose to challenge them in Taney County. The Bald Knobbers came to a rather ignominious end when three of their number in Christian County were hanged by the state for murder in 1889.

Over the last two decades, a few historians have written short treatments of the Bald Knobbers. In these works, the authors have not presented a careful and close analysis of just who was involved with the Bald Knobbers and Anti–Bald Knobbers. Yet a detailed analysis is terribly important when one wishes to advance an argument about what the "real" goals and functions are of an organization.[2] Unfortunately, this subject is difficult to research because it is awfully hard at times to separate myths and legends—told and retold over more than a century—from the facts.

Nonetheless, when one researches the organization more closely, the entire episode appears to be much more about local politics and regional loyalties than about law and order. A significant number of the Bald Knobbers in Taney County were ex-Union soldiers who were both newcomers to the county and Republicans. Kinney, himself a member of the Democratic party, who ran for county office twice in the 1880s, had come to realize that his vision of the future had more in common with that of the Republicans. Correspondingly, Kinney almost always cast his lot with the Republicans in Taney County. The men who op-

---

2. David P. Thelen, *Paths of Resistance: Tradition and Democracy in Industrializing Missouri* (Columbia: University of Missouri Press, 1991), 87–92. Thelen contends that the Bald Knobbers fit into his overall argument about rural Missourians resisting industrialization and modernization without doing the necessary research to make sure the fit is a good one. Another recent version of this argument of the Bald Knobbers as modernizers appears in Kristin Kalen and Lynn Morrow, "Baldknobbers Sought to Bring Their Kind of Capitalism, Order to Ozarks Counties in 1880s," *Springfield News-Leader,* December 19, 1989, 3F. Of all attempts to interpret the Bald Knobbers saga, my argument is the closest to that made in their brief treatment of the episode by Lawrence O. Christensen and Gary R. Kremer in *A History of Missouri, Volume IV, 1875–1919* (Columbia: University of Missouri Press, 1997), 23–24. While Christensen and Kremer cite other factors such as "the frustration of being unable to effect change through normal political and governmental channels," they do see the Bald Knobbers as being part of a partisan attempt to gain control over the county.

posed them in the Anti–Bald Knobbers were ex-Confederates who were Democratic in their politics and longtime residents of Taney County. Like other vigilante organizations at the same time, the Bald Knobbers and Anti–Bald Knobbers in Taney County appear to have been most interested in political and social control over their communities. The Christian County Bald Knobbers, however, were a quite different group of men; they appear to have had radically different long-term goals—if they had any real goals at all.[3]

In addition to briefly telling the story of the Bald Knobbers vigilante band of the 1880s, this essay analyzes the membership of the three major organizations in the drama—the Taney County Bald Knobbers, the Taney County Anti–Bald Knobbers, and the Christian County Bald Knobbers—providing insight into this famous episode in the history of the Missouri Ozarks. In the process, we will see that, as much as new generations of Missouri historians might try to get away from the traditional topics of politics and the Civil War, it is impossible to do so in this case. Much of the explanation for the actions of the Bald Knobbers and Anti–Bald Knobbers involves these important political and regional loyalties.

In order to understand the Bald Knobbers episode fully, one must return to the brutal events of the Civil War in Taney County more than twenty years earlier. During the war, Taney County, like most of the state's southernmost counties, had been rocked by skirmishes between

---

3. Kristin Kalen and Lynn Morrow, "Nat Kinney's Sunday School Crowd," *White River Valley Historical Quarterly* (fall 1993): 8. Kinney's running for office on the Democratic ticket is misleading to the casual observer. Kalen and Morrow argue that Kinney would have preferred to run as a Republican but that his "volatile personality and proclivity towards violence" clashed with the "more educated, professional, progressive" leaders in the county's Republican party at the time. Kinney's move to run as a Democrat infuriated Republican leaders but should not be misconstrued as Kinney being a truly dedicated Democrat. As Kalen and Morrow put it, Kinney was the Democratic candidate for state representative "by default" so that the Democrats could "mount a credible political race" in 1884 and 1886. He lost both times and apparently never stopped associating with his Republican allies in the Bald Knobbers. For more on the causes of violence and night riding in rural America during the late nineteenth century, see William Lynwood Montell, *Killings: Folk Justice in the Upper South* (Lexington: University Press of Kentucky, 1986); Christopher Waldrep, *Night Riders: Defending Community in the Black Patch* (Durham, N.C.: Duke University Press, 1993); and Altina L. Waller, *Feud: Hatfields, McCoys, and Social Change in Appalachia, 1860–1900* (Chapel Hill: University of North Carolina Press, 1988).

Union and Confederate cavalry and guerrillas. Taney County was a Confederate-leaning county situated just south of the Unionist Republican strongholds of Springfield and Ozark. Because of its proximity to these areas, Taney County found itself under close scrutiny by Union commanders in Springfield and was subject to frequent murderous raids by Union units seeking Confederate "bushwhackers." The most famous Confederate bushwhacker in the area, Alf Bolin, was killed in 1863; according to local legend, his severed head was displayed on a pole in the town of Ozark. Union troops had committed other atrocities during the war, including the burning of the county seat, Forsyth, in 1863. Several of the leaders of these guerrilla-hunting Union cavalry units would later play important roles in the Bald Knobbers band twenty years later.[4]

Most of the Southern sympathizers of the county were forced to flee southward—especially during the last two years of the war. The population of the county declined from thirty-five hundred in 1861 to less than one thousand by 1865. Those that remained for the duration of the war were primarily Union sympathizers. In the clearly fraudulent election of 1864, only twenty-nine votes were cast, all for Abraham Lincoln and another Republican, Missouri official F. M. Gideon.[5] The experiences of those who fled embittered them for the rest of their lives. It is not surprising that the Southern sympathizers who returned to the county following the war made up the core of what would later be the Anti–Bald Knobbers.

The upheaval in the county that started during the war continued in the years following the war. Thus, one of the most important legacies of the Civil War in Taney County was the creation of a culture of violence and political terrorism. From the war years onward, the county was a violent and dangerous place to live. Historians have long pointed to the relative peacefulness of the county before the war and its wild,

4. Lucille Morris Upton, *Bald Knobbers* (Caldwell, Idaho: Caxton Printers, 1939), 29; Elmo Ingenthron, *Land of Taney: A History of an Ozark Commonwealth* (Point Lookout, Mo.: School of the Ozarks Press, 1974), 89–123; Lynn Morrow, "Where Did All the Money Go? War and the Economics of Vigilantism in Southern Missouri," *White River Valley Historical Quarterly* (fall 1994): 6. In particular, one of those characterized as a "bushwhacking villain" would be Madison Day, who later served as sheriff and coroner for the county.
5. Morrow, "Where Did All the Money Go?" 4–9; Ingenthron, *Land of Taney,* 218.

lawless nature after the war as the reason for the rise of the vigilante band. These historians overemphasize the prewar years and ignore the important experience of the war for changing the people and their attitudes towards violence. During the war, residents of Taney County learned that "might makes right" in wartime politics. Most postwar migrants to the county—who came from other rural parts of the state or from upper South states—would have had similar wartime experiences. Both Unionists and Confederates had learned to hate the other passionately and believe the other was truly evil. This malevolence thus justified any action necessary to defeat them. Taney Countians continued to believe in these ways after the war.[6]

In the years following the Civil War, political participation by ex-Confederates was limited by the "ironclad" loyalty oath provided for in the state constitution of 1865 that prevented many Missourians from being involved in politics.[7] During this period, Republicans controlled Taney County's politics by default. In a county that had voted Democratic by a two-to-one margin before the war, the Democrats could only muster 8 votes out of 114 (7 percent) cast in the election of 1866. In 1868, Democrats cast only 57 out of 261 votes (22 percent) cast, and in 1870 that number rose only slightly to 83 out of 314 (26 percent).[8] When the ironclad oath was no longer required for voting in 1872, the situation changed dramatically. Democrats regained control of most county political offices and continued to grow stronger throughout the 1870s. The 1870s and early 1880s were a time when the parties were pretty evenly matched in Taney County. The Republicans tended to win the state and national contests in the county—usually by a narrow margin—but often lost the races for important local offices such as prosecuting attorney, sheriff, county clerk, and school commissioner. In the presidential election of 1876—the high-water

6. In describing this "culture of violence," I am contending that the *war* created a "might makes right" culture. Unlike some scholars, I am not contending that rural people of southern extraction were any more prone to violence than those from other parts of the country. In fact, I would argue that this outbreak of violence represents quite a discontinuity with the past behavior of Taney Countians before the war.

7. William E. Parrish, *A History of Missouri, Volume III: 1860 to 1875* (Columbia: University of Missouri Press, 1973), 121–23.

8. Missouri State Archives, Elections Division, Election Returns, box 11, folder 22, and box 12, folder 5.

mark for Democrats in postwar national elections in Taney County—
there were 368 votes (51.2 percent) for Republican Rutherford B. Hayes,
versus 351 votes (48.8 percent) for Samuel Tilden, the Democratic
candidate. In the same election, the majority of county offices went to
Democratic candidates.[9]

This state of affairs clearly did not sit well with Republicans in the
county, who wished to regain control over the local government. In
the early 1880s, the Republicans began to complain about the incredible rise in the county's debt. At the end of the Republicans' time in
control of county government (between 1870 and 1872), Republican
county officials floated bonds worth $17,650 to pay off debts accrued
during Republican administrations.[10] What these bonds were used for
by county officials is unclear—no major renovations were planned or
completed during this time. Once the Democrats took over, Republicans began to accuse them of embezzling funds derived from these
bonds from the county treasury. While one could certainly accuse
Republicans of playing politics, there is considerable circumstantial
evidence of embezzlement by Democratic officials during the 1870s.
During the period from 1872 to 1884, the county debt skyrocketed to
$42,000. Some of the Democratic county officials had suspicious
gains in personal wealth during the period (one prominent county official, in particular, had erected a new mill in the early 1880s). The tax
rates paid by Taney County residents were quite exorbitant compared
to those of neighboring counties, which upset many within the county.[11]

Together, these events contributed to the rise of the Bald Knobbers.
Republicans were angry that they had lost control over the county and
were infuriated by what they saw as clear wrongdoing by Democrats.
Furthermore, the prevalent culture of violence had led to a huge increase in the number of murders in the county in the postwar years
and to a subsequent large number of suspicious (to Republicans at
least) acquittals. Republicans believed that the rising murder rate was
the result of a corrupt justice system that the Democrats controlled.

9. This is according to the election results and list of county officers published in
the *State Almanac and Official Directory of Missouri, 1878* (Jefferson City: State of
Missouri, 1878); and the *Official Directory of Missouri, 1879* (Jefferson City: State
of Missouri, 1879).
10. Ingenthron, *Land of Taney,* 226–27.
11. Morrow, "Where Did All the Money Go?" 11–12.

Believing the opposing party's motives and nature were malevolent, the Republicans in the county convinced themselves that the Democrats alone were to blame for all of these problems (conveniently ignoring the fact that at least a few Republicans also appeared to play roles in the fraud and had served on the juries that acquitted those accused of murder). The Republicans apparently felt there was a need to take radical steps to take control of the county before everything collapsed. The acquittal of Al Layton (a cousin of Democratic county official Thomas A. Layton) in the murder of local store owner James Everett was the last straw for these men. This frustration and rage led them to extralegal action and the formation of the vigilance committee later known as the Bald Knobbers. One of their first actions was the lynching of Frank and Tubal Taylor. The Taylor brothers, two outlaws who had shot another local store owner, John Dickenson, and his wife, were taken from the jail and hanged on April 8, 1885. Pinned to Frank Taylor's shirt was a note that read, "BEWARE! These are the first Victims to the Wrath of Outraged Citizens—More will follow. THE BALD KNOBBERS."[12] From this point onward, the committee began its activities, which included physically assaulting political opponents and those whom they believed were politically or morally bankrupt (not surprisingly, most of those attacked were of Southern background and, presumably, voted for the other party in county elections).

There also appears to have been a profound cultural distance between the Bald Knobbers and their victims. Most of the Bald Knobbers were from other places and did not pursue traditional Ozarkian ways of life. A close analysis of the backgrounds of thirty-seven of the more prominent Bald Knobbers gives insight into this cultural distance and provides a solid evidence upon which to make claims about the goals of the organization.[13] The group, reported by some to have had as many as nine hundred members, appears to have comprised only eighty to one hundred active members in Taney County. As mentioned earlier, the Bald Knobbers were composed almost entirely of men who were sympathetic to the Union cause. In fact, nine of this

12. Hartman and Ingenthron, *Bald Knobbers*, 52–54.
13. The lists of prominent Bald Knobbers, Anti–Bald Knobbers, and Christian County Bald Knobbers were compiled from contemporary newspaper accounts as well as from secondary historical articles written about the group during the last seventy-five years.

group had fought for the Union army in the Civil War, whereas only one of the Bald Knobbers appears to have fought for the Confederacy. Many of the Bald Knobbers were quite active in the Taney County chapter of the Grand Army of the Republic, the society of Union veterans.

The Bald Knobbers involved men of all ages; in 1886, the youngest member was twenty-four and the oldest was sixty-one. The group was primarily composed of men of family-raising age, however. In 1886, 46 percent of the Bald Knobbers were in their thirties, and 29 percent were in their forties. The average age of the Taney County Bald Knobbers was just over thirty-eight years. Therefore, they would have been men who were concerned about the future of the county for their families' sake. It is reasonable to assume that men of this age would be most likely to take steps they felt necessary to safeguard the future for their children.[14]

The Bald Knobbers also came from a wide variety of places. Although 44 percent of them were born in Missouri, the vast majority of even this group came from other parts of the state and were not native to Taney County. Thirty-three percent of the Bald Knobbers came from the southern states of Arkansas, Tennessee, and North Carolina. Yet the Bald Knobbers also had members from outside the traditional places of origin for Ozark settlers; 10 percent of the Bald Knobbers came from Illinois and Indiana. The Bald Knobbers also had a few members who came from places much farther away from the Ozarks: two from the state of New York and one from England. What stands out most about the places of origin for these men is how few of them were natives of Taney County. In the entire group, only one of them appears to have lived his entire life in Taney County. It is clear that these were outsiders wishing to change what they believed were the corrupt ways of the native Taney Countians.

The occupations of the Bald Knobbers demonstrate just how different they were from the average Ozarker. While a large number of Bald Knobbers (nearly a third) claimed to be farmers in the census of 1880, their primary occupations were in other areas by the middle

14. The biographical data of the Taney County Bald Knobbers analyzed here is compiled from U.S. Census data for Taney County from 1880 and 1900 as well as from newspaper obituaries that appeared in the *Taney County Times* and *Taney County Republican* during the 1880s and 1890s.

1880s. By 1887—after the Republicans had returned to power in county government—42 percent of these men worked for county government. These men worked for the sheriff's department, held elective offices in county government, or worked in the prosecutor's office. The main reason these Bald Knobbers appear to have been involved in the group was the seeking of political jobs and power. To them, regaining county government had a personal economic and political payoff. Another third of the Bald Knobbers were involved in small business, were engaged in agricultural commerce or processing, or were lawyers. These men would have been most interested in stabilizing county government for business reasons. Of the remaining Bald Knobbers, less than 10 percent appear to have pursued farming as their only occupation in the 1880s—quite an unusual statistic considering most Ozarkers were farmers. The remaining Bald Knobbers had a wide variety of occupations: Two of them owned the newspaper (a Republican party organ); one acted as a minister (but would later be a long-serving Republican state legislator); and one was a teacher. So in addition to being concerned about the future for their families, these outsiders also had self-interested reasons for leading the charge for a change in county government.

These men viewed longtime residents as backward, uncultured, and immoral people who must change their ways to continue living in the county. In fact, many of the Bald Knobbers' activities were nothing more than public shaming rituals, targeting political opponents who abused their wives and children, drank too much, or did something else that the self-appointed stewards of morality viewed as beyond the pale. The group conveniently ignored the fact that many of these same moral faults were exhibited by those within their own band (a weakness for strong drink was certainly one of Kinney's many failings).

One of the early victories for the Bald Knobbers was when several of their number succeeded in persuading the circuit judge to bring a state auditor in to examine the county's finances. The auditor came in November 1885 and told members of the county government that he would complete the audit in January 1886. In December 1885, the courthouse burned to the ground; the most cursory investigation turned up evidence of arson.[15] Now the Bald Knobbers believed the corrupt government of the county had gone so far as to burn the

---

15. Hartman and Ingenthron, *Bald Knobbers*, 90–91.

courthouse down to conceal evidence of their wrongdoing. The Republicans believed that the Democrats in power had stooped to this level to avoid detection of their misdeeds. To them, this was certainly proof of their opponents' malevolence. In the months following the fire, the conflict between the Bald Knobbers and their opponents intensified, resulting in numerous gunfights.

One of the things that especially outraged the Bald Knobbers was the common practice in the hill country of having a common-law wife. Nat Kinney was particularly outspoken about this "immoral" practice. Contrary to the natives, these men believed that common-law marriages were wrong and should stop immediately. One can see here a major cultural difference between the more middle-class Bald Knobbers and the longtime residents of the county. The Bald Knobbers felt that the "hill people" lacked the character and morals to do the right thing both politically and in their own lives—this had to change, they believed. Kinney went so far as to call the struggle to change the ways of the people "a war between civilization and barbarism."[16]

Kinney's comments upset many of the older and more traditional families in the area. They responded by forming their own organization shortly after the founding of the Bald Knobbers. They called their organization the Home Guards, but it quickly became known locally as the "Anti–Bald Knobbers." The Anti–Bald Knobbers were incensed by the way Kinney portrayed those who disagreed with him as immoral and uncivilized. The Anti–Bald Knobbers were very different from those on the other side of the conflict. An analysis of these twenty or so men reveals them to be quite a bit older than the Bald Knobbers, with the average age being forty-five. In fact, 40 percent of the known Anti–Bald Knobbers were over the age of fifty. Half of these men were born in Missouri, but most of these individuals were locals, native to Taney County. The other half of the organization's members came primarily from southern states. Only two Anti–Bald Knobbers appear to have come from non-southern states, and both of them were from Illinois. The Anti–Bald Knobbers were composed

16. Harvey N. Castleman, *The Bald Knobbers: The Story of the Lawless Night-Riders Who Ruled Southern Missouri in the 80's* (Girard, Kans.: Haldeman-Julius Publications, 1944), 7.

primarily of older, longtime residents of the county—just the type of hill people the Bald Knobbers were trying to change.[17]

The differences in occupations between the two groups is also striking. Two-thirds of the Anti–Bald Knobbers were involved in agricultural commerce as either farmers or mill owners. Two of the Anti–Bald Knobbers were involved in county government in the early 1880s (as a sheriff and a prosecutor), so they, like many of their Bald Knobber counterparts, had a personal stake in the outcome of the political conflict. The Anti–Bald Knobbers also included in their ranks a minister, a small businessman, and a newspaper owner. In short, the Anti–Bald Knobbers were the common hill folk who were resisting the sort of cultural and political changes that the Bald Knobbers wanted to institute. These men held meetings and wrote angry letters about the state of affairs in Taney County to Springfield newspapers (they were forced to do so because the Forsyth paper was owned by two Bald Knobbers, who refused to print letters by their opponents). They also planned the assassination of Nat Kinney.[18] Many in the county, while they did not join the relatively small group of Anti–Bald Knobbers, clearly would have agreed with the goals of this group.

The biggest achievement of the Anti–Bald Knobbers was their success in convincing the state government to get involved in the dispute between themselves and the Bald Knobbers. After Nat Kinney shot and killed Andrew Coggburn, a well-known Anti–Bald Knobber, the group met on March 1, 1886, and decided to appeal to Governor John S. Marmaduke, a Democrat. The Anti–Bald Knobbers felt sure that Marmaduke would be happy to help them oust the Republican Bald Knobbers from power. Interestingly, Alonzo S. Prather, one of the original Bald Knobbers, attended the meeting. Prather, now disenchanted with Kinney, had changed sides in the conflict.

The Anti–Bald Knobbers claimed in their petition that the county was "enjoying a reign of terror from the depredation of a band of men organized under the name of Bald Knobbers." The news of this meeting

17. The biographical data of the Anti–Bald Knobbers analyzed here is also compiled from U.S. Census Data for Taney County from 1880 and 1900 and newspaper obituaries that appeared in the *Taney County Times* and *Taney County Republican*.

18. Examples of these vitriolic letters appear in the *Springfield Daily Herald*, March 6, and April 14, 1886. For more on the meeting of the Anti–Bald Knobbers, see Hartman and Ingenthron, *Bald Knobbers*, 104–6.

had gotten out, and by the following morning, Kinney and his men were shouting threats at known Anti–Bald Knobbers in the streets of Forsyth. John J. Reynolds, a former Democratic county judge, took the Anti–Bald Knobbers' petition to the governor four days later. The petition to the governor claimed that the county government was now in the hands of the vigilantes and that the common citizens' civil rights were frequently violated. Reynolds asked that the local militia (formed illegally by the Anti–Bald Knobbers) be recognized and that the state militia be sent in to "put an end to the Bald Knobbers' reign of terror." Marmaduke's reaction was less enthusiastic than Reynolds had expected. Marmaduke promised to send a representative in the next few days to look into the situation.[19]

About a week later, upon hearing that the governor was considering sending in the state militia, the Bald Knobbers sent three representatives to meet with the governor to try to convince him that the situation in the county was not as dire as he had been led to believe. Supposedly, the vigilantes convinced the governor that the Anti–Bald Knobbers were actually more concerned about their back taxes than justice. The governor soon ordered the local militia to disband.[20]

Eventually, Missouri's adjutant general James Jamison visited Forsyth in April 1886. In a heated meeting, Jamison met with members of both sides and told them they must disband or face the state militia being sent in to bring order and to force both sides to disband. He argued that both organizations were unlawful and refused to favor either side. Jamison met with Kinney alone and convinced him he was serious, even going so far as to threaten to throw Kinney in jail if the organization did not disband within forty-eight hours. Kinney and Jamison made a joint public statement calling for the disbanding of the Bald Knobbers. The following day, a committee of the group drafted resolutions disbanding the organization. Claiming that "peace and quiet now prevail supreme," the committee signed the resolutions and sent them to the governor.[21]

19. Hartman and Ingenthron, *Bald Knobbers*, 105–7; F. McConkey, *The Bald Knobbers or Citizen's Committee of Taney and Christian Counties, Missouri* (Forsyth, Mo.: Groom and McConkey, 1887), 23.

20. Hartman and Ingenthron, *Bald Knobbers*, 112.

21. "Report of Adjutant-General of Missouri for 1886" (Jefferson City, Mo.: Tribune Printing Company, State Printers and Binders, 1887), 7–8; Hartman and In-

However, the Bald Knobbers, despite their claims to the contrary, did not disband in April 1886. The beatings, whippings, and barn burnings continued unabated in Taney County. The Anti–Bald Knobbers continued to send letters to the adjutant general requesting assistance and claiming that the disbanding was "a farce."[22] Many Bald Knobbers insisted these night assaults were committed by men who were impostors or outlaws. Nonetheless, many in the community believed they heard the same voices in the middle of the night and that the official disbanding had only been to please the governor. While Kinney never again publicly appeared as the chief of the Bald Knobbers, many believed he still led the same men on raids of their political opponents' houses at night. The action that really brought the activities of the Taney County Bald Knobbers to an end was the murder of Nat Kinney in a store in Forsyth on August 20, 1888, by William Miles, an Anti–Bald Knobber. The Anti–Bald Knobbers had planned for nearly three years to kill Kinney and had finally done so. Kinney's death appears to have brought the organized activity of the Bald Knobbers in Taney County to an end.[23]

The Christian County chapter of the Bald Knobbers has often been presented as part of the same story as their Taney County counterparts. Although some scholars have chosen to treat the Christian County Bald Knobbers as part of the Taney County group, a close analysis of their membership and actions demonstrates that the two groups apparently shared little in the way of goals, membership, or basic nature—despite their having the same name. Unlike the Taney County group, the Christian County Bald Knobbers did not seem to have a

---

genthron, *Bald Knobbers,* 116–21; Castleman, *Bald Knobbers,* 17–18. A copy of the disbandment resolution can be found in the *Springfield Daily Herald,* April 14, 1886.

22. J. J. Reynolds, Forsyth, Missouri, to James Jamison, Jefferson City, Missouri, May 10, 1886, State Archives, Adjutant General's Records, box 88, file 7, "Miscellaneous Articles Bald Knobbers." This folder contains many letters sent to Jamison from March through August of 1886. All but two of these letters are from the Anti–Bald Knobbers. The letters by the Anti–Bald Knobbers become increasingly histrionic after Jamison's visit in April, arguing that they needed protection and that more violence was sure to break out if the state did not intervene soon. The letters from the Bald Knobber supporters downplay the threat and argue that the situation was not nearly as dire as the Anti–Bald Knobbers said it was.

23. *Springfield Daily Republican,* August 22, 1888; and Hartman and Ingenthron, *Bald Knobbers,* 213–15.

long-term political goal at all. Christian County had been a Republican stronghold since the Civil War, and there was no need for political terrorism to reclaim Christian County from the other party. In fact, the Christian County Bald Knobbers were formed primarily because of the presence of two illegal saloons in Chadwick at the terminus of the recently completed Springfield and Southern Railroad. It appears that most of the Bald Knobbers in Christian County wished to clean up Chadwick, for it was providing too much temptation for the wayward in the county. Like the Taney County Bald Knobbers, members of the Christian County chapter argued that the county had become too lawless; they even believed that the outlaws who were run out of Taney County by the Bald Knobbers had moved north into Christian County and needed to be taught a lesson. In short, it was these two fairly short-term goals that brought the Christian County Bald Knobbers together.

Unlike their Taney County counterparts, these men appeared to be interested more in establishing law and order in their county than in any sort of long-term political goal—at least in the beginning. The Christian County Bald Knobbers wore a mask that had been designed by the Taney County Knobbers but seldom worn by them. This fearsome mask included horns on top of a cambric skullcap.[24] The Christian County Bald Knobbers did very little during the active period of the Taney County Bald Knobbers (April 1885–April 1886). The Christian County chapter became active after the "official" demise of the Taney County chapter, in the summer of 1886. Led by David "Bull Creek" Walker, the Christian County vigilantes raided the two illegal saloons in Chadwick in July and August of 1886, pouring out the beer and whiskey into the main street in Chadwick.

However, this goal of enforcing law and order appears to have gone by the wayside quickly during the first few months of activity by the organization. The Christian County Bald Knobbers' activities went well beyond simply trying to clean up Chadwick. By the end of the summer of 1886, the vigilantes spent most of their time seeking vengeance against those who had criticized their group or its members in public. Many of their nightly beatings and assaults were to settle these types of personal scores. Within a few months, the Christian County

24. Castleman, *Bald Knobbers*, 9–10.

group degenerated into committing primarily these types of activities.[25] The vigilantes had become little more than criminals, committing just the type of crimes they had decried when they formed their group. Like their Taney County counterparts, the Christian County vigilantes became a force to be feared by those who opposed them or even by those who had said an unkind word about them to someone in passing.

As a close analysis of the backgrounds of more than sixty members demonstrates, the Christian County group consisted primarily of much younger men than in Taney County. These men clearly got a great thrill out of terrorizing their personal enemies. The average Christian County Bald Knobber was barely over twenty-nine years of age, meaning that they were generally much younger than their Taney County counterparts.[26] In fact, 63 percent of the Christian County group were young men in their teens and twenties. Of the remaining men, 23 percent were in their thirties and only 14 percent were over the age of forty. In regard to birthplace, 65 percent of these men were from Missouri, the vast majority of them having been born in Christian County. Twenty-four percent of the Christian County Knobbers came from the southern states of Tennessee, Arkansas, and Kentucky. Only 11 percent of the Christian County group came from the non-southern states of Illinois and Indiana. The Christian County group also appears to have had less to do with wartime activities and loyalties. Of course, the average member of this group would have been too young to have taken part in the Civil War. Only three members out of sixty known Christian County Bald Knobbers fought for the Union (Walker was one of the exceptions), and none of the Christian County Knobbers fought for the Confederacy. As far as occupations are concerned, the Christian County Bald Knobbers may have been the most typical Ozarkers of the three groups, with 93 percent of them working as farmers and farmhands; the only other occupations represented among their number were those of minister and merchant. Therefore, the connections between the Taney County group and the Christian County group were tenuous with regard to membership

25. Hartman and Ingenthron, *Bald Knobbers*, 139–53.
26. The biographical data of the Christian County Bald Knobbers analyzed here is drawn entirely from the U.S. Census Data for Christian County from 1880.

and goals; essentially the two groups shared the name "Bald Knob-bers," but not much else.

By March 1887, the reputation of the Christian County vigilante group had declined to the point where many in the county were ask-ing David Walker to follow the lead of the Taney County group and disband it. On March 11, 1887, despite attempts by Walker that very evening to convince members of the Christian County Bald Knobbers to disband, the group embarked upon a night assault on one of their perceived enemies, William Edens. Edens had been attacked once be-fore for speaking against the Bald Knobbers, and he had continued to criticize the group. The assault led to the deaths of William Edens and Charles Green, who were shot by the Bald Knobbers.[27]

It was this event that brought Ozark vigilantism to state and na-tional attention. Eventually, more than seventy of the Christian County Bald Knobbers were arrested and charged with a great number of crimes. However, only a few of the band were actually charged with the murders. Journalists from newspapers all across the nation cov-ered the trials of David Walker, William Walker, Wiley Mathews, and John Mathews.[28] All four were found guilty of murder and sentenced to hang. It appears that most residents of Taney and Christian coun-ties felt that the executions were pointless and wanted the sentences commuted, but Governor Francis refused to intervene. The May 10, 1889, executions of David and William Walker and John Mathews (Wiley Mathews escaped from the jail at Ozark four months before the executions) were national news as well.[29]

Many in the media believed that the executions would be the end of vigilantism and lawlessness in the Ozarks. Unfortunately, the hang-ings of Christian County Bald Knobbers did not end the culture of vi-olence that prevailed in southwest Missouri for the remainder of the

27. Hartman and Ingenthron, *Bald Knobbers*, 155–60. For a contemporary ac-count of the Edens-Green murders, see the *Springfield Leader*, March 17, 1887.

28. *Springfield Daily Herald*, March 20, 26, and 29, 1888. The most famous series of articles appeared in the *New York Sun* in December 1888. This series was later reprinted in the *Kimberling City Gazette* in August and September 1963.

29. *Springfield Daily Republican*, April 16, 1889; and Castleman, *Bald Knobbers*, 23–27. See also *Taney County Times*, May 16, 1889. For a more recent version of events, see Will Townsend, "The Day That Three Bald Knobbers Were Hanged," *Springfield News and Leader*, November 23, 1975, F2; and "Newspapers Tell Story of Hangings a Century Ago," *Ozark Headliner*, May 11, 1989, 11.

nineteenth century. This is particularly true in Taney County. During the next several years there continued to be gunfights between the former Bald Knobbers and the former Anti–Bald Knobbers. The most notorious of these gunfights led to the deaths of Sheriff Galba Branson and Ed Funk in 1889. Lynchings continued as well, including most particularly that of John Wesley Bright in March 1892.[30] Contrary to Kinney's claim, peace and quiet did not prevail after the disbanding of the Taney County Bald Knobbers in 1886 or even after the hangings of the Christian County Bald Knobbers in 1889. Law and order had not been restored, and the culture of violence continued. However, in Taney County, former Bald Knobbers had now gained control of county government—which was apparently what they were after all along.

Evidence of their success in achieving this goal can be seen in the election returns from Taney County during the Bald Knobber era and after. After the political terrorism and intimidation of the Bald Knobbers, Republicans in the county captured all of the county offices. While a Democrat or two would win a county office every now and then, the Republicans now ruled the political roost in Taney County. In 1890, the average margin of victory of Republicans in the county was two to one.[31]

An unfortunate legacy of the Civil War was this prevailing culture of violence and lawlessness in the Ozarks. The historian Richard Maxwell Brown has gone so far as to argue that violence and vigilantism during the Gilded Age were "legacies of the violent emotions and methods bred by the Civil War."[32] The war taught Taney County residents that the way to "win" a political dispute was to mobilize as many people as possible and to perpetrate violence against those who disagreed with them. It is therefore important to place the Bald Knobbers into historical context. The Bald Knobbers were not employing a new approach to local politics; instead, they were only showing they had learned very well the lessons from the Civil War and were applying them to the political present. The Bald Knobbers of Taney and

30. Hartman and Ingenthron, 245–85.

31. *Official Directory of Missouri,* 1883, 1885, 1887, 1889, and 1891; *Taney County Times,* November 15, 1888, and November 13, 1890.

32. Richard Maxwell Brown, *Strain of Violence: Historical Studies of American Violence and Vigilantism* (New York: Oxford University Press, 1975), 9.

Christian counties are best understood as a product of this culture of violence, not a departure from it. It should be no surprise that the Bald Knobbers in both counties purportedly began as an attempt to stem the tide of violence but eventually succumbed to it. In fact, one could argue that nighttime vigilantism, the vehicle that these men chose to effect political and cultural change, was shaped by this culture of violence emanating from the war. Given the history of the region during the war, it was just this type of violent solution that one would expect them to choose.

In light of this analysis, the events of the Bald Knobber era are consistent with the violent history of the region during the Civil War era. Regarding Taney County at least, instead of wondering why such violent clashes erupted between the Bald Knobbers and their enemies, perhaps we would gain more from posing a different question: Why was there relatively *little* violence during the antebellum era—what was different about the county then? Presumably it had as much, if not more, of a frontier element in its population and society than it did after the war. Did the war change the Ozarkers' ways that profoundly? Evidence from the present study suggests that the experiences of the Civil War and Reconstruction may indeed have impacted Ozark society in such a major way.

Unfortunately, the execution of the three Christian County Bald Knobbers was not likely to change much in Taney County. It would require more to transform the ways of the people who lived through the Civil War in the Ozarks. Nat Kinney was wrong in arguing that his Bald Knobbers band had won the "great struggle against the forces of evil." Some would view Kinney's band as merely a part of a much larger struggle against violence in the Ozarks—one that would last longer, even into the early twentieth century. In fact, some would argue that the activities of Kinney's Bald Knobbers, the Anti–Bald Knobbers, and the Christian County Bald Knobbers worked against their stated purpose—to restore law and order and stop violence. Their actions actually encouraged lawlessness and perpetuated the culture of violence.

Like members of the Ku Klux Klan in the South some two decades earlier, these men felt frustrated at every turn by the political realities of the 1880s. As George Rable has theorized in his study of violence in the South during Reconstruction, this extreme frustration and rage could lead men of the nineteenth century into committing violent extralegal acts to further their political ends. Interestingly enough, one could make the argument that, unlike the Ku Klux Klan of the immediate postwar years, the Bald Knobbers were quite successful in fulfilling their long-term goals of making Taney County a Republican stronghold. As the noted local historian Elmo Ingenthron put it, the violence of the 1880s "ushered Republicanism" into the county. Republicans had used the political terrorism of the Bald Knobber band to transform the only hotly contested county in southwestern Missouri into one that was solidly in their column from the middle 1880s to the present day. Nat Kinney argued that by 1886 the Bald Knobbers had won the "great struggle against the forces of evil." According to the Republicans of the Taney County Bald Knobbers, by the end of the 1880s, evil had been vanquished and good had finally triumphed.[33]

33. George C. Rable, *But There Was No Peace: The Role of Violence in the Politics of Reconstruction* (Athens: University of Georgia Press, 1984), 9–15, 101–21; Ingenthron, *Land of Taney,* 228; and Castleman, *Bald Knobbers,* 18.

Race, Citizenship, and the Origins of Organized Labor in Antebellum St. Louis

DANIEL A. GRAFF

On December 3, 1835, the newly formed United Benevolent Society of Journeymen Tailors launched the first strike by unionized workers in the city of St. Louis. Taking advantage of the perennial labor shortage in the rapidly growing river city, the journeymen presented their employers with a new price list for cutting and making garments. When the master tailors rejected the proposed wage hike and instead sought to cut costs by demanding an increase in the number of apprentices, the journeymen walked out. They immediately established a cooperative, the "Tailors Union Shop," and solicited the public's business in the city's leading newspapers. Over the next three months, the journeymen held firm until, one by one, the master tailors succumbed to the union's terms. On March 16, 1836, the journeymen tailors publicly announced a complete victory, declaring "perfect satisfaction in regard to the misunderstanding between themselves and the Master Tailors of this city."[1]

The author would like to thank the following for their assistance in improving this essay or the larger work of which it is a part: his professors at the University of Wisconsin–Madison, in particular Jeanne Boydston, Steve Kantrowitz, and David Zonderman (now at North Carolina State University); his graduate student colleagues in the Wisconsin History Department and the Teaching Assistants Association (AFT #3220), especially Eric Morser, Steve Burg, Sean Adams, and Brett Barker (all now moved on to greener pastures); individuals who provided constructive critical feedback on an earlier version of this essay at the 1999 North American Labor History Conference in Detroit, especially James Barrett, Mary Blewett, Jonathan Prude, and Dave Roediger; and, most importantly, for reasons personal, political, and professional, his partner, Nicole MacLaughlin.

1. For coverage of the strike, see the *St. Louis Commercial Bulletin and Missouri*

The 1835 tailors' dispute ushered in an era of unprecedented class conflict in early St. Louis, and over the next decade journeymen mechanics organized multiple craft unions, made plans to establish a city-wide labor council, and challenged traditional political allegiances by fielding an independent workingmen's ticket. In many aspects, the 1835 tailors' strike, as well as the local labor movement that emerged in its wake, paralleled the craft conflicts exploding in other cities in the 1820s and 1830s, disputes well chronicled by labor historians. Throughout the antebellum United States, growing economic competition propelled by transportation and financial innovations spurred the uneven, yet dramatic erosion of a traditional artisan mode of production, with its emphasis on craft-based regulation of labor and product markets, "just" prices and wages, and a harmony of interests. Increasingly in these years, entrepreneurial master mechanics squared off against their increasingly unionized journeymen employees over fundamental questions of production, work organization, and profits.[2]

Labor historians have paid considerable attention to the rhetoric that characterized these confrontations, in particular the efforts of both sides to claim fidelity to craft tradition and the legacy of artisan

---

Literary Register, December 7, 14, 18, 1835, and March 16, 1836; see also the *Missouri Republican,* December 17, 1835, and February 27, 1836. For evidence of the high demand for tailors in St. Louis, see the advertisements in the *St. Louis Commercial Bulletin,* August 17, 24, September 7, 1835.

The 1835 tailors' strike is generally recognized as the first instance of organized labor conflict in St. Louis. See John R. Commons et al., *History of Labour in the United States* (New York: Macmillan, 1918), 2:352–53; Halvor Gordon Melom, "The Economic Development of St. Louis, 1803–1846" (Ph.D. diss., University of Missouri, 1947), 304–7; and Gary Fink, "The Paradoxical Experiences of St. Louis Labor during the Depression of 1837," *Missouri Historical Society Bulletin* 26 (1969): 60–61. Russell M. Nolen mistakenly omits the tailors' dispute from his chronicle of early strikes in "The Labor Movement in St. Louis prior to the Civil War," *Missouri Historical Review* 34 (1940): 18–19.

2. For more details on the first labor movement of St. Louis, see Daniel A. Graff, "Forging an American St. Louis: Labor, Race, and Citizenship from the Louisiana Purchase to Dred Scott" (Ph.D. diss., University of Wisconsin–Madison, 2004). Among the multiple studies of artisan republicanism and the breakdown of craft production in the early to mid-nineteenth century, two representative and influential studies are Sean Wilentz, *Chants Democratic: New York City and the Rise of the American Working Class, 1788–1850* (New York: Oxford University Press, 1984); and Steven J. Ross, *Workers on the Edge: Work, Leisure, and Politics in Industrializing Cincinnati, 1788–1890* (New York: Columbia University Press, 1985).

republicanism inherited from the American Revolution. In their printed appeals for public support, both parties in the 1835 St. Louis tailors' strike certainly employed such language. The striking journeymen, for example, expressed confidence "that the public will sustain us in our endeavors to obtain a livelihood by an honorable course . . . [while] we maintain our independence towards those . . . taking advantage of our necessities." The employers countered that if any "society of mechanics" had the power to raise wages and control the labor market at will, "then there is an end to our independence," perhaps intentionally leaving ambiguous whether "our independence" referred to the employers specifically or to the community or the republic at large. In short, the experiences and responses of St. Louis craft workers in the 1830s represent a microcosm of the labor and political discord impacting urban America during the Jacksonian period, and this essay draws upon those studies of other cities that have been so important in recovering the tensions and conflicts surrounding early industrialization within the United States.[3]

At the same time, however, this essay draws equally from scholarship critical of these community-based studies of working-class formation. Critics such as Peter Way have argued that an emphasis on craft journeymen and their struggles paints a romanticized, heroic picture of the working-class past, one that excludes the majority of those—such as canal diggers, sweatshop workers, and teamsters, to name just a few—whose "common labor" fueled the industrial revolution yet who reaped few personal rewards for their efforts.[4] But it is

---

3. *St. Louis Commercial Bulletin,* December 18, 1835, January, 15, 1836. For an introduction to the scholarship on early U.S. industrialization, particularly from the perspective of the crafts, see Wilentz, *Chants Democratic;* Ross, *Workers on the Edge;* Alan Dawley, *Class and Community: The Industrial Revolution in Lynn* (Cambridge: Harvard University Press, 1976); Susan Hirsch, *Roots of the American Working Class: The Industrialization of the Crafts in Newark, 1800–1860* (Philadelphia: University of Pennsylvania Press, 1978); and Bruce Laurie, *Working People of Philadelphia, 1800–1850* (Philadelphia: Temple University Press, 1980). For a synthesis emphasizing the centrality of craft conflict and breakdown to understanding labor history, see Bruce Laurie, *Artisans into Workers: Labor in Nineteenth-Century America* (New York: Hill and Wang, 1989).

4. Peter Way, "Evil Humors and Ardent Spirits: The Rough Culture of Canal Construction Laborers," *Journal of American History* 79 (1993): 1397–428; Peter Way, "Labour's Love Lost: Observations on the Historiography of Class and Ethnicity in the Nineteenth Century," *Journal of American Studies* 28 (1994): 1–22; Peter Way,

more than the exclusion or marginalization of nonartisan labor that has drawn criticism from scholars; it is also the emphasis on crafts-men as class-conscious actors defined largely, at times solely, in rela-tion to their employers. As historians of women in particular have demonstrated, journeymen were agents whose strikes, unions, and political participation were shaped as much by their gender as by class interests, significantly complicating, and in many ways compromising, their responses to an emerging economic order prioritizing private property, entrepreneurship, and labor as a commodity.[5] Just as impor-tant, as David Roediger has most forcefully asserted, most studies of artisans tend to neglect, if not completely ignore, the increasing racism exhibited by white workingmen during a period defined as much by the politics of slavery and sectionalism, urban race riots, and the min-strel stage as by the rise of labor unions, strikes, and class rhetoric.[6]

These critiques have all contributed to labor historians' growing sense of the complicated nature and conflicted meanings of work, wages, identity, and politics during the early to mid-nineteenth cen-tury. However, the insights have not been applied to the intensive study of a single community over several years, which is still the best avenue for understanding the complexity of political and economic developments in the nineteenth century, specifically the importance of the local context within which labor struggles and class formation historically developed. This essay, and the larger research project from which it stems, seeks to do just that, through an exploration of the un-derstudied interior metropolis of St. Louis.[7]

Common Labor: Workers and the Digging of North American Canals, 1780–1860 (New York: Cambridge University Press, 1993).

5. See, for example, Mary Blewett, *Men, Women, and Work: Class, Gender, and Pro-test in the New England Shoe Industry, 1780–1910* (Urbana: University of Illinois Press, 1988); Jeanne Boydston, *Home and Work: Housework, Wages, and the Ideology of Labor in the Early Republic* (New York: Oxford University Press, 1990); and Ava Baron, "Gender and Labor History: Learning from the Past, Looking to the Future," in Ava Baron, ed., *Work Engendered: Toward a New History of American Labor* (Ithaca: Cornell University Press, 1991).

6. David Roediger, *The Wages of Whiteness: Race and the Making of the American Working Class* (New York: Verso, 1991); see also Eric Lott, *Love and Theft: Blackface Minstrelsy and the American Working Class* (New York: Oxford University Press, 1993); Noel Ignatiev, *How the Irish Became White* (New York: Routledge, 1995).

7. This and succeeding paragraphs draw from material more fully explored in Graff, "Forging an American St. Louis," chapters 2 and 3.

This essay in particular looks at the complicated interconnections of race and class, as St. Louis offers a perfect site to explore how slavery and race shaped the thoughts and actions of the workers who forged the city's first labor movement. For while St. Louis was developing much like New York, Philadelphia, and Cincinnati (and increasingly connected to its eastern counterparts via steamboats, railroads, and the goods and people they transported), only St. Louis resided in a slave state. This significantly complicated the city's transition to a market economy rooted in wage labor, and it just as significantly colored its politics throughout the antebellum era. The 1835 tailors' strike, for example, emerged in the midst of an ongoing racial panic gripping the city of St. Louis, and this larger context governed the trajectory and resolution of the conflict.

The 1835 St. Louis tailors' strike—and most of the labor struggles emerging in its wake—represented a conflict between white employers and white workingmen. But it was fought and won on the terrain of race. By 1835, white St. Louisans had fundamentally accepted an understanding of race that associated African Americans, especially free blacks, with disorder and public danger. Using the local press as a public forum, the master tailors attempted to redirect this discourse toward the white journeymen and to associate their strike with the hazards presumably posed by the presence of free persons of color in the city. The tactic failed—not because racial discourse was unpersuasive in antebellum St. Louis, but rather because it had become so deeply persuasive. By the time of organized labor's emergence in St. Louis, the white community simply could not be successfully mobilized against itself.

Over the previous fifteen years, the St. Louis elite had worked to impose municipal order, labor discipline, and racial separation upon a diverse workforce through the practice of racial policing. Racial policing consisted of two interrelated components: one, the demonization of free blacks as agents of disorder; and two, the enlistment of white men of "the lower sort" in the enforcement of racial order. Those efforts reached a peak in late 1835, as city leaders publicly fretted about an alleged influx of abolitionists, vagrants, gamblers, and free blacks intent on liberating the slaves of St. Louis, murdering their white masters, and destroying the town. The master tailors' characterization of their striking workers represented an attempt to transfer the community mobilization against free blacks onto another subordinate (though admittedly less subordinate) group, white workingmen. The failure of that strategy revealed the constraints upon employers in disciplining their white employees in the face of white workingmen's assertions of active citizenship, not least through active participation in racial policing. In short, then, to understand fully the 1835 tailors' strike, as well as the emergence of the labor movement that followed in its wake over the next half dozen years, we must place it in the context of an emerging politics of citizenship, race, and order in antebellum St. Louis.

Throughout the tailors' dispute, both the striking workers and their employers waged a battle for public support in the pages of the local press. One week after the journeymen announced the formation of the tailors' cooperative in early December 1835, they published a second notice encouraging the community to patronize their fully operating "Union" shop. In a clear sign that they were organized, dedicated, and intent on expanding their "challenge" to the master tailors, the journeymen solicited "ten or fifteen workmen." Significantly, the call for workers emphasized that "none but *regular men* need apply." The striking journeymen's call for only "regular men" mocked the paternalist pretensions of master artisans and employers, whose advertisements seeking to employ journeymen customarily called for those who were "sober" and "industrious," and often closed with the sentence "None other need apply."[8] By advertising their cooperative venture in the same newspaper favored by the city's leading merchants and employers, the striking journeymen challenged not only the master tailors' businesses, but also their heretofore unquestioned claim to determine what traits constituted good workers—and, just as important, good citizens. For the striking journeymen, "regular men" were those who refused to buckle at the boss's claims of superiority and supported the efforts of the United Benevolent Society of Journeymen Tailors, actively expressing their citizenship through these acts of independence and resistance.

8. *St. Louis Commercial Bulletin,* December 14, 1835; unless otherwise noted, italics are presented as in the original. For examples of "help wanted" ads offering employment to journeymen, see ibid., July 27, September 7, 25, October 21, November 19, 1835, May 2, 1836. Each ad called specifically for those possessing sobriety and industriousness, while two contained the sentence "None other need apply."

The journeymen's notice sparked a quick rebuke from the six leading tailoring firms in St. Louis, who published a long manifesto denouncing the strike and strikers as disorderly, unlawful, and violent, and calling upon the community to suppress the workers' insubordination.[9] On one level, the journeymen's militant language and the master tailors' alarmist response seem reminiscent of many other craft disputes in the Jacksonian era. However, given the context of the specific history of St. Louis, as well as the timing of the tailors' strike, such rhetoric carried implicitly racial meanings.

Calling attention to "the conduct of journeymen tailors in this city . . . [that] has become so intolerably oppressive, as to make it necessary for us to appeal to the public," the employers charged their workers with pursuing a "violent and unlawful course" and a "crusade against order and law." In condemning the journeymen tailors, the masters refused to distinguish between the act of unionization itself, the tactic of the strike, or the workers' particular demands. Displaying a strong paternalism, the master tailors quite simply expressed incredulity at their employees' audacity. To the master tailors, the cooperative was a ridiculous venture, since the strikers were "offering to work for less than they get as journeymen, and taking upon themselves all the risk and the responsibility." "As it is impossible that they can [make] a living in this manner," the manifesto continued, "it is evident that their only object is to force the master tailors to submit to their extortions."[10]

The master tailors also attacked the journeymen's work habits and leisure pursuits, calling them "a discredit to our city." According to the master tailors, their employees were lazy, drunken vagrants with no stake in society or concern for the community. Contrasted to "the steady and industrious workmen" the masters would have liked to employ, the journeymen were described as "a set of roving, dissipated,

9. Ibid., December 18, 1835. To be more specific, the employers published three separate notices in this issue, including one each from the master tailors of Louisville and Cincinnati, whose journeymen were also striking. Because the six St. Louis tailor firms signing the notice expressed their complete agreement with the declarations from the other two cities, I have treated the three notices as a single text reflecting the arguments and strategy of the St. Louis employers. Whether or not the journeymen in the three cities were coordinating strike activity is unclear.

10. Ibid.

unsettled men, having no fixed residence, and no character to lose." Not only did the journeymen tailors defame the craft by "encouraging each other in defrauding their employers and the public" through enforcing all workshops "to come down to the same standard," but also they engaged in dubious acts outside of work. In the words of the master tailors, "They have insisted upon occupying our back shops on Sunday, for the purpose of drinking and playing cards, and when we object to their immorality, they threaten to leave our employ." The "immoral and overbearing conduct of our journeymen," the masters continued, had turned their workshops into "scenes of riot and debauchery, at night, and on the Sabbath." Nearly overnight, the city's most "competent workmen" (as praised by the city's tailoring firms in their advertisements just three months before) had transformed into a motley crew of intruders bent on disrupting the community.[11]

The employers' characterization of their journeymen employees as shiftless and unruly suggests the emergence in St. Louis of struggles over time, work, and leisure characterized by many labor historians of the nineteenth-century United States. But the masters' extreme denunciations went beyond the rhetoric of industrial morality to tap idioms and images specifically associated with free African Americans in St. Louis. In the masters' words, the journeymen tailors' actions were "calculated to destroy that good order upon which society is founded." If not stopped, they predicted, the journeymen's walkout "will strike at every root of social order." Deploying language normally reserved for demonizing free blacks, the master tailors attempted to frighten other employers and city elites into opposing the walkout, by force if necessary. As they declared, "We ask that protection of law and public sentiment to which every industrious citizen is entitled. Our case is that of all other mechanics; if our journeymen can take the law into their own hands, can trample on justice and morality, work when they please, and ask their own prices, other workmen will follow their example." The master tailors closed their appeal by calling upon the city to "put down a lawless band of depredators, who . . . if not checked, will corrupt the whole body of the working classes who may be weak enough to be visited by their bad example." Faced with an

11. Ibid. For expressions of craft pride that boast of superior wares and workers, see the tailor ads in ibid., July 6, September 21, 30, 1835.

unfamiliar situation—the first strike by unionized journeymen in the city's history—the master tailors responded as local elites had often done in early St. Louis to threats, real or imagined, from subordinate groups: they called for coordinated action by the city and "the public" to suppress the subversive activity.[12]

While the harsh attacks on the journeymen's character may seem familiar in the context of craft conflicts in the 1830s, to fully understand their resonance in St. Louis, we must look to the already well-established public discourse of race in the developing city. The employers' denunciation of the journeymen and their calls for public suppression of the walkout bear a striking similarity to the maligning of and mobilization against the free black community by local leaders and prominent citizens in the years following St. Louis's integration into the United States in the wake of the Louisiana Purchase in 1803. Conceptions of free blacks as disorderly, insubordinate, and violent made their first appearance in the territorial era, but they were explicitly codified in the 1820 constitution of Missouri, which obligated the legislature "[t]o prevent free negroes and mulattoes from coming to, and settling in this state, under any pretext whatsoever."[13]

The constitutional mandate to exclude free blacks from Missouri emerged from a struggle over slavery and citizenship animating the state's founding constitutional convention, where elite proslavery ad-

12. Ibid., December 18, 1835. Perhaps the master tailors, self-described as "mechanics," represented an aspiring, yet uncertain class anxious to claim the mantle of leadership traditionally enjoyed by St. Louis merchants and professionals—a leadership whose privileges included defining municipal order and mobilizing the community against agents threatening that order. For an introduction to the scholarship on industrial morality, see Herbert G. Gutman, "Work, Culture, and Society in Industrializing America, 1815–1919," *American Historical Review* 78 (1973): 531–88; David R. Roediger and Philip S. Foner, *Our Own Time: A History of American Labor and the Working Day* (New York: Verso, 1989), 1–42; and David Brody, "Time and Work during Early American Industrialization," *Labor History* 30 (1989): 5–46.

13. This essay draws extensively upon the rich literature on free and enslaved urban African Americans in the nineteenth-century United States. The standard treatments are Richard C. Wade, *Slavery in the Cities: The South, 1820–1860* (New York: Oxford University Press, 1964); Ira Berlin, *Slaves without Masters: The Free Negro in the Antebellum South* (New York: Pantheon Books, 1974); and Leonard P. Curry, *The Free Black in Urban America, 1800–1850: The Shadow of a Dream* (Chicago: University of Chicago Press, 1981).

vocates squared off against antislavery forces intent on securing white manhood suffrage and ballot voting. Forged from these conflicts was an "internal Missouri Compromise" granting all white men full citizenship while guaranteeing the permanent preservation of slavery (the state government was practically forbidden from abolishing the institution). The 1820 Missouri constitution thus constructed a political-economic order with a firm racial line separating white citizens from black slaves, and it marked free blacks as unwelcome intruders. As one local leader declared in light of the divisions concerning slavery and suffrage, all white St. Louisans still agreed that a "free black population ought not be tolerated!"[14]

But in spite of the constitutional restriction barring their entry, free blacks flocked to St. Louis. Especially with the widespread introduction of steamboats by the 1820s, St. Louis captured an increasing amount of the interior commerce of the republic, as well as the provisions trade for both westward migrants and the U.S. army's frontier outposts. Poised at the intersection of the Mississippi, the Missouri, and the Ohio—the interior rivers whose currents acted as both boundaries separating and conduits linking much of the free and slave states and territories of the nation—St. Louis beckoned a diverse workforce consisting of whites of various origins, free blacks, and black slaves, many of them hired out and living on their own. In 1830, for example, St. Louis's small but growing population of nearly six thousand was classified as 75 percent white, 20 percent slave, and 5 percent free black. Hence, fully one in four St. Louis residents were designated as "negro or mulatto."[15]

14. *Missouri Gazette and Public Advertiser,* April 12, 1820. For a fuller discussion of the "internal Missouri Compromise," see Graff, "Forging an American St. Louis," chapter 2.

15. For the population figures cited throughout this essay, I have used the tables in Maximilian Ivan Reichard, "The Origins of Urban Police: Freedom and Order in Antebellum St. Louis" (Ph.D. diss., Washington University, St. Louis, 1975), Appendix A, 320–31. Reichard integrates successive U.S. censuses, city directories, and St. Louis newspaper reports to create reliable estimates from sketchy data. Calculations such as percentage of the whole and percentage increases over time are mine. For the economic growth of early St. Louis, see Melom, "Economic Development"; Richard C. Wade, *The Urban Frontier: The Rise of Western Cities, 1790–1830* (1959; reprint, Urbana: University of Illinois Press, 1996), 161–202; and Glenn E. Holt, "The Shaping of St. Louis, 1763–1860" (Ph.D. diss., University of Chicago, 1975).

The 1830s represented a takeoff period in the urbanization of St. Louis, as the city's population exploded by nearly 300 percent over the course of the decade. Although by 1840 whites made up a larger share of the population (87 percent) than in 1830, all three categories of residents showed significant growth. The free black community, for example, nearly doubled in size during that decade, climbing to 510 (from 287 in 1830). In 1840, fully 13 percent of the 16,000 inhabitants of St. Louis were classified as negro or mulatto. And because the city's river economy fostered a transient labor force of remarkable mobility and diversity, the free black or slave population at any given time might be larger than the official estimates indicate.[16]

In order to maintain racial order, labor discipline, and the security of slavery in the face of such a potentially disruptive workforce, St. Louis's political and economic leaders built upon the "internal" Missouri compromise embodied by the 1820 state constitution, which created the political and legal foundation for the emergence of a system of racial policing. In the decades following 1820, the state constitution represented a precedent to which white St. Louis leaders repeatedly referred as they attempted to prevent social, economic, and political alliances among the working population in the initial years of the city's rapid economic growth. Deploying a variety of legal and extralegal strategies, local elites increasingly demonized the free black population as the cause of all disorder in expanding St. Louis.

First and foremost, St. Louis elites secured the passage of state laws and local ordinances to govern the working population. Even before statehood, the territorial government enacted an elaborate slave code determined to reassure local slaveholders in the protection of their property. The 1804 law prohibited slaves from leaving their owner's house without a pass, placed tight restrictions on slave gatherings, and denied owners from allowing any slave to "go at large, and trade as a free man" or to "hire him or herself out." Moreover, this initial slave code legislated the behavior not only of owners and slaves, but also of other members of the community, prohibiting "any white person, free negro, or mulatto" from meeting with, harboring, or trading any com-

16. Reichard, "Origins of Urban Police," Appendix A, 325. Reichard ignores nativity and includes European immigrants in the white totals. Significant numbers of European immigrants did not begin coming to St. Louis until the following decade; by 1850, amazingly, roughly one-half of St. Louis residents would be foreign-born.

modities with any slave, without the master's permission. Establishing a pattern that would last for decades, the local government of St. Louis enacted an ordinance in 1811 that built upon and detailed more fully the restrictions and penalties sketched out in the territorial slave code. The ordinance prohibited slaves from riding horses, outlawed anyone from selling or giving slaves liquor, forbade "every free person of color, giving balls, amusements or public diversion" and from admitting slaves without written permission, and imposed fines on "every white person who shall associate with slaves at their Balls or other amusements."[17] In sum, territorial and local legislation in St. Louis constructed strict boundaries on the mobility and sociability of slaves, outlawed their social interaction with free persons, and closely monitored the free black population.

Although at times these laws recognized a distinction between slaves and free persons of color, the overall thrust of the early legislation governing slavery treated the two groups as nearly indistinguishable. The 1804 slave code, for example, authorized death for any "negro or other slave" conspiring to revolt, while also prohibiting masters of ships from transporting "any servant whatsoever, or any negro or mulatto, or other slave out of this district." In addition, no "negro or mulatto" could serve as a witness in court against a white person.[18] This conflation of free blacks with slaves in the laws regulating slavery suggests that, at least in the minds of territorial-era lawmakers, race was a more important indicator of difference than the line separating slaves from free persons; moreover, it reveals an era before free blacks had become singularly defined as the agents of disorder. That would change in the wake of the internal Missouri Compromise.

Seizing the mandate granted by the 1820 state constitution, the Missouri general assembly revised the territorial slave code in 1825 and established a separate code for "free negroes and mulattoes." For

17. "A Law Entitled a Law Respecting Slaves," passed by the Governor and the Judges of the Territory of Indiana, October 1, 1804, *Laws of a Public and General Nature of the District of Louisiana, of the Territory of Louisiana, of the Territory of Missouri, and of the State of Missouri, up to the Year 1824*, 27–33; "An Ordinance Concerning Slaves in the Town of St. Louis," February 5, 1811, *Ordinances of the Board of Trustees of the Town of St. Louis, 1811 to 1823* (typescript edition at the St. Louis Public Library, n.d.), 1–5.

18. "Law Entitled a Law Respecting Slaves," 1804, 27–33.

the most part, the 1825 slave law merely integrated various laws passed since 1804 into a single code. The new free black code, on the other hand, declared, "hereafter, no free negro or mulatto, other than a citizen of the some one of the United States, shall come into this state under any pretext whatsoever." Free blacks unable to prove either their U.S. citizenship or their right of local residence could be jailed, fined, and ordered to depart the state, while anyone bringing a free black into the state without a "certificate of citizenship" could be fined five hundred dollars.[19] By the 1820s, it is clear that state lawmakers in Missouri increasingly saw free blacks as a problem, and they attempted to either banish them from the state or deny them any modicum of respect or safety in their communities.

In the meantime, the St. Louis city council and mayor established a city patrol in 1826, whose duty was "to apprehend all persons, of every colour, who may be found disturbing individual repose, or the general peace." The patrol was directed to keep "an especial eye upon negro houses, and other places of rendezvous for slaves and coloured people." This patrol ordinance also placed further restrictions on black assemblies of any kind ("other than those for the worship of God"), requiring written permission from the mayor.[20] Taken together, the overall effect of the flurry of state and local legislation represented nothing less than a legal assault upon the free black community St. Louis.

In 1835, the legal harassment of the free black community peaked with the state legislature's revision of the code for "free negroes and mulattoes." Henceforth, all free blacks in Missouri were required to apply for a license to remain in the state. Any "negro or mulatto acting as a free person" without proof of local residency or citizenship from another state could be treated as a runaway slave; at minimum, the individual faced a hefty fine and expulsion from the state. Even more

19. "A Law Respecting Slaves," January 15, 1825, *Laws of the State of Missouri, Revised and Digested, 1825,* 741–46; "An Act Concerning Negroes and Mulattoes," January 7, 1825, ibid., 600–602. In a sign that the lawmakers understood the crucial labor performed by free blacks, primarily in the growing St. Louis economy, the free black code exempted boat workers and servants of visitors, as long as they stayed no longer than six months at a time.

20. "An Ordinance Establishing and Regulating a Patrol for This City," February 9, 1826, *Ordinances of St. Louis, Revised, 1828,* 59–62.

draconian than the code it replaced, the revised code required county courts to bind out all free black children as "apprentices and servants" until the age of twenty-one. But, as opposed to the law governing white apprentices, masters were not obligated to teach "coloured apprentice[s] to . . . read and write" or give them "a knowledge of arithmetic." In addition, no black apprentice could be placed "in company with a free white apprentice, to be taught any trade or occupation, except by the consent of the parents" of the white child.[21]

By the mid-1830s, then, state and local lawmakers had constructed a legal foundation for the maintenance of slave subordination, labor discipline, and racial order. But legislation was one thing; enforcement was another. Noting that such attempts to restrict and monitor every aspect of black life represented "enacting legislation impossible of enforcement," one historian of early St. Louis has concluded that those "[c]itizens who valued order were not willing to spend the energy and resources necessary to enforce all the laws all the time."[22] There is certainly some truth to this statement, but local leaders in St. Louis were plagued less with a lack of will and more by economic self-interest. On the one hand, elites in St. Louis—fearful of lower-class interracial activity and its impact on the sustainability of slavery—effectively demonized the free black population as unwelcome intruders intent on creating chaos or fomenting violence by their sheer presence within the city. On the other hand, these same individuals recognized the value of the services that free black workers provided, whether as servants in their homes or laborers loading and unloading the steamboats that brought the city wealth and prominence.

Rarely did employers or city officials publicly acknowledge the centrality of free black workers to the city's economy, but one instance is illuminating in this respect. In June 1831, the city council passed an ordinance demanding that all free black residents obtain a license for residency by September 15. Four days after the deadline had passed, the board extended the due date to December 1, explaining, "it is not the intention of this board to put any of that class of persons to unnecessary

21. "An Act Concerning Free Negroes and Mulattoes," March 14, 1835, *Revised Statutes of Missouri, 1835*, 413–17. See also the law on apprentices, March 17, 1835, *Revised Statutes of Missouri, 1835*, 68.
22. Reichard, "Origins of Urban Police," 114, 94.

trouble or expenses."[23] Torn between the need for free black labor and the simultaneous belief that free black labor undermined the social order, elite St. Louisans whipsawed back and forth between accepting and rejecting free blacks as legitimate, if admittedly marginalized, participants in the local economy.

The result was not the active enforcement of the slave and free black codes, but periodic outbursts in the form of "citizens' meetings," extralegal conventions called by local leaders to address alleged problems of disorder, disease, and violence. These meetings often produced resolutions denouncing free blacks and self-hired slaves, appointed committees of vigilance to enforce resolutions or existing laws, and threatened free blacks with organized repression or exile. Less common, but just as important, local elites coordinated extralegal mob actions that targeted segments of the free black population for violence.

As early as 1824, for example, a group of "several citizens" called the public's attention to the problem of "Disorderly Negroes." The group denounced slaves *"going at large and hiring their own time"* and threatened to arrest and sell any whose masters did not assume responsibility for their behavior immediately, in accordance with the state's slave code. As these anonymous individuals put it, self-hiring slaves, "in conjunction with the free Negroes, seduce, & corrupt our servants, by their idle dissolute and thievish habits."[24] This public notice suggests the following: these were wealthy individuals (they had servants); they had a knowledge of state law; and they possessed the social standing necessary to have the city's oldest and most prominent newspaper, the *Missouri Republican,* publish their declaration (one that included a threat to take the law into their own hands). Such meetings and public announcements represented the central mechanisms of racial policing as they developed in the 1820s and 1830s.

Alongside these practices of racial policing emerged a rhetoric that identified "half-free slaves" and free blacks as the agents of disorder, insubordination, and violence—not simply in regard to slave discipline, but in terms of the community generally. In a show of support for the "citizens" protesting "disorderly negroes" above, the *Missouri Republican's* editor reprinted the state law that forbade self-hiring slaves

23. Ibid., 107–9 (quotation from the Board of Aldermen on 109).
24. *Missouri Republican,* July 12, 1824.

and empowered "any persons" of the community to apprehend viola-
tors and take them to the county justice of the peace. But the editor
went beyond that to elaborate on "the evils resulting from the neglect"
of slave owners who permitted slaves to hire their own time. According to this influential St. Louisan, these slaves "take upon themselves at once the airs of freemen, and often resort to very illicit modes
to meet their monthly payment. Being left to their own choice, they
refuse to work for those who would keep them under salutary discipline. They become unsteady and vicious, and corrupt their associ-
ates, and perhaps at length resort to theft as an easier mode of paying
their masters."[25] Revealed here are the anxieties of an employing class
concerned with labor discipline and social stability, and finding their
cause in the alleged liberties of the free and "half-free" black population.

Several months later, again in the *Republican*, a letter signed simply
"MANY" returned to the problem of slaves hiring their own time. The
letter denounced the "servants of this place" as "vicious" and concluded that "the prime source of their bad habits is the liberty, which
they have to a great extent hitherto enjoyed, of hiring themselves out
(thus having the control of their own time)." Possessing "a general license to commit iniquity," self-hiring slaves staged "noisy assemblage[s]," bringing together "all classes and descriptions of whites and
blacks." The writers urged the city to disperse any "mixed assembly,"
and they also hoped that "those who rank themselves with the grade
of *masters* will never degrade themselves by mingling in such assemblies."[26] Clearly, elites feared the actions not only of slaves and free
blacks, but also of whites who refused to obey the laws prohibiting interracial liaisons unsanctioned by leading citizens.

But while elite St. Louisans concerned for social order scrutinized
the actions of slaves and whites for signs of suspicious or threatening
activity, they increasingly singled out free blacks as the prime agents
of disorder. Wherever free blacks were found, intoned the editor of the
Missouri Herald in 1827, the slave population became "most depraved
and licentious." Strongly supporting the efforts of the American
Colonization Society to relocate ex-slaves from the United States to

25. Ibid., July 19, 1824.
26. Ibid., October 4, 1824.

Africa, the editor demanded the removal of free blacks from St. Louis in the interest of "our national and individual safety." Any attempt to "ameliorate the situation of the [free] negro" would only fail, he continued, for "in proportion as he approximates the white man, he becomes dangerous. . . . [T]he white man will never suffer him to rise to the same civil, political, or social level in which he himself moves and lives." Put simply, prominent white St. Louisans argued that the mere presence of free blacks created disorder. As the resolution of one public meeting bemoaned, a free black population represented "one of the greatest evils that can be inflicted on a community in a slave state."[27]

Free blacks suffered unceasing criticism for being "rowdy" or "boisterous," especially on Sundays. As early as 1817, for example, pastor Timothy Peck complained of congregations of free blacks drinking and dancing on Sundays, in his words, "quite to the annoyance of all seriously-disposed persons." Fourteen years later, the editor of the *Missouri Republican* derided the "African church" and complained that the peace of "the whole neighborhood is effectually destroyed by the unusual length of time to which their meetings extend, and the yellings which invariably attend them." A county grand jury convened in 1832 to consider the problem of "negro assemblages" and free black "balls" that continued to attract slaves as well as whites of "low character" and "vicious habits." The grand jury concluded that such gatherings inevitably led to "bacchanalian scenes" of excessive drinking and interracial liaisons, tending to "familiarize the blacks with a practical equality with the white person which is destructive of that subordination and submissiveness that must be preserved."[28] Increasingly,

27. *Missouri Herald,* February 21, 1827, quoted in Reichard, "Origins of Urban Police," 105–6; public meeting resolution quoted in Lloyd A. Hunter, "Slavery in St. Louis, 1804–1860," *Missouri Historical Society Bulletin* 30 (July 1974): 244. By 1831 (and perhaps earlier), the American Colonization Society had an active chapter in St. Louis; prominent members included nine-term mayor William Carr Lane, Hamilton Gamble (the Missouri secretary of state in the 1820s), and former congressman Edward Bates.

28. Peck quoted in Hunter, "Slavery in St. Louis, 1804–1860"; *Missouri Republican,* September 20, 1831, and "St. Louis County Grand Jury Presentment," *Missouri Republican,* January 31, 1832, both quoted in Reichard, "Origins of Urban Police," 112. The uncritical characterization of free blacks as inherently disorderly has endured in the scholarship on early St. Louis. Janet Hermann, for example, refers to black boat workers as "a rowdy lot whose boisterous conduct disturbed the respect-

St. Louis leaders concluded, the preservation of the necessary "subordination and submissiveness" required not only the tightening of restrictions on free-black-initiated gatherings, but also the total destruction of the free black community.

In sum, in the first fifteen years of Missouri's statehood, St. Louis elites, elected officials, and newspaper editors constructed a racialized rhetoric of disorder in their attempts to impose order in early St. Louis. Ever fearful of slave insubordination or flight, and always wary of biracial social interaction, they effectively demonized the free black population as unwelcome intruders intent on creating chaos or fomenting violence by their sheer presence within the city. By 1835, the language of disorder was so thoroughly racialized that, when the mayor called a public meeting to mobilize the community against another purported menace, (presumably white) gamblers run out of cities to the south and allegedly headed upriver to St. Louis, a local editor termed the gamblers "even worse than free negroes."[29] In short, to classify disorder in 1830s St. Louis, the obvious reference point was the free black population.

The efforts at racial policing peaked in 1835, just weeks before the outbreak of the tailors' strike. The state legislature revised its free black code, which henceforth required the registration of every free black by county courts and established strict guidelines for those eligible to remain within Missouri. Following up on the state legislature's new mandate, St. Louis courts began processing free black applications for residency and banished many free persons of color from the city. The new state legislation and the city's determination to enforce it represented local responses to the larger national crises over slavery and mob violence occasioned by the rise of the abolitionist movement throughout pockets of the urbanizing North. Demanding the immediate and uncompensated abolition of slavery, antislavery agitators like William Lloyd Garrison sparked great controversy throughout the republic, especially when the American Anti-Slavery Society launched

---

able citizens," and Donnie Bellamy states that "rowdyism by free blacks" caused consternation within the white community. See Janet Hermann, "The McIntosh Affair," *Missouri Historical Society Bulletin* 26 (1970): 124–25; and Donnie Bellamy, "Free Blacks in Antebellum Missouri, 1820–1860," *Missouri Historical Review* 67 (1973): 209.

29. *Missouri Republican,* May 14, 1835, quoted in Reichard, "Origins of Urban Police," 122.

its pamphlet campaign through the U.S. mail, threatening to flood all corners of the country with antislavery propaganda in the summer of 1835.[30]

In the midst of the legal assault upon the free black community, the local press mounted a vigorous antiabolition campaign, filling their pages with horrific stories of the work of Garrison and other anti-slavery advocates. Reprinting (and celebrating) incidents of antiabolition mob actions from Utica, New York, to Charleston, South Carolina, St. Louis editors warned white residents that the "mad schemes of the Abolitionists" were surely spreading westward. By September, when the capture of a white "slave kidnapper" outside of St. Louis coincided with the appearance of a local weekly newspaper featuring antislavery editorials, the city seemed on the verge of a racial panic.[31]

Characteristic of previous city actions addressing alleged problems of racial control, city leaders called for a "citizens' meeting" to nip the problem of abolitionism in the bud. Convening on October 24, 1835, and many times over the next several weeks, the "citizens" formed two working committees, one to address abolitionists and the other to confront "the free colored portion of our population." Their resolutions represented the logical culmination of the practice of racial policing in St. Louis. Justifying action in the name of "the Constitution of this State," the "citizens" declared: "[E]xperience has proved, that [it] is highly injurious to the good order, well-being, and safety of this community, to permit free persons of color to reside permanently therein." Therefore, they passed resolutions to "guard . . . against the

30. "An Act Concerning Free Negroes and Mulattoes," March 14, 1835, *Revised Statutes of the State of Missouri, Revised and Digested by the Eighth General Assembly, 1834–1835*, 413–17. For examples of the enforcement of the ordinance, see the "Mayor's Court" decisions in *St. Louis Commercial Bulletin*, October 14, 1835. Historians have marked 1835 as a peak year of the abolitionist movement's rise to prominence nationally. See the standard accounts in Leonard L. Richards, *"Gentlemen of Property and Standing": Anti-Abolition Mobs in Jacksonian America* (New York: Oxford University Press, 1970), 47–81; and James Brewer Stewart, *Holy Warriors: The Abolitionists and American Slavery* (New York: Hill and Wang, 1976), 50–73.

31. *St. Louis Commercial Bulletin*, September 2, October 19, 21, 23, 1835. The *St. Louis Observer*, nominally serving the Presbyterian community in the St. Louis region and beyond, had been active since 1833, but only in mid-1835 did editor Elijah P. Lovejoy begin consistently opposing slavery. See the issues beginning September 10, 1835.

ill consequences which have resulted from allowing free persons of color to reside among us." Committees of vigilance for each ward were appointed to mobilize the white community to locate all free blacks living illegally in St. Louis, compile a list, and then force their removal. Even steamboat captains arriving at the port were requested to submit lists of free blacks aboard. Whether or not the resolutions were enforceable, they represented the most dramatic attempt yet to regulate and repress free black St. Louisans.[32]

Analyzing the crisis in October 1835, the editor of the *St. Louis Commercial Bulletin* could have been describing the practice of racial policing as it had evolved over the previous fifteen years, in particular the association of free blacks as the agents of disorder, insubordination, and violence. He summarized his point of view in blunt terms:

> [Regarding the] just cause of repugnance entertained by our citizens toward the free blacks, which infest our city in hordes, we believe there now exists but one sentiment. That they should be expelled [from] the city, is the solemn declaration of all we have heard express an opinion on the subject. Their excesses have become so flagrant and enormous, that it is time some active measures were adopted to secure the future peace and safety of our city. . . . The nightly riots in our streets, and the use of infamous language, and [the] impudent bearing of these *"gentlemen in black,"* call loudly for correction, and we sincerely hope measures will be taken . . . which will effectually rid us of a population so useless and offensive.[33]

Such was the polarized racial climate within which the tailors' strike developed in late 1835, and the master tailors' attempt to activate the community against the journeymen bears a striking similarity to the ways city elites were currently mobilizing the white community against the free black population. Both free blacks and the white journeymen tailors were characterized as disorderly; both were accused of engaging in poor work habits and "riotous" behavior at night and on Sunday; and both were targeted for public suppression in the name of

32. The official proceedings of the "citizens' meeting" were printed in the *St. Louis Commercial Bulletin*, November 2, 1835.
33. Ibid., October 26, 1835.

preventing their insubordination from spreading to other members of the working classes. But the master tailors proved unable to enlist the white community in the suppression of the journeymen's strike.

In a political climate in which disorder was so thoroughly racialized—identified exclusively with free blacks—appeals against white workingmen in the name of order failed to resonate within the broader white community. In contrast to the mobilization against free blacks, city leaders did not pass ordinances limiting labor actions by white workingmen, did not convene grand juries to investigate the problems of journeymen's societies, and did not summon "the citizens" for a public meeting to denounce the journeymen and appoint committees to suppress the strike. In short, the white community refused to rally against the striking journeymen tailors.

Tellingly, the editor of the city's leading business newspaper displayed an unprecedented caution in his coverage of the tailors' dispute. The pro-entrepreneurial *Commercial Bulletin,* whose editor had recently mocked a group of Boston printers for engaging in a walkout, remained silent during the course of the journeymen tailors' strike in St. Louis. During the local dispute, the newspaper even ran the ad for the Tailors Union Shop in the same column as two "help wanted" ads by local master tailors (who were, in effect, calling for strikebreakers)— an implicit recognition of the editor's neutrality. On the other hand, the editor fully endorsed the community's mobilizations against abolitionists and free blacks, declaring, "They are watched, their slightest movement will bring upon them a summary punishment,—*they will be put down!*" But when the master tailors requested the public to "put down a lawless band of depredators" in the form of their striking journeymen, they were unable to enlist any editorial support within St. Louis.[34]

Instead, in the midst of the racial crisis gripping St. Louis, elites themselves might face challenges from below. One local businessman, for example, was accused by a white drayman named McLaughlin of paying a "colored drayman" in "Abolitionist Pamphlets" rather than in cash. The businessman, Thomas P. Green, felt compelled to take out an ad in a local newspaper to deny the charge. Admitting that he had hired both men, Green exclaimed, "I paid both alike with money, both

34. Ibid., October 7, 21, December 18, 1835, January 18, 1836.

McLaughlin and the negro who were hauling together." To dispel any doubts among the community, Green emphasized, "I am politically and religiously opposed to the views of the abolitionists," considering them "as injurious alike to the well being of our country and slave population."[35]

The journeymen tailors capitalized on this racially polarized climate by holding out until the masters accepted their economic demands and retracted their public denunciation of the workers, the "groundless charge they laid at our door," as the journeymen called it. Clearly, for the journeymen, the issue was about more than simple craft issues, for they also refused to allow the masters to "abuse and slander us at their pleasure." When the journeymen declared victory in the struggle, they publicly announced that the employers had "recalled the charge . . . and otherwise complied with our demands."[36] In short, the journeymen tailors had fought and won the economic struggle and, just as importantly, the war of rhetoric with their employers. The reputation of the journeymen tailors, these "regular men," had been vindicated.

Only a month after the amicable settlement of the tailors' strike, a labor protest of a different sort caught the attention of St. Louis residents. Francis McIntosh, a boat worker characterized as a "free negro" or "mulatto" from Pittsburgh, helped two coworkers flee from police who were trying to arrest them for disorderly conduct. The officers seized McIntosh instead and charged him with obstruction of justice. But when the authorities threatened him with a severe and lengthy punishment, the black boat worker unveiled a knife, stabbed both captors, and fled. As one officer lay dying in the street and another collapsed from a serious wound, the commotion attracted the attention of several passersby, who apprehended McIntosh and escorted him to jail. But the violence had only begun. Before the hour was up, an angry crowd assembled outside the prison, overpowered the jailor, whisked McIntosh from his cell, paraded him to the outskirts of town, and tied him to a tree, where they burned him alive. As hundreds, perhaps thousands, looked on, an alderman brandished a pistol and

35. Ibid., October 23, 1835.
36. Ibid., January 15, February 5, 12, 1836.

threatened to shoot anyone attempting to stop the brutal proceedings.[37]

Although local authorities convened a grand jury to investigate the lynching, its members—at the behest of the presiding judge and with nearly unanimous support from the local press—refused to indict, closing the legal proceeding on the sordid affair. But the lynching of Francis McIntosh had significant repercussions, culminating in the exile of white antislavery editor Elijah P. Lovejoy, who denounced both the action of the vigilantes and the inaction of local officials. In the most well-known aspect of this series of events, Lovejoy, who resumed publishing his *Observer* across the Mississippi River in nearby Alton, Illinois, was shot and killed while defending his printing press from an antiabolition mob in 1837.[38]

The murderous mob action ending McIntosh's life represented an extreme example of the practice of racial policing. In the wake of McIntosh's stabbing of two police officers and his subsequent lynching at the hands of a vengeful mob, the local press sought to justify the crowd action and define McIntosh as the only true criminal in the violent proceedings—thereby converting the free black victim of a white mob into the embodiment of the danger and disorder inherent

37. The actions and subsequent lynching of Francis McIntosh occurred on Thursday, April 28, 1836, and were reported and discussed in the *St. Louis Commercial Bulletin*, April 29, May 2, 4, 9, 1836; *Missouri Republican*, April 30, May 7, 12, 1836; *Missouri Argus*, April 29, May 6, 1836; *St. Louis Observer*, May 5, 1836; and other local newspapers. One of the fullest accounts is from a diary written by an anonymous St. Louisan in 1836, a copy of which is held by the Missouri Historical Society in St. Louis. This entry is quoted extensively in Hermann, "McIntosh Affair," 126–27. McIntosh's actions can be seen as those of a worker expressing labor solidarity; I explore this idea further in Graff, "Forging an American St. Louis," chapter 3. For other scholarly accounts, see Hermann, "McIntosh Affair," 123–43; Reichard, "Origins of Urban Police," 139–50; and Bonnie E. Laughlin, " 'Endangering the Peace of Society': Abolitionist Agitation and Mob Reaction in St. Louis and Alton, 1836–1838," *Missouri Historical Review* 95 (2000): 1–22.

38. The actions of the judge and jury were reprinted in *St. Louis Commercial Bulletin*, May 23, 1836; *Missouri Republican*, May 26, 1836; *Missouri Argus*, May 27, 1836. The two standard scholarly biographies of Lovejoy also provide narratives of the lynching of Francis McIntosh. See John Gill, *Tide without Turning: Elijah P. Lovejoy and Freedom of the Press* (Boston: Starr King Press, 1958), 60–70; and Merton L. Dillon, *Elijah P. Lovejoy: Abolitionist Editor* (Urbana: University of Illinois Press, 1961), 81–82.

in the free black population. When the *Missouri Argus* referred to the "diabolical acts," or the *Missouri Republican* described the "atrocious crime," or the *Commercial Bulletin* detailed the "heart-rending tragedy," in other words, they meant McIntosh's fatal stabbing of Deputy Constable Hammond, not the mob's consequent act of tying McIntosh to a tree and setting the fire that burned him to death.[39] The St. Louis press presented McIntosh as a violent intruder with no apparent motivation or human feeling whose lynching was just punishment for his infamous crime.

The judge of the Circuit Court of St. Louis County, who presided at the proceedings investigating the lynching, brought the denunciation of McIntosh to a climax in his charge to the grand jury. In a speech reprinted in the major St. Louis newspapers, Luke Lawless attacked "the atrocious and savage demeanor" of McIntosh, whose actions represented just the most recent example of "atrocities committed in this and other states by individuals of negro blood against their white brethren." The black race, Lawless argued, possessed a "fiery, unreasoning instinct . . . uniformly marked by ruthless, remorseless revenge." And with the specter of abolitionism haunting St. Louis and the nation, "the free negro has been converted into a deadly enemy." Lawless recommended against indicting anyone for the murder of Francis McIntosh, and the grand jury agreed.[40]

Based on the response of the local press, Judge Lawless's speech to the grand jury articulated perfectly the opinions of the community's leaders. One editor urged readers, especially any sympathetic to the cause of abolition, to study "the powerful charge of Judge Lawless, and note the action upon it of one of the most intelligent of Grand Juries." To the white leaders of St. Louis, Francis McIntosh personified the demonization of the free black population, and the mob responded efficiently, if overzealously, to snuff him out. In the analysis of the editor of the *Commercial Bulletin*, "there was a sensation abroad, honest but misguided, which developed into a general burst of indignation and determination on revenge upon the foul murderer." Even the *St. Louis Observer*, whose editor, Elijah P. Lovejoy, denounced the vigilante

39. *Missouri Argus*, April 29, 1836; *Missouri Republican*, April 30, 1836; *St. Louis Commercial Bulletin*, May 2, 1836.
40. *Missouri Argus*, May 27, 1836.

action, referred to McIntosh as "a hardened wretch certainly, and one that deserved to die." The editor of the *Argus* urged the community to "drop the curtain" on "this awful scene" and hoped that another punishment of this kind would not be necessary. Still, he sought to use the lynching as a lesson in the logic of racial policing. "It is certainly as well," he concluded, "for impudent free negroes to be *cautious*."[41]

The lynching of Francis McIntosh represented the climax of the racial panic gripping St. Louis in the mid-1830s, but it did more than simply reinforce the central premise of the practice of racial policing—the association of free blacks with violence, danger, and disorder. More than that, the violent death of McIntosh called upon the entire white community, both literally and metaphorically, to act as the agents of that racial policing. And white workingmen, just emerging as an identifiably distinct social group within St. Louis, represented an important segment of that white community. The journeymen tailors' strike confirmed the thorough racialization of the rhetoric of disorder in St. Louis, a development that uniquely benefited white workingmen, who mobilized to defend and advance their interests in the name of respectability and good order. The lynching of Francis McIntosh showed further that white workingmen were more than beneficiaries of the racial policing regime—they were called upon as its most ardent advocates and participants.

The enlistment of white men of the lower sort in the elite-initiated effort to maintain racial and labor order dated back to the territorial era, when ordinances required all "free white male inhabitants" aged eighteen and over to serve in the town's slave patrol and night watch. But elites concerned as much about labor discipline as about racial hierarchy were not entirely comfortable with the enlistment of white workingmen as the agents of economic and social order. Many of the state laws and city ordinances enacted during these years, while primarily dedicated to the repression of the black population, also contained provisions penalizing whites for harboring, hiding, trading with, or socializing with slaves and free blacks. Clearly such codes prohibiting interracial liaisons targeted that portion of the white community whose working lives and social worlds intersected most

41. Ibid., April 29, May 27, May 30, 1836; *St. Louis Commercial Bulletin,* May 2, 1836; *St. Louis Observer,* May 5, 1836.

frequently with the black population of the city. Similarly, despite the fact that slave patrols and night watches operated under the supervision of the mayor or his appointed captains, elites not infrequently expressed anxiety about the reliability of lowly white men in positions of even limited authority. As late as 1829, for example, a correspondent to the *Missouri Republican* worried that the night watch was dominated by poor white men, who might convert the patrol into "the propagator of vice, instead of its corrective."[42]

Despite the lingering concerns of privileged St. Louisans, by the mid-1830s white workingmen had become thoroughly integrated into the racial policing machinery, playing subordinate but active roles in the citizens' meetings and vigilante actions organized by white elites against slave and free black insubordination. Especially in moments of community crisis, such as in the fall of 1835 and the spring of 1836, the white elite of St. Louis relied as much on journeymen tailors as on leading merchants to repel the threats of disorder represented by New England abolitionists, wandering vagrants and gamblers, and free black boat workers like Francis McIntosh.

The murderous mob action ending McIntosh's life represented the most extreme example of the practice of racial policing, as leading members of the community authorized a group of white men to take revenge against a free black intruder who dared defy the racial and labor order of St. Louis. Although none of the contemporary accounts identified the mob's participants by name, more than one noted that leading citizens were present. As one resident who stayed a safe distance from the lynching recorded in his diary, "one of the most respectable citizens of this city[,] who was anxious to learn who was engaged in the horrid business, says he saw one of the aldermen walking around and swearing that he would shoot any person who would dare to loose the chain which bound the negro. This I believe to be

---

42. See the series of ordinances concerning the slave patrol, first passed in 1811, and the night watch, initially signed into law in 1818, plus related ordinances passed in 1826, 1831, and 1835, in *Ordinances of the Board of Trustees of the Town of St. Louis, 1811 to 1823*, passim; St. Louis Ordinances, No. 1–314, April 22, 1823–March 25, 1836 (St. Louis Public Library microfilm). For elite fears of lower-class white men serving as agents of order, see the *Missouri Republican*, March and April 1829, quoted in Maximilian Reichard, "Black and White on the Urban Frontier," *Missouri Historical Society Bulletin* 33 (1976): 10–13.

true statement of the case. Part I saw myself. The rest I would not go to see." The same witness noted that there were "only a few active persons . . . [who] drove away the Sheriff[,] broke open the prison, and brought out the negro. This was the work of not more than 15 or 20, [and] the rest were passive spectators." The demographic makeup of the active participants remains unknown, and whether the vigilantes included white workingmen is thus unclear. But clearly the "passive spectators" who witnessed the brutal murder included white workingmen. The press estimated the crowd to be in the thousands, and though this may be an exaggeration for a town of no more than ten thousand in 1836, the hyperbole suggests that the size of the mob appeared overwhelming and therefore difficult to gauge.[43]

Whatever the social breakdown of either the small group of men who actually lynched Francis McIntosh, or the much larger group of residents who witnessed the brutal murder, the analysis of the event by the local press painted a picture of a unified white community that mobilized in defense of the city's racial order. In the repeated retellings, the violent burning to death of a human being became rationalized as the necessary and proper act of the entire community. The mob was characterized as "the tossing multitude," "the assembled multitude," and "an excited assemblage," while the lynching was the result of "the over-excited zeal of the populace to render justice to the dead." The editor of the *Missouri Republican* even described the lynching as though it were a citizens' meeting convened to address the problems of racial order in the city: "There was no tumult, no disturbance of any kind; but the crowd retired quietly to their several homes." When the nearby *Alton Telegraph* ran a story critical of the lynching, the editor of the *Missouri Argus* took offense at the "unwarrantable language" challenging "the execution of a free negro at this place." The St. Louis editor dismissed the version as "so obvious an effort to disparage our citizens" and defended the lynching as a fitting punishment "decided by a portion of the makers of Law—citizens of St. Louis & of the United States." One observer even described the setting of the lynching as though it were a theatrical production witnessed by the

43. Anonymous physician's diary, entry for July 6, 1836, quoted in Hermann, "McIntosh Affair," 126–27. The *Missouri Republican*, April 30, 1836, reported that "several thousand persons witnessed the revolting spectacle," while the *Missouri Argus*, April 29, 1836, described "the gathering thousands" present.

entire community: "The scene was on sloping ground and the tree to which he was bound was at the foot of the slope. The whole side of the hill was covered with the dense crowd."[44] In short, the articulate members of the white community in St. Louis mobilized to defend such an extreme example of racial policing by redefining it as an act of the community in the name of social order.

Again it was Judge Lawless, in his charge to the grand jury, who provided the most elaborate justification for the lynching as an expression of the white community's united sentiment. In addressing the jurors, Lawless posed a "preliminary question, namely, whether the destruction of McIntosh was the act of the 'few' or the act of the 'many.'" If the lynching "was perpetrated by a definite, and compared to the population of St. Louis, a *small* number of individuals, separate from the mass . . . you ought to indict them without a single exception," he declared. But if "the destruction of the murderer . . . was the act . . . of the many—of the multitude—in the ordinary sense of the words—not the act of ascertainable malefactors, but of congregated thousands, seized upon and impelled by that mysterious, metaphysical, and almost electric phrenzy . . . then I say act not at all in the matter—the case transcends your jurisdiction—it is beyond the reach of human law. The attempt to punish it, would, in my opinion, be fruitless, and perhaps worse than that. The foundations of society might be shaken—the social elements in this City and County thrown into most disastrous collision. For, how are we to indict—upon what evidence—two or three thousand offenders?"[45]

Lawless, in his charge to the grand jury investigating the lynching of Francis McIntosh, perfectly articulated the practice of racial policing in 1836 St. Louis. Initiated by elites, racial policing demanded the full engagement of the city's entire white citizenry, whether as physical enforcers or as active witnesses. And in Lawless's vision, there was really no distinction between the two. If the entire community had not been responsible for the death of McIntosh, then the "foundations of society" would tumble and "the social elements" of St. Louis would surely

44. *Missouri Argus,* April 29, May 6, 1836; *Missouri Republican,* April 30, 1836; *St. Louis Commercial Bulletin,* May 2, 1836; S. W. McMaster, *Sixty Years on the Upper Mississippi: My Life and Experiences* (1893), selections reprinted in the Missouri Historical Society's *Glimpses of the Past* 4 (1937): 40–41.

45. *Missouri Argus,* May 27, 1836.

clash. Taking seriously Judge Lawless's threats of social disorder, the grand jury concluded that McIntosh's death was "the act of the populace, an assemblage of several thousand persons, for which, five or ten individuals could not be made responsible; so far from it, it was satisfactorily shown, that any decided opposition to or an attempt to prevent the perpetration of the act by that number of persons, would have endangered their lives."[46] The grand jury's decision not to indict represented the official closing of the ordeal of Francis McIntosh in 1836 St. Louis. Taken as a whole, the actions of McIntosh, the mob, the local press, Judge Lawless, and the grand jury all confirmed the acceptable boundaries of racial and labor solidarity at the point of organized labor's emergence in 1830s St. Louis.

A small number of historians have written on the rise of the first St. Louis labor movement in the decade beginning in 1835, while a comparable number have addressed the increasingly violent conflicts over slavery and abolition during this same period. None, however, have addressed the developments in tandem or probed the possible connections linking the two. As a result, the histories of the evolving politics of class and race in St. Louis have been written as parallel yet never intersecting narratives, with little to no overlap in the characters, events, or plots.[47] But as much as the 1835 journeymen tailors' strike was premeditated, organized collectively, and resolved peacefully—while Francis McIntosh's action was apparently spontaneous, singular, and ended in violence—the two disparate events shared more than coincidental timing. The triumph of the journeymen tailors and

46. Ibid.
47. Despite its high ranking in terms of population, commercial activity, and manufacturing output from the mid-nineteenth century on, St. Louis remains an understudied city in comparison with New York, Philadelphia, New Orleans, and Chicago. On the labor movement, in addition to the studies already cited in the notes throughout this essay, see also Walter R. Houf, "Organized Labor in Missouri Politics before the Civil War," *Missouri Historical Review* 56 (1962): 244–54. A recent synthesis of the history of St. Louis, James Neal Primm, *Lion of the Valley: St. Louis, Missouri*, 2d ed. (Boulder, Colo.: Pruett Publishing, 1990), weaves the history of slavery, racial violence, and sectionalism into his narrative of the city's economic and political growth up to the Civil War, but he completely ignores the history of organized labor or conflicts between employers and free workers until the explosive general strike of 1877.

the lynching of Francis McIntosh were inextricably linked, exposing not only the racial boundaries of labor solidarity in rapidly developing St. Louis, but also the centrality of racial violence in shaping the trajectory of the city's first labor movement. In the years to come, the labor solidarity forged by white workingmen was not simply premised on the exclusion of nonwhite workers—it was fundamentally rooted in the active, often violent repression of those nonwhite workers. Francis McIntosh's brief act of resistance on the levee in 1836 did indeed play a part in the forging of labor solidarity in antebellum St. Louis, but it was a twisted labor solidarity with deadly consequences that would endure throughout the nineteenth century and beyond.

The practice of racial policing, initiated by the elites and designed to enforce slave subordination, racial separation, and labor discipline in the city, effectively demonized the free black population as contagions of public disorder and violence. At the same time, however, by claiming the allegiance of all white men as members of the community responsible for racial policing, elites laid the foundation for the rise of a white workingmen's movement and the full inclusion of white men in the polity. In the wake of the 1835 tailors' strike, white workingmen in St. Louis engaged in a wave of labor organizing and political protest that culminated in the formation of an independent political party in 1840. Simultaneously, they continued to participate in racial policing practices designed to intimidate, harass, and marginalize the black working population. Central to these white workers' demands was the sense that they, as citizens responsible for keeping racial control in the city, deserved greater participation in the political process.

This is not to suggest that white workers gained the upper hand in their struggles with employers. As David Roediger has noted, "the wages of whiteness" more often than not proved spurious to white members of the working class. By foreclosing avenues of biracial labor solidarity, white working-class race consciousness in effect foreclosed alternative visions to the emerging industrial order. At the same time, though, we need to recognize the constraints placed upon employers and political leaders in their attempts to impose an elite vision of municipal order and labor discipline within a racially charged environment. The 1835 tailors' strike in St. Louis suggests that at least some employers were more than willing to suppress, with violence if necessary, the actions of their white journeymen employees. But without the support of city authorities or significant members of the white community, they were forced to accommodate at least some of their workers' demands.

The practice of racial policing in St. Louis, violently acted out in the lynching of Francis McIntosh, also suggests the local terrain upon which racial and class constructions were forged in industrializing America. While white workingmen in St. Louis, as elsewhere, were beginning to contrast their evolving political and economic status against caricatures of black slaves portrayed in folklore and on the minstrel stage, they were also constructing political identities through daily, direct, and often violent contact with African Americans inhabiting the same workshops, neighborhoods, and streets. Many times that contact was mediated through legitimate government or vigilante channels involving night watches, city patrols, citizens' meetings, and mob actions in the cause of racial control. Such a multiplicity of avenues for political participation outside the arena of party organization and formal elections suggests the complexities we encounter in understanding citizenship and its relationship to race and class in nineteenth-century America.

Race, Power, and the Building Trades Industry in Postwar St. Louis

DEBORAH J. HENRY

Well before the end of World War II, the federal government, along with leaders in private industry and public officials at the state level, began work on a postwar economic stabilization program. War demobilization and reconversion to a peacetime economy required extensive planning to avoid a return to the prewar economic crisis.[1] The nation's construction industry played a vital role in this planning. Both the American Federation of Labor (AFL) and the Associated General Contractors of America lobbied for federal policies supporting public works projects, urban slum clearance, and low-income housing development to stimulate the economy and provide jobs for returning veterans.[2] Like other major urban centers, St. Louis became part of the nation's economic stabilization program by embarking on its own aggressive postwar urban renewal and revitalization plan, a plan that was ultimately funded in large part by the federal government. Leaders in St. Louis's construction industry, both labor and management, worked closely with local civic, business, and government leaders to initiate

1. "Construction as a Source of Jobs following Cutbacks in War Production: Problems and the Challenge They Present," War Productions Board, October 13, 1944, series 4, box 25, Industry Reference file, American Federation of Labor Papers, State Historical Society of Wisconsin, Madison; James F. Byrnes, Director, Office of War Mobilization and Reconversion, "War Production and VE-Day," Second Report, April 1, 1945, Student Research file on Demobilization and Reconversion, folder 16, box 2, Papers of J. Anthony Panuch, Harry S. Truman Library, Independence, Missouri.
2. "A.F. of L. Presents Postwar Program," *Constructor,* May 1944, 34; "Construction and the Nation's Future," *Constructor,* April 1945, 23–25.

this plan. This coalition, in partnership with the federal government, worked to ensure the realization of its ambitious city improvement and revitalization goals. The realization of these goals, however, fundamentally depended on the labor supplied by St. Louis's construction industry.

The city's post–World War II urban renewal agenda created thousands of construction jobs, jobs traditionally and securely held by white workers. African Americans had been trying to penetrate the lily-white building trades in St. Louis since the early twentieth century, but without any real measurable success. St. Louis's growing black community, however, empowered by its World War II experiences, expanded its efforts to secure black labor's share of urban renewal's construction jobs in the postwar years. These efforts unfolded in a racially segregated city encumbered by Jim Crow practices. They unfolded, as well, alongside the development of a powerful urban renewal coalition determined to accomplish its aggressive urban renewal agenda. Despite the racially inclusive language of the urban renewal coalition and the sustained efforts of the black community and some white liberals, skilled black building trades workers were unable to penetrate the ranks of white labor in the building industry during St. Louis's post–World War II urban renewal program. Rather than risk compromising the construction progress of their aggressive goals, St. Louis's urban renewal coalition left the collective power over construction jobs in the hands of the city's white building trades unions.

To provide a context for the racial divides defining St. Louis's construction industry, we should examine the city's racialized social and political patterns in the postwar years. Jim Crow's insidious patterns of segregation permeated post–World War II St. Louis. Just months before the German surrender on May 8, 1945, and the subsequent decision in August by the United States to force Japan's surrender with the use of atomic bombs, Fannie Cook, a prominent white advocate for racial equality in St. Louis, summarized the city's segregated living conditions: "the Negro . . . is highly educated, moderately educated, uneducated; skilled or unskilled, good or wicked; yet all these attributes rank only second—a late, lagging second. First, he is a Negro. . . . We have two sets of churches, two sets of schools, two sets of residential districts, two sets of hotels, two sets of movie houses, with the shabby set invariably for the Negro. Where we have only one set, the

Negro is frequently barred, as in the use of most down-town eating places and hotels." An article appeared in the May 1947 issue of the *St. Louis Argus* echoing Cook's observations. The author stated, "Segregation is still our pronounced pattern of civic, racial, political and economic living. This means that Negroes live under heavy restrictions in employment, in education, in residential accommodations, in restaurant and hotel service, in cultural advantages, and in recreational opportunities."[3] .

Two years later, in July 1949, the *St. Louis Argus* reported that the 1949 national convention of the National Education Association voted to reconsider St. Louis as the location for the group's forthcoming national convention in 1950. Delegates voiced their opinion "that St. Louis is a 'Jim Crow' city where Negro delegates could not be assured adequate hotel and restaurant facilities." Once the association announced its decision to hold the annual conference in Chicago rather than in St. Louis, C. B. Broussard, president of the St. Louis Urban League and a member of the Mayor's Council on Human Relations, publicly expressed his regret that the city's lack of interracial progress had denied St. Louis the opportunity to host the prestigious National Education Association.[4] Efforts to ameliorate these racial realities in St. Louis gained momentum during the World War II era.

An expanding black population throughout the 1940s and its increasingly militant voice in the postwar years exacerbated racial tensions in St. Louis. City leaders took steps to address these tensions. In September 1943, Republican mayor Alois Kaufmann created the St. Louis Race Relations Commission, appointing seventy-two members, black and white, male and female. The commission's explicit charge was "the promotion of good will between white and colored citizens of the City of St. Louis and to that end to inquire into their mutual

3. Fannie Cook, interview for KMOX Radio, December 24, 1944, transcript, box 28, folder 10, Fannie Cook Papers, Missouri Historical Society; Frank L. Williams, "St. Louis Negroes in Their Environment," *St. Louis Argus*, May 16, 1947, 10. The *St. Louis Argus*, founded in 1912, was one of two black St. Louis newspapers (the *St. Louis American* was founded in 1928); see Lorenzo J. Greene, Gary R. Kremer, and Antonio F. Holland, *Missouri's Black Heritage*, rev. ed. (Columbia: University of Missouri Press, 1993), 171.

4. "St. Louis Given Black Eye by Racial Discrimination," *St. Louis Argus*, July 15, 1949, 1; "Education Ass'n Moves to Chicago in Protest," *St. Louis Argus*, February 3, 1950, 1.

and respective problems in the fields of housing, health and sanitation, employment, education and recreation in the City." A February 1946 progress report summarizing the work of the Commission acknowledged the work of the Commission in areas of discrimination in schools, housing, recreation facilities, public accommodations, and health and medical facilities. But the Commission regarded fair employment practices "as one of first priority." Members of the Commission's Employment Committee regularly met with St. Louis employers and expressed its official position in support of a Fair Employment Practice Ordinance for St. Louis City. The commission's employment efforts realized incremental success in some areas but did nothing to alter employment practices in the construction industry.[5]

Except for the hiring of black workers as common laborers or hod carriers, skilled jobs in St. Louis's powerful unionized building trades remained securely in the hands of white labor. These jobs were historically and traditionally the preserve of white labor, and the Race Relations Committee became increasingly aware of these racial boundaries. Reflecting on the commission's work, the *St. Louis Argus* reported in March 1946 that members of the commission were realizing the fact that "the so-called Negroes' problem is really the 'white people's problem.'"[6]

Although such sentiments were making progress among members of the commission, views about race within the broader community

5. "St. Louis Race Relations Commission," Bulletin No. 1, December 1944, box 9, folder 12, Fannie Cook Papers, Missouri Historical Society. "Progress Report," St. Louis Race Relations Commission, February 6, 1946, series 6, box 68, National Urban League Collection, Library of Congress. See also financial support solicitation letter from Finance Committee, St. Louis Race Relations Commission, January 19, 1944, box 9, folder 3, Fannie Cook Papers, Missouri Historical Society.

6. "Race Relations Commission," *St. Louis Argus,* March 29, 1946, box 30, folder 25, Fannie Cook Papers, Missouri Historical Society. Hod carriers carry loads of brick and mortar from a storage site to the bricklayer on the job. Many whites refused to perform this hard, dirty work, and the local union of hod carriers and laborers held the most liberal attitudes about admitting blacks. In 1928 the International Hod Carriers', Building and Common Laborers' Union of America (IHCB & CLUA) reported ten thousand blacks among its total national membership. In 1965 the union changed its name to Laborers' International Union of North America (LIU). For more on blacks and labor in the construction industry, see "Legal Status of Labor Unions as They Affect Negroes" [ca. 1940], RG 228, box 427, Records of the Commission on Fair Employment Practices, National Archives, Washington, D.C.

were strained. Tensions continued to run high in postwar St. Louis when it came to matters of racial progress. Organized by the Peoples Movement, a mass civil rights meeting held September 14, 1947, rallied citizens at large to fight segregation and discrimination in theaters and other public places. Those attending the rally "adopted a resolution calling for the drafting of a civil rights bill to be presented to the Board of Aldermen" as a necessary action "to meet the rising tide of undemocratic practices and discrimination in the city."[7] Although energy and expectations ran high in 1947 for the support of such a bill, these initial efforts met with rejection. City government forced St. Louis's black community to wait for the passage of a civil rights bill. Racial violence incited by measures to integrate city swimming pools spurred further efforts to ameliorate racial tensions.

In the spring of 1949, Mayor Kaufmann's successor, the Democrat Joseph M. Darst, ordered the city's previously segregated playgrounds and swimming pools open to blacks. Darst released his order without advance notice, and such an action was not without its consequences. According to one city leader, the racial violence that ensued after the integration order "shocked the City, and came dangerously close to reaching proportions which could have shocked the whole country."[8] The mayor's office quickly rescinded the order, and swimming pools closed for the summer of 1949. Within a week of the incident, Darst established a committee to study the situation, and in January 1950 he signed Board Bill No. 275 into law. The bill provided for the formal creation of the fifteen-member St. Louis Council on Human Relations and charged the council with the responsibility of determining recommendations for the improvements of black/white relations in St. Louis City.[9] The council recommended a gradual integration of public swimming pools and reopened them as segregated through the

7. "Will Seek Anti Bias Ordinance," *St. Louis Argus,* September 19, 1947, 1; "Public Forum on Civil Rights Bill Wednesday," *St. Louis Argus,* October 17, 1947, 1; see also "Seek St. Louis 'Bill of Rights,'" *St. Louis Argus,* September 12, 1947, 1.

8. Speech, George Winston Cloyd, written for a religious program stressing social education and action, [ca. 1952], box 2, folder 4, George Winston Cloyd Papers, Missouri Historical Society.

9. Letter of Joseph M. Darst to George W. Cloyd, January 23, 1950, box 1, folder 10, George Winston Cloyd Papers, Missouri Historical Society. See also "H. L. Simmons Elected Chairman of New Human Relations Council," *St. Louis Post-Dispatch,* February 3, 1950.

first half of the 1950 swimming season.[10] Despite these events, however, the St. Louis Board of Aldermen continued to reject a civil rights bill for St. Louis through the late 1940s and during the entire decade of the 1950s. It was not until May 26, 1961, by a vote of twenty to four, that the St. Louis Board of Aldermen passed legislation banning racial discrimination in public places based on color.[11]

Within this environment of postwar racial segregation and discrimination, city leaders grew increasingly eager to move forward on an urban revitalization plan to clean up the riverfront, redevelop the city's central core, and improve the quality of life for city residents. Despite two low-rent housing projects in the late 1930s and early 1940s and several civic improvement projects provided for by municipal bond issues during the 1920s and 1930s, large areas of St. Louis remained either obsolete or blighted.[12] With the economic restrictions of the Great Depression behind them and with relief from federal controls over nonessential building during the war, city leaders turned their attention to urban renewal. As early as 1942, city planners began a concentrated effort to develop and plan the implementation of inner-city revitalization plans. Local leaders and urban planners believed the decline of the central city could be traced to the physical problems of blight and to the resulting decline in property values and quality of life in the city. In their report issued in December 1942, St. Louis's City Plan Commission asserted that decadence was due to the city's progressive population loss, which resulted in foreclosures, higher taxes, and tax delinquency. The report argued that correction of the "unprecedented magnitude" of the city's deterioration required a "broad vision, sound policy and firm enforcement of the measures and controls selected, and enforcement characterized not by momentary vigor and enthusiasm but by sustained application over a long

10. "Attendance Report for Outdoor Swimming Pools," [ca. 1951], box 1, folder 12, George Winston Cloyd Papers, Missouri Historical Society. Full integration of all open-air pools did not occur until ordered by the U.S. District Court in July 1950. See John A. Wright, *Discovering African-American St. Louis* (St. Louis: Missouri Historical Society Press, 1994), 86.

11. "Valid in Area after Month Delay," *St. Louis Argus,* May 26, 1961, 1.

12. James Neal Primm, *Lion of the Valley: St. Louis, Missouri,* 2d ed. (Boulder, Colo.: Pruett Publishing, 1990), 486–87. The definition for a "blighted" area was "one that had become unprofitable to both the private investor and the municipality." See Dennis R. Judd, *The Politics of American Cities: Private Power and Public Policy,* 3d ed. (Glenview, Ill.: Scott, Foresman, 1988), 263.

period of time." The commission stressed the necessity of "Joint action by public authority and private interests" to "overcome these difficulties and rebuild St. Louis in a logical and practical manner."[13]

With city leaders focused on this physical approach to understanding urban renewal, St. Louis embarked on an aggressive, central city urban renewal and redevelopment path after 1945. Meanwhile, the social problems often associated with urban renewal—racial conflict, employment discrimination, and unequal distribution of political and economic power—received little attention.[14] Moving forward within a physical approach paradigm, the urban renewal coalition identified housing as its first priority. To further an understanding of the city's initial attention on urban renewal projects directed toward low-income housing and the subsequent need for construction labor, whether white or black, requires a consideration of demographic shifts in population, along with unprecedented housing deficiencies.

The early decades of the twentieth century found St. Louis with a decelerating population growth. In 1910 the population grew by 19.4 percent, in 1920 the growth was 12.5 percent, and in 1930 the growth was only 16.3 percent. During the decade from 1930 to 1940 the population of the city experienced its first actual net loss, -9.7 percent. At the same time, St. Louis's black population disproportionately swelled. From 1900 to 1910 the black population grew by 23.8 percent. A decade later the rate of growth more than doubled reaching 58.7 percent by 1920. Although the city experienced a population net loss of -9.7 percent during the 1930s, the black population grew by 16.2 percent.[15] The prospect of jobs generated by the production boom of World War II and the promise of central city renewal and redevelopment provided stimulus for a large black migration to the city from poor, rural areas of Mississippi, Arkansas, Tennessee, Alabama, and southeast Missouri.[16] Following this same trajectory, in the decade from 1950 to 1960, St. Louis's total population declined by 12.5 percent,

13. "Saint Louis after World War II," Saint Louis Missouri City Plan Commission, December 1942, 13, 19, 27, Missouri Historical Society.

14. Jon C. Teaford, *The Rough Road to Renaissance: Urban Revitalization in America, 1940–1985* (Baltimore: Johns Hopkins University Press, 1990), 11.

15. "The Negro in the St. Louis Economy," Urban League of St. Louis, 1954, 14, Missouri Historical Society.

16. Teaford, *Rough Road*, 125–27; "Negro in the St. Louis Economy," 20. See also Kenneth T. Fox, *Metropolitan America* (New Jersey: Rutgers University Press, 1985), 8–9; and Primm, *Lion of the Valley*, 490.

but the nonwhite population grew from 18 percent of the city's total population in 1950 to 29 percent in 1960.[17]

The expanding numbers of poor blacks in search of housing, coupled with urban renewal goals that included demolishing many "blighted" residential properties, exacerbated the overcrowded and substandard housing problems already a reality for most of the city's black residents. During the summer of 1950, the St. Louis Housing Authority conducted a survey of living conditions in the Jefferson–Cass–Carr–20th Street section of the city. Overcrowding was prevalent in this district. More than three-quarters of black families lived in homes classified as dilapidated, only one in sixteen black homes had indoor running hot and cold water, and less than 30 percent of black homes had an indoor flush toilet for private use. More than half only had access to outdoor facilities.[18]

Historian Neal Primm cites a 1937 study that "revealed that obsolete housing areas chiefly within fifteen blocks of downtown, with one-fifth of the city's area and one-third of its population, accounted for three-fourths of the illegitimate children, one-half of the infant deaths, and two-thirds of the tuberculosis and delinquency in the city." These statistics attest to the squalid conditions for St. Louis's black population living within the area immediately surrounding the downtown business district. Prior to beginning any commercial urban redevelopment within the downtown core, the surrounding blighted residential areas would have to be razed and residents relocated. Low-rent housing became the major objective of City Hall. After several failed attempts, both houses of Congress finally passed legislation designed to aid local efforts aimed at slum removal. Passage of the 1949 Housing Act, and specifically Title I of the act, provided federal funds to assist with urban slum clearance goals and the construction of low-rent housing.[19]

17. "Analysis of Selected Population Characteristics: St. Louis City, 1950–1960," St. Louis: Metropolitan Population Project, 1961, 1 and 6, Missouri Historical Society.

18. Saint Louis Federation of Block Units, "Report to St. Louis on the Negro Child ... Negro Employment ... Negro Housing ...," Urban League of St. Louis, February 12, 1951, 8, series 3, box 61, National Urban League Collection, Library of Congress.

19. Primm, *Lion of the Valley,* 486; Judd, *Politics of American Cities,* 263–68. For many African Americans in St. Louis, as in other cities, urban renewal was another name for "Negro removal." See Joseph Heathcott and Maire Murphy, "Corridors of

Passage of the 1949 Housing Act created the legislative space for urban renewal and occurred as a result of a compromise between liberals and conservatives. Liberals focused more on the social crisis resulting from slums and advocated slum clearance, along with the construction of new low-income housing projects. Conversely, conservatives viewed the urban crisis in economic terms. The presence of "blight" in central cities' commercial and residential areas weakened economic vitality. The conservative coalition included such groups as the National Association of Real Estate Boards, United States Savings and Loan League, National Association of Home Builders, the Producers Council, and the United States Chamber of Commerce. Members were most interested in protecting their urban business interests from capital loss resulting from blighted areas. Conservatives eventually agreed to the continuation of a public housing program, but only in exchange for the agreement that "private enterprise would be the main vehicle for redevelopment."[20] This meant that once slum clearance was completed by the city, land would be sold to private commercial interests, who would then enter into building contracts with private contractors. Although initially designed for slum clearance and the construction of low-income housing, amendments to the 1949 Housing Act in 1954 and 1960 shifted the focus to commercial development. By the early 1960s local authorities were able to manipulate guidelines allowing for the allocation of two-thirds of the federal funds received to be used for commercial development.[21] Consequently,

---

Flight, Zones of Renewal: Industry, Planning, and Policy in the Making of Metropolitan St. Louis, 1940–1990," forthcoming in the *Journal of Urban History;* Arnold R. Hirsch, *Making the Second Ghetto: Race and Housing in Chicago, 1940–1960* (Cambridge: Cambridge University Press, 1983), 250–53, 273–74; Douglas S. Massey and Nancy A. Denton, *American Apartheid: Segregation and the Making of the Underclass* (Cambridge: Harvard University Press, 1993), 55–57; and Thomas Sugrue, *The Origins of the Urban Crisis: Race and Inequality in Postwar Detroit* (Princeton: Princeton University Press, 1996), 48–55, 86–88.

20. Judd, *Politics of American Cities,* 263. See also June Manning Thomas, *Redevelopment and Race: Planning a Finer City in Postwar Detroit* (Baltimore: Johns Hopkins University Press, 1997), 55; and Jon C. Teaford, *Cities of the Heartland: The Rise and Fall of the Industrial Midwest* (Bloomington: Indiana University Press, 1993), 214–15. Liberals included such groups as the National Conference of Catholic Charities, American Council on Education, American Association of Social Workers, and League of Women Voters. See Judd, *Politics of American Cities,* 265.

21. Judd, *Politics of American Cities,* 268–69.

public policy that was favorable to commercial real estate ultimately determined the advance of post–World War II urban renewal and re-development projects in St. Louis and in other aging midwestern cities.[22]

With federal funding in place, plans moved forward with high-rise building designs that were adopted to minimize land costs. The city proceeded with its new low-rent housing projects, projects constructed with frugal measures and on undersized lots that could not comfort-ably accommodate large numbers of families with many children. Cochran Gardens, a project located just north of the central business district, was completed in 1953 and provided 704 dwelling units. Pruitt and Igo apartments were built on the northwest edge of the down-town district, and occupancy began in 1954 and 1955 respectively. Together, they comprised thirty-three eleven-story buildings, provid-ing 2,850 family units. The fourth project located on the downtown district's near north side was Vaugn Apartments, sitting just east of Pruitt-Igo. Vaugn opened in 1957 and consisted of 656 dwelling units in four nine-story buildings. Another low-rent housing project, the Darst-Webbe complex, located just south of Chouteau Avenue on the city's South Side, opened in 1956 and 1957 and provided an addi-tional 1,238 low-income units. Collectively, between 1953 and 1957, new postwar public housing dwellings totaled nearly 5,500 units.[23]

These low-rent housing projects were all located in black neighbor-hoods or within close proximity to black neighborhoods. The projects were also constructed with a predominantly white labor force and with money partially provided by the federal government and St. Louis City. Throughout this period of intense, low-rent housing con-struction in the 1950s, blacks were only able to secure jobs as laborers, hod carriers, or as an occasional brick mason. Although Jim Crow patterns and practices permeated the social, cultural, political, and ed-ucational lives of St. Louis's black residents, more importantly, em-ployment restrictions determined by race denied opportunities for

22. Teaford, *Rough Road,* 6.

23. Other cities also embarked on their own large-scale, low-income housing pro-grams. For studies on Philadelphia, Chicago, and Detroit, respectively, see John F. Bauman, *Public Housing, Race, and Renewal: Urban Planning in Philadelphia, 1920–1974* (Philadelphia: Temple University Press, 1987); Hirsch, *Making the Second Ghetto;* and Sugrue, *Origins of the Urban Crisis.*

economic uplift. The denial of economic opportunities, in turn, negatively influenced every other aspect of black life in St. Louis. Some areas of economic opportunity were more racially restricted than others and the building trades was one. Unionized skilled building trade jobs remained exclusively white, denying black workers access to these high-wage jobs and the promise of sustainable economic opportunities. The urban renewal coalition's racialized hiring practices on these projects represented a blatant disregard for the economic needs of St. Louis's black community and its building trades workers.

The post–World War II years of urban renewal arose from a legacy of conflict over the absence of black skilled labor on construction projects that were built for blacks and located in black neighborhoods. First, built in the early 1930s, the mission of Homer G. Phillips Hospital was to serve the African American community. St. Louis blacks had lobbied City Hall as early as 1915 to provide a health care facility on the north side of the city. Medical care received at the segregated City Hospital #2 was inadequate and poorly funded. The city ignored these demands until Mayor Henry Kiel needed support for passage of an $87 million bond issue in 1923. Kiel negotiated with Homer G. Phillips, a popular community leader and black attorney, for black votes. In exchange for black support of the bond issue, Kiel promised $1 million of the $87 million for a hospital to serve the black community. Along with overwhelming white voter support, the bond issue easily passed. The bond issue resulted in improvements to sewers and city streets and provided for the new construction of Aloe Plaza, Soldiers Memorial, and Kiel Auditorium.[24] But city officials resisted fulfilling the campaign promise of building a new hospital in the black community and under black administration.

Not until 1932 did construction begin on the hospital, a year after the death of Homer G. Phillips. The actual construction process presented another challenge. Although construction occurred for the new hospital in the black community and was intended to provide full-service medical care for blacks, black construction workers were denied access to jobs. The city contended that qualified black workers were not available, when in reality the practice simply supported discriminatory hiring practices of the city's white construction unions

24. Primm, *Lion of the Valley,* 447–49.

affiliated with the St. Louis Building and Construction Trades Council.[25] Throughout the construction process, protests from the black community continued, but construction proceeded without the use of any skilled black labor. Forty-four black painters, thirty-five black electricians, thirty-one black carpenters, and twenty black plasterers applied for work through the city. All had either performed comparable work on other projects in St. Louis or carried union cards from locals in other cities. Despite this availability and desire to work, the city denied black building trades workers jobs.[26]

A second example of prewar conflict over the absence of black labor on construction projects in black neighborhoods involved construction of the city's first federally assisted, low-rent housing project, Carr Square Village. Construction began on the project in 1939.[27] In 1941 the National Association for the Advancement of Colored People (NAACP) filed a lawsuit against the St. Louis Housing Authority and its contractor for failure to meet a federal goal of 3.2 percent participation for skilled black workers on federally assisted projects. These two experiences, coupled with the denial of building trades jobs for black labor during the construction buildup for World War II, increased the black community's frustration, anger, and determination to place expanded pressure on St. Louis's white construction industry to open its doors to black labor.[28] The racialized hiring practices of the postwar urban renewal coalition exacerbated the tensions.

Regardless of the transformation of a public policy program of urban renewal that supported the goals of private business interests, the accomplishment of these urban real estate development goals depended on the labor of the local construction industry. Maximizing the economic profitability of development projects was largely con-

25. The St. Louis Building and Construction Trades Council was the umbrella organization for the American Federation of Labor in St. Louis for building trades workers. Individual craft locals, such as the electricians, painters, cement finishers, and plumbers, affiliated with the Building Trades Council. The council represented a powerful labor force in St. Louis.

26. George Lipsitz, *The Sidewalks of St. Louis: Places, People, and Politics in an American City* (Columbia: University of Missouri Press, 1991), 52–54.

27. "Annual Report of Field Industrial Secretary," March 1–December 31, 1941, RG 16, series 1, box 6, Urban League of St. Louis Records, Washington University; Primm, *Lion of the Valley*, 486.

28. Deborah J. Henry, "Structures of Exclusion: Black Labor and the Building Trades in St. Louis, 1917–1966" (Ph.D. diss., University of Minnesota, 2002).

tingent on a construction labor force working in concert with builders and commercial real estate developers. Without an available construction labor force on the job, working, and free of strife and conflict, the city's aggressive urban renewal goals could not be met. Any activism by black labor in pursuit of construction jobs generated by St. Louis's urban renewal program, whether for public or private goals, promised to upset the industry's existing state of racial exclusivity and could risk obstructing the course of urban development in St. Louis. The prospect, however, of economic opportunities in the form of urban renewal construction jobs mobilized St. Louis's black community. Several actions were taken to strengthen the position of black workers in order to challenge the obstinate resistance to their presence in the skilled building trades.

The first action addressed the need to provide quality building trades education for black students. Apprenticeship training represented the traditional way for workers to gain access to the trades, and in St. Louis segregated schools barred blacks from building trades education leading to apprenticeship opportunities. Access to unionized, skilled building trades jobs usually occurred through vocational education and hiring as an apprentice. During the years covered by this essay, public schools in St. Louis were segregated. In fact, Article IX, Section 1 of the new Missouri Constitution ratified by Missouri voters in 1945 reinforced the legal status of school segregation throughout the state. Working within these restrictions, blacks in St. Louis organized in 1931 to lobby for a separate vocational high school for black students.[29] By the late 1930s, Booker T. Washington Technical High School provided vocational education for black students, while Herbert S. Hadley Vocational School provided the same for white students. Hadley, however, was the only school offering education for the construction trades. A report prepared in February 1941 by F. J. Jeffrey, the assistant superintendent of the St. Louis Public Schools, stated:

> it has been the policy of the St. Louis schools to build courses around employments that show possibilities of entrance jobs for the boys and girls who spend two or three years in completing

29. "Minutes of the Meeting of the Committee to Study the Use of the Franklin School," Joint Committee of the Department of Neighborhood Service and Recreation and Department of Race Relations, December 18, 1931, box 4, folder 8, Fannie Cook Papers, Missouri Historical Society.

pre-employment training. Vocational schools or technical high schools in the city, regardless of race involved, need not be uniform in their offerings. . . . Since we have two general vocational schools in St. Louis, it should be easily understood that all courses at the Booker T. Washington Technical High School would not necessarily be repeated at the Hadley Technical High School, [and] not all courses of the Hadley be repeated in the Booker T. Washington. . . . The Superintendent of Instruction, the Assistant Superintendent to vocational education, and the principal and faculty of the Booker T. Washington Technical High School, are ready at all times to recommend the expansion of our vocational and technical training along any line that will not lead to disappointment to the trainee, and that will not require an unreasonable expenditure of Board of Education funds.[30]

Jeffrey's statement provided justification for the absence of building trades education in the black school. Young blacks would remain barred from this education as long as schools remained segregated in St. Louis; moreover, they were barred from access to building trades jobs.

The St. Louis Race Commission surveyed both Hadley and Washington schools and concluded that vocational training education at Washington for blacks did not equal that provided at Hadley for white students. Edwin B. Meissner, chairman of the St. Louis Race Relations Commission, appeared before the St. Louis Board of Education on March 9, 1948, reporting on these inequalities in education. The Race Relations Commission requested "as emphatically as words can convey, that you [the Board of Education] take prompt and adequate action to equalize at least the facilities and personnel in both colored and white vocational training schools." The Race Relations Commission went further, suggesting that if funds were not available to upgrade Washington Technical High School, that the unused facilities at Hadley "be utilized for the training of Negro students." The commission contended that this action "would not be a violation of the Missouri State Statutes appertaining to segregation in schools. It would be in compliance with that transcending portion of the law which pro-

30. F. J. Jeffrey, assistant superintendent, "Vocational Training for Colored," series 6, box 69, National Urban League Collection, Library of Congress.

vides that equality of privileges be established for both White and Negro students."[31]

Later that same year, in October 1948, the director of industrial relations with the Urban League of St. Louis reported the same conditions of unequal education in vocational training before the Missouri Equal Rights Committee.[32] Again, relief for black students did not occur. Throughout the 1950s and during the 1960s those working to eliminate the inequalities in vocational education for blacks persevered in their efforts. Even with the 1954 Supreme Court ruling in *Brown vs. Board of Education,* access to equal and integrated vocational education did not occur for the city's black students. Even though integration was ordered at Hadley, a prerequisite to enrolling in the school's building trades classes required employment by the student with a contractor. The greatest employment opportunities were with the city's largest contractors, and these contractors only employed union workers. Since these unions denied membership to blacks, such "closed shop" agreements between contractors and the city's white-controlled building trades unions only promised the continued denial of employment opportunities for black students seeking jobs in the building trades. In both implicit and explicit ways, blacks were shut out of Hadley Technical High School in the postwar years and, moreover, shut out of access to skilled craft jobs with local building trade unions.[33] William E. Douthit, director of industrial relations for the Urban League of St. Louis, reported in November 1959 that, to his knowledge, "there were no Negroes apprenticing in the skilled labors crafts, in the City of St. Louis, even though the apprenticeship program is supported by government funds and taught on the grounds of the St. Louis Public School System." Again, in February 1961 the Urban League reported that there were "no Negro apprentices in the following: electricians, plumbers and steamfitters, carpenters, cement finishers,

31. Edwin B. Meissner, chairman, St. Louis Race Relations Commission, "Statement to Meeting of Board of Education," March 9, 1948, series 6, box 68, National Urban League Collection, Library of Congress.

32. "Statement by Chester E. Stovall, Director of Industrial Relations, Urban League of St. Louis, before the Missouri Equal Rights Committee," October 15, 1948, series 6, box 67, National Urban League Collection, Library of Congress.

33. "Desegregation of the St. Louis Public Schools," St. Louis Public Schools, Instruction Department, 1956, 60, box 2, Irving Alexander Williamson Sr. Papers, Missouri Historical Society.

lathers, plasterers."[34] Without blacks moving through the apprentice-ship process, fewer and fewer trained black workers would be available for building trades jobs. Those blacks already holding building trades skills took another avenue to strengthen the position of black labor.

With the assistance of the Urban League of St. Louis, these workers organized themselves as the Skilled Building Mechanics Association (SBMA) in the spring of 1947. The association's goals included the broadening of building trades jobs for blacks and ongoing petitioning of the Board of Education to provide improved trades training at Washington High School. By May 1958 the SBMA's membership exceeded three hundred skilled black workers and continued its work to integrate the field of building trades jobs. This collective strength of this large membership provided a more commanding voice for the city's black building trades workers. Frustration over the city's award of public contracts exceeding $25,000,000 and without the employment of "a single Negro skilled building mechanic" prompted the association to charge in March 1959 that "There are three areas in which blame can be either divided or placed: The City of St. Louis and its subsidiary boards and commissions which let the contracts; the contractors who receive the contracts and the Building and Trade unions which hold the jobs." By the end of the year, the SBMA launched a campaign "to encourage the training of young men interested in becoming skilled craftsmen in the building trades."[35]

In addition to these efforts, black workers began appealing to the National Labor Relations Board (NLRB). Created by the National Labor Relations Act of 1935 (more commonly known as the Wagner Act), the responsibilities of the NLRB included the investigation of complaints filed for unfair labor practices. Section 8 (3) of the act

34. Herbert Simmons, "Hearings on Jobs to Be Continued," *St. Louis Argus,* November 6, 1959, 1; "Apprenticeship and Training Opportunities for Negro Youths in Selected Urban League Cities," Department of Industrial Relations, National Urban League, February 15, 1961, series 4, box 27, National Urban League Collection, Part II, Library of Congress.

35. "Skilled Negroes Form Council," *Urban League Bulletin,* spring 1947, 3, series 13, box 27, National Urban League Collection, Library of Congress; "Builders Urge New Age Firm to Reconsider," *St. Louis Argus,* May 16, 1958, 1; "A Basic Issue," *St. Louis Argus,* March 27, 1959, 6B; "Skilled Mechanics Ass'n Recruiting Area Prospects," *St. Louis Argus,* December 25, 1959, 1.

made it illegal for employers to engage in discriminatory hiring practices wherein labor union membership determined employment.[36] Throughout the 1920s, 1930s, and 1940s, St. Louis's construction industry had progressively become a "closed shop." Construction projects bound by the union "closed-shop" status only employed workers who were union members. In order to retain employment, closed-shop provisions required these workers to remain union members or lose their jobs. Such provisions in labor contracts between construction companies and building trade unions in St. Louis presented another obstacle for black labor.[37] As part of his statement before a congressional committee holding hearings in St. Louis during October 1947 to investigate problems blocking urban housing programs, the executive secretary of the Urban League of St. Louis stated:

> As to the Negro participation in the Building Trades unions in St. Louis, it has been a long and hard struggle with only a gesture of success in other than the Hod-Carriers and Common Laborers Local. To say that 120,000 Negro citizens can produce only a dozen Carpenters, Plasterers, Brick Masons, Plumbers, able to qualify for membership in the Building Trades Unions, ignores the Negro mechanics' glorious history in construction work back even in slavery days.[38]

The report further summarized the number of Negro electricians, plumbers, painters, brick masons, and plasterers that held either city licenses and/or union cards from locals in other cities. Nonetheless, as long as closed shop provisions remained in place, building trades unions continued to deny membership to blacks. At the same time, other members of the urban renewal coalition—contractors, private capital, St. Louis City Hall—refused to force change to these exclusionary practices, reinforcing white workers' control over the city's skilled building trades jobs.

36. Paul D. Moreno, *From Direct Action to Affirmative Action: Fair Employment Law and Policy in America, 1933–1972* (Baton Rouge: Louisiana State University Press, 1997), 113.

37. For more information on various forms of union status, see "Union Shops Hold Gains," *Carpenter,* December 1941, 41.

38. "29th Annual Report of the Work of Urban League of Saint Louis, 1947," series 13, box 26, National Urban League Collection, Library of Congress.

Blacks worked with the NLRB to correct the discriminatory hiring practices in St. Louis's construction industry, in which only union members received a referral for employment. Beginning in the early 1950s, black workers began filing their complaints of discriminatory hiring practices with the NLRB. With the support of the Urban League of St. Louis and James P. Troupe, a member of the St. Louis Housing Authority and the agency's only black member, in March 1953 four unionized black brick masons filed a complaint with the NLRB against the Stephen Gorman Bricklaying Company for discriminatory hiring practices. Although they held union cards from other cities, the AFL-affiliated brick masons' local refused to hire them. Gorman Bricklaying, the masonry contractor on the Wendell Pruitt Housing Project, would not hire workers unless referred by the brick masons' union local. Commissioner Troupe insisted that future contracts on housing projects not be awarded unless the contractor immediately began hiring black workers. After all, Federal Housing Authority regulations stipulated that skilled black workers must make up at least 4 percent of the workforce on all housing projects receiving federal funds. The St. Louis Housing Authority, however, refused to adopt a resolution proposed by Commissioner Troupe wherein he recommended that "contracts not be awarded to firms ignoring the federal regulation."[39] Regardless of this federal regulation and the St. Louis Housing Authority's awareness of discriminatory hiring practices, contracts remained in place with both general contractors and subcontractors working in noncompliance with the 4 percent hiring quota. Legal force exercised by black workers seemed to be the only remedy, if only in an incremental way. The formal complaint filed with the NLRB by the four brick masons proved to be an effective tool. By the end of April 1953 Gorman Bricklaying Company hired two of the seventeen aggrieved black workers initially applying for jobs on the Wendell Pruitt project.[40]

In the late summer of 1954, a carpenter, George Newsome, filed a complaint with the NLRB, wherein he accused the MacDonald Construction Company of unfair labor practices on the Joseph M. Darst Public Housing project. For six weeks, Newsome tried without success

39. "Brickmasons Complain to Labor Board," *St. Louis Argus,* March 20, 1953, 1; "Housing Authority Not Fair," *St. Louis Argus,* March 20, 1953, 14.

40. "Roland Hayes . . ." *St. Louis Argus,* May 1, 1953, 1.

to obtain a work permit from the United Brotherhood of Carpenters and Joiners of America, St. Louis Local 1596. Head of the local, Erwin C. Meinert, advised Newsome that members had voted against his admission. After intervention by the NLRB, attorneys representing both Local 1596 and MacDonald Construction Company agreed to the hiring of Newsome, contingent on the withdrawal of his suit.[41] Nearly four years later, in June 1958, George Newsome and his brother John were admitted as members of Local 47 of the United Brotherhood of Carpenters and Joiners of America. The brothers and others in St. Louis's black community viewed the event as "encouraging." For many, it raised "high hopes for an easing of the bars which have heretofore existed." When asked if the Carpenters' District Council of St. Louis would hire additional black workers, Dick Adams, the powerful business manager for the council, stated that "'right now we aren't accepting any more applications' . . . there are 'almost 8,500' white carpenters in the St. Louis area alone."[42] Although it was intended to explain refusals of future applications, this statement's argument, based on the labor market's saturation, only reinforced the point that white carpenters controlled the labor market in St. Louis. The admission of only two black workers to Carpenters' Local 47 did not signal a change in that control.[43]

In fact, just over a year later, George Newsome alleged that the secretary of the local carpenters' union told him that he needed to find his own jobs, rather than rely on the carpenters' hiring hall for opportunities. After traveling to Chicago to secure employment, Newsome saw an ad in the *Chicago Tribune* seeking carpenters in St. Louis. George Newsome made these facts public before a St. Louis aldermanic committee investigating racial discrimination on city construction projects. During the hearing, Newsome further stated that, to his knowledge, he did not know of any Negro ever enrolled as a carpenter apprentice in St. Louis. Finally, he contended that "it was easier to

41. "First Carpenter Goes to Work on Housing Job," *St. Louis Argus*, September 24, 1954, 1.

42. "Brothers Join Local Here Wed.," *St. Louis Argus*, June 13, 1958, 1; "A Crack in the Dike," *St. Louis Argus*, June 13, 1958, 14.

43. The St. Louis Carpenters' District Council was the umbrella union organization with which all carpenter locals in the St. Louis metropolitan area affiliated. Some locals in outlying areas also held membership in the council. The carpenters represented the largest and most powerful group of building trades workers in the city.

enter the skilled building crafts in cities in the deep south than it was in the city of St. Louis." Other black workers—specifically carpenters, a bricklayer, and an electrician—provided further support for Newsome's statement when they also testified concerning the hardships encountered in their efforts to obtain work in the building trades.[44] These workers all found support in the Urban League of St. Louis.

In addition to its work to obtain apprenticeship education for young blacks, during the early 1950s the Urban League of St. Louis expanded its efforts to strengthen the position of already skilled black building trades workers. The league's Industrial Committee had been steadfast in its efforts to open building trade jobs as early as the 1920s and throughout the Depression years.[45] These early efforts by the league to integrate black workers in the building of public housing and municipal projects had not realized any sustained progress. But the massive construction of low-rent housing projects in the 1950s provided expanded opportunities for the Urban League to assert its voice. With both the federally financed Cochran Gardens and Pruitt public housing projects under construction in 1952, Chester E. Stovall, the Urban League's director of industrial relations, encouraged "all Negro skilled laborers" to "go to these projects and apply for employment, particularly brick layers, cement finishers and carpenters."[46]

Such actions clearly reflected the availability of skilled black workers, and the subsequent nonhiring of these workers only accentuated the discriminatory hiring practices on federally assisted projects. Representing the Urban League, Stovall brought these discriminatory employment concerns before the city's Institute of Human Rights hearings that were held in early December 1952 to consider issues around health, housing, employment, and education in St. Louis City. Stovall recommended that the mayor's St. Louis Council on Human Relations "take an affirmative stand and urge the contractors now constructing the federal-financed Public Housing projects to employ non-white skilled workers as prescribed by law."[47] Although the Council on Human Relations had been in place since January 1950 and was

44. Simmons, "Hearings on Jobs," 1.
45. Henry, "Structures of Exclusion."
46. "Seeks to Place Skill Laborers," *St. Louis Argus,* December 5, 1952, 1.
47. "Urge Jobs for All at Institute," *St. Louis Argus,* December 12, 1952, 1.

charged with leadership in race relations, St. Louis's black community did not feel it had been very useful in ameliorating racial problems in the city. In theory, the council held the necessary power and authority to achieve significant improvements for black St. Louisans, but in reality, the council's unwillingness to aggressively move forward rendered it ineffective. After the Urban League's proposal to the council at the Institute of Human Rights hearings, St. Louis's black press challenged the council to establish its legitimacy. A statement published in the *St. Louis Argus* concluded, "It remains to be seen if the Council will finally begin to take its job seriously."[48]

The complexities of the urban renewal process itself, however, made it difficult for the Council on Human Relations to exert any real effectiveness. The multiple "layers" within the process created an environment conducive to finger-pointing and denial of wrongdoing when it came to the hiring of black construction workers. A policy statement issued by the St. Louis Land Clearance for Redevelopment Authority provides an example of these "layers."[49] On the eve of construction startup on the massive Mill Creek Valley redevelopment project, an editorial addressing the subject of black hiring practices appeared in the *St. Louis Argus*. The editorial insisted that the Board of Commissioners of the Land Clearance for Redevelopment Authority issue a statement concerning the policy of hiring black workers for the project. The Board of Commissioners responded, and an excerpt from its statement reads as follows:

48. "Another Chance for the Council," *St. Louis Argus,* December 19, 1952, 14.

49. Passage in mid-1951 of the Land Clearance for Redevelopment Law by the Missouri legislature enabled St. Louis City to establish the St. Louis Land Clearance for Redevelopment Authority as an operating agency "to acquire and clear land and then sell it to developers at fair market values even though the cost of securing and clearing the land may have been greater than the price to the developer." Passage of another law, the Missouri Urban Redevelopment Corporation Law, offered "private investors and developers incentives to clear blighted areas and construct office structures, stores, industrial plants and homes on a large scale." See "St. Louis Development Program," St. Louis City Plan Commission, June 1973, A10, Missouri Historical Society; "Facts about Urban Renewal in St. Louis," St. Louis Land Clearance for Redevelopment Authority, October 1962, 3–4, series 3, box 61, National Urban League Collection, Library of Congress; and "A Place to Live, Part Two: Public Programs and Issues in Renewal," Washington University Civic Education Center, spring 1962, 12, Television Collection, 1957–1963, Missouri Historical Society.

Individuals to be employed for jobs in the demolition and construction stages in the Mill Creek Valley Project . . . or any other project, should not be selected or restricted because of race, creed or color. . . . With respect to DEMOLITION contracts executed by the Land Clearance Authority with private contractors, the contract will contain the following proviso: "There shall be no discrimination by reason of race, creed, color or national origin against any employee or applicant for employment qualified by training and experience for work under this contract." Failure to comply with the provision will result in the prompt stoppage of all payments. The Construction stage takes place after the land is sold by the Land Clearance Authority. Construction will be undertaken by private industry, and not by the Land Clearance Authority or Governmental Agency; however, the Land Clearance Authority will exert every influence to cause the redevelopers to hire workmen without regard to race, creed or color.[50]

Property designated as "blighted" and subject to slum clearance and redevelopment fell under control of the Land Clearance for Redevelopment Authority. Demolition of structures on this property occurred under contracts with demolition contractors issued by the city's Redevelopment Authority. Yes, the aforementioned proviso could be made a part of said contracts, but before a discriminatory hiring complaint could be registered, investigated, and heard, more likely than not, the land clearance portion of the work would be completed. This phase of work was also the one most likely to hire black workers, anyway, because it was low-paying, labor-intensive work. St. Louis did have a black laborers local, so there were unionized black common laborers available for hire to perform work during the demolition process. The demolition contractors engaged in this work would have been subject to the "closed shop" bargaining agreements prevailing in St. Louis. Under these circumstances, it was relatively easy for St. Louis's Land Clearance for Redevelopment Authority to comply with federal hiring guidelines. But once the land was cleared and the city agency sold the land to private developers, hiring practices became increasingly decentralized and far more difficult to control.

50. "Text of Declaration," *St. Louis Argus,* October 1, 1954, 1.

Private developers purchasing property from the Land Clearance for Redevelopment Authority entered into contracts with general contractors. These general contractors were signatories to collective bargaining agreements with the St. Louis Building Trades Council. Collective membership in the Building Trades Council consisted of the various AFL building trades' locals who supplied the labor hired by general contractors. These locals determined who would gain membership in their respective locals and whether they would be white or black. Once the St. Louis Land Clearance Authority sold the cleared land to private interests, they relieved themselves of responsibility for discriminatory hiring practices. When the Land Clearance Authority issued as part of their statement that they would "exert every influence to cause the redevelopers to hire workmen without regard to race, creed or color," the members left their role vague and ambiguous. What did the Land Clearance Authority mean by "every influence" and how would this city agency exercise these "influences"? Since the financial package for these redevelopment projects included city and federal dollars, the greatest influence that the Land Clearance Authority could exert, of course, was legal enforcement of nondiscriminatory hiring practices. Despite their formal statement in support of nondiscriminatory hiring practices on urban renewal projects, the only formal *action* taken by the St. Louis Land Clearance and Redevelopment Authority was pursuit of a core city urban renewal agenda, accomplished with the conspicuous absence of black labor. Although the Urban League of St. Louis continued to challenge the mayor's Council on Human Relations to intercede in efforts to secure skilled jobs for black labor, the complexities of the urban renewal process required a commitment by the entire urban renewal coalition to accomplish such goals.

The Urban League also policed local craft unions and criticized them for their "undemocratic" practices. The local practices excluding blacks were brought to the attention of the National Urban League as well as to the federal government's National Housing Agency. The St. Louis Urban League served as the conduit between the National Urban League, local contractors, local and national trade union organizations, the local black community, and local, state, and federal government agencies. Even with this conduit in place, however, substantive change did not occur.

Finally, the NAACP joined in supporting St. Louis's black community in placing pressure on government officials and the construction industry for a fair share of the jobs generated by urban renewal projects. Paralleling the actions taken by the four brick masons, who filed their discriminatory hiring complaint with the NLRB in 1953, the legal committee of the St. Louis chapter of the NAACP took action. In early April 1953, the legal committee advised the St. Louis Housing Authority of its preparations underway to engage in legal action against the authority for engaging in prejudicial hiring practices on housing construction projects. In a letter to John J. O'Toole, executive secretary of the Housing Authority, the legal committee expressed its willingness "to discuss the matter with him in an effort to arrive at a 'just and prompt solution of the problem, thus, avoiding the necessity of legal proceedings.'"[51] Over the next several years, the NAACP legal committee and City Hall continued in their conversational exchanges, but without any sustained changes in construction jobs for black workers. As the scope of St. Louis's urban renewal agenda expanded, so did the demand for jobs. Black workers wanted construction jobs not only on public housing projects, but on the massive Mill Creek development project and other urban renewal projects, as they occurred one-by-one.[52]

The schedule for the Mill Creek construction project extended over a nine-year period, with startup expected in 1958. Initial estimates for the project's complete cost totaled $500,000,000. Funds for the project came from the federal government, municipal funds from St. Louis City, and private financing.[53] Even before demolition of the blighted area began, the NAACP launched its campaign to guarantee the pres-

51. "Threaten Suit over Work Bar," *St. Louis Argus,* April 3, 1953, 1.

52. The large Mill Creek urban development project, which consisted of both residential and commercial elements, received much criticism for the relocation of previous residents, mostly black. "Mill Creek Renewal Project Running ahead of Schedule," *St. Louis Globe Democrat,* July 4, 1966, Newspaper Clippings, 1950–1969 Collection, Missouri Historical Society.

53. The Mill Creek project covered approximately one hundred city blocks (465 acres) on the city's West Side. The net cost of "slum" clearance, after sale of the land, totaled approximately $34,400,000. The city paid $11,400,000 of this cost with the federal government providing the remainder. Private investment in this project alone exceeded $250,000,000. See "Facts about Urban Renewal in St. Louis," St. Louis Land Clearance and Redevelopment Authority, October 1962, 6–7, series 3, box 61, National Urban League Collection, Library of Congress.

ence of black labor in the nine-year construction process.[54] A year later, in March 1959, there remained no resolution, and the absence of skilled black building trades workers on the Mill Creek project, as well as on other urban renewal projects, endured. Before those attending a protest meeting, the St. Louis NAACP chapter "called for a sweeping investigation of the wholesale absence of Negroes on programs paid for with bond issue or municipal monies." Ernest Calloway, a former president of the local chapter, insisted that St. Louis City fulfill its responsibility to enforce Municipal Ordinance 47957, "which forbids employment discrimination because of race or color on all public works projects paid for in whole or in part by municipal funds."[55] The protest meeting led to incremental actions or promises to remedy the problem.

Charles Farris, executive director of the St. Louis Housing and Land Clearance Authority, noted the authority's inclusion of some of the Fair Employment Practice Ordinance language in the Mill Creek contracts. Farris stated that he expected the Urban Redevelopment Corporation, formed to purchase the land and develop the plaza project, "would live up to all laws governing the land." Farris further tried to legitimate his agency's commitment to nondiscriminatory hiring by calling attention to a meeting earlier in the month that resulted in the hiring of a black carpenter by McCarthy Brothers Construction Company on the Darst Public Housing project. Still in noncompliance relative to the hiring of unskilled laborers, Farris promised to follow through to ensure contract compliance by McCarthy. He also promised to "keep on their (contractors) backs to see that they comply" on the Mill Creek project.[56]

54. "Seek 'Fair' Share for Construction," *St. Louis Argus*, March 21, 1958, 1.

55. "Protest Meeting Highlights Issue," *St. Louis Argus*, March 27, 1959, 1. In addition to the NAACP, the mass protest meeting was composed of representatives from the Urban League of St. Louis, the black Skilled Building Mechanics Association, the St. Louis Fair Employment Practices Commission, the St. Louis Council on Human Relations, the St. Louis Board of Aldermen, the Jewish Community Relations Council, the Missouri House of Representatives, the Committee on Racial Equality, the St. Louis Federation of Block Units, the Frontiers of America, the Catholic Interracial Council, the *St. Louis American* newspaper, the National Alliance of Postal Employees, the Mound City Engineers, and the *St. Louis Argus* Publishing Company.

56. Quoted in "Protest Meeting Highlights Issue," *St. Louis Argus*, March 27, 1959, 1. For a discussion of Charles Farris's work as executive director of the St. Louis Housing and Land Clearance Authority, see Heathcott and Murphy, "Corridors of Flight."

Promises and wrangling continued concerning noncompliance by contractors and their subcontractors, but active enforcement of both federal and municipal laws aimed at discriminatory hiring practices never occurred during the 1950s. Complaints continued to be filed with City Hall and the NLRB into the 1960s. The aggressive construction goals, however, of urban renewal and redevelopment moved forward, and they did so with a lily-white skilled labor force, barring the occasional appearance of a "token" black worker here and there. In late 1951, a meeting held between members of a citizens' group and the St. Louis Housing Commissioners clearly reflected the agenda of the urban renewal coalition. The explicit agenda, "declaring [that] the Commission was mainly concerned with bricks and mortar," ultimately reinforced white privilege and power in the process, despite legislation aimed at racial inclusiveness. During the same meeting, "Members of the Commission repeatedly emphasized the fact they were largely interested in getting buildings constructed and not concerned about social aspects." Arthur Blumeyer, the chairman of the St. Louis Housing Commissioners, stated that "contractors make their bids under specifications which cite the Housing Act requirements on labor, but said enforcement is left up to the contractor."[57] So went the ongoing finger-pointing. Discriminatory hiring practices were always the fault or responsibility of a different party. No individual, group of individuals, governmental agency, or legislative body ever assumed the active and sustained enforcement of nondiscriminatory hiring practices during the urban renewal process.

Two years later, in 1953, the *St. Louis Argus* issued a scathing response to Mayor Joseph M. Darst's four-year report on his administration. The report's disregard for St. Louis's black population prompted the black press to denounce Darst and his administration. Although the *St. Louis Argus* editorial commented on several aspects of Darst's report, which he had titled "An American City," in the area of employment the editorial stated: "Being a real estate man, Mayor Darst should know that the Housing Act provided that in the construction of hous-

57. "City Housing Body Hears from Citizens," *St. Louis Argus,* December 28, 1951, 1. The citizens' group included representatives from the Catholic Interracial Council, Negro Business League, Council of Jewish Women, National Council of Negro Women, Civil Liberties Union, National Council of Christians and Jews, Metropolitan Church Federation, and Teamsters Union, Local 688, AFL.

ing projects assisted by the federal government at least a certain percent of skilled workers should be Negro citizens. St. Louis's great construction program has been carried on without aid of skilled Negro workers. Indeed, they have been refused such jobs. . . . There are other instances of Negro workers being discriminated against where federal contracts were involved, but construction of housing is the Mayor's primary interest."[58] All the while that groups of blacks and concerned white citizens took actions to strengthen the position of black labor during the period of urban renewal in St. Louis, organized labor itself worked to ameliorate its own internal problems. Although organized labor recognized the external challenge of black activism pushing for access to skilled jobs, this challenge did not seem as threatening to the stabilization of the trades as other internal challenges.

In May 1945 the *St. Louis Labor Tribune* published an article reporting on the unanimous vote by the St. Louis Building and Construction Trades Council to support Mayor Kaufmann's plans for slum clearance and housing projects. Throughout the period of postwar urban renewal, the *St. Louis Labor Tribune* consistently reported on labor's support of urban renewal projects. The Building Trades Council went so far as to contribute $15,000 in 1955 to a $110,639,000 bond issue campaign to help defray publicity and advertising costs. The passage of this particular bond issue brought with it an additional $586,145,000 from private capital and the state and federal government for a total of $696,784,000 to fund more capital improvements.[59] The council's support for bond issues is not surprising in that slum clearance and urban renewal translated into a stable employment pattern for white members of AFL craft unions. Not only did organized labor support urban renewal, but also labor leaders rallied their members to vote in favor of pending local and state legislation designed to expedite and ease the urban renewal process. Mayor Kaufmann's

---

58. "An American City," *St. Louis Argus,* April 3, 1953, 14.

59. "AFL Building Trades Supports Mayor's Slum Housing Project," *St. Louis Labor Tribune,* May 30, 1945, 1; "Building Trades Council Urge Bond Issue Passage as Vitally Essential for City Progress," *St. Louis Labor Tribune,* May 12, 1955, 1; "AFL Central Trades Supports Both $110,639,000 Bond Issue and $16,395,000 Bond Issue," *St. Louis Labor Tribune,* May 19, 1955, 1. Still in publication, the *St. Louis Labor Tribune* is a weekly newspaper circulated to all members of local unions affiliated with the AFL-CIO.

appointment in 1947 of John J. Church, former executive secretary of the St. Louis Building and Construction Trades Council, to the newly created nine-member St. Louis Plan Commission further strengthened the urban renewal coalition between local government and the construction industry. Established in 1945, the commission assumed the legal authority to administer the city's "master community plan." The mayor also appointed Church to the Anti-Slum Commission and the Bond Issue Supervisory Committee.[60]

Aside from labor's external public support of the urban renewal process and the promise of jobs for some thirty thousand white building trades workers, significant challenges within organized labor threatened to unsettle the ability of the building trades to successfully meet construction demands. These challenges appeared more ominous and seemed to pose an even greater threat to the stability of the building trades than the presence of black activism around jobs. In St. Louis's secure Jim Crow environment, the possibility of blacks encroaching on the racialized practices of the construction industry did not appear to suggest a real threat to white jobs. The building trades either ignored or addressed in a minimalist way black labor's activism, leaving time and resources to focus on what seemed to be labor's real challenges.

Confrontation over the issue of wages represented the first of these challenges. The carpenters, as well as other trades, battled with contractors to secure higher wages for apprentices and journeymen.[61] Carpenters constituted the largest trade union in St. Louis and frequently set the pace for other crafts. It was not unusual for wage disputes to lead to informational picketing and strikes, strikes respected by all trades, which effectively shut down construction projects. Struggles for power over who would dictate established union wage scales escalated between members of the St. Louis Building and Construction Trades Council and the Master Builders Association of St. Louis, a

60. "John J. Church Named by Mayor to New St. Louis Plan Commission," *St. Louis Labor Tribune*, May 9, 1947, 1; "St. Louis: Report to the Community, 1947–1948," City of St. Louis, 1948, 77, Missouri Historical Society.

61. "Twenty Dollars a Day Sought by AFL Hoisting Engineers in City, Top Rate for U.S.," *St. Louis Post-Dispatch*, November 14, 1945; "Building Strike Scheduled Today by Two Unions," *St. Louis Globe-Democrat*, May 1, 1947; "Contractors Yield to AFL Carps in Wage Disputes," *St. Louis Argus*, June 11, 1947, 1.

group composed of about twenty-seven of the largest construction firms in St. Louis.[62] Public opinion over the high cost of construction on housing and urban renewal projects, and the association made between high construction costs and high labor costs, led labor organizations to defend their wage scales. In defense of their wage scales, labor pointed the finger at contractors and their "hidden costs," resulting in large profits for construction firms.[63]

Jurisdictional disputes also challenged the stability of the building trades worker. These jurisdictional disputes between crafts led to frequent work stoppages and antagonistic relationships between various craft unions and their members. They occurred when two or more trades laid claim to a particular segment of work. The multitasked nature of the work and the multitude of various craft workers looking to expand their individual share of work on a given project left the construction process prone to such disputes. A jurisdictional dispute in June 1951 reflects the economic impact of such disputes on both workers and urban renewal projects. Carpenters and laborers walked off the job over a dispute concerning which workers "should carry the wooden forms into which concrete is poured after it is fabricated by the carpenters." The dispute threatened the jobs of nearly twenty-five thousand building trades workers and the shutdown of millions of dollars of work in progress.[64]

Prefabricated building products presented yet another destabilizing element for the building trades. Picketing at job sites by labor over the delivery and use of prefabricated building products incited conflicts between labor and management. Throughout the twentieth century, the use of prefabricated building products increasingly expanded.

62. A labor agreement with this group, the Master Builders Association of St. Louis (MBA), bound all member firms to the agreement. The MBA and the Municipal Contractors Association (MCA) were both organized in the World War I era. Each organization affiliated with the newly formed Associated General Contractors of America. MBA members were large general contractors, and the MCA members provided heavy construction services such as the building of sewers, roads, bridges, and power plants. In 1950 they merged as the Associated General Contractors of St. Louis.

63. "St. Louis A.F. of L. Carps Ask: Who Are the Profiteers in the Building Industry?" *St. Louis Labor Tribune*, May 14, 1947, 1.

64. "Laborers Strike at Jobs Not Hit by Carpenter Walkout," *St. Louis Star-Times*, June 15, 1951, 16.

When these products were manufactured in a nonunion shop and were then delivered to a union job site, tensions flared. Not only did these products represent work now taken out of the hands of the craft worker, but also the prefabricated nature of the products often made it unclear as to which trade should install the product, which frequently led to jurisdictional disputes. The end solution sometimes resulted in the use of a "composite crew," possibly electricians and carpenters working together to install the prefabricated product. Management's aim was to take advantage of the newest technology and manufacturing techniques in order to deliver construction projects in the shortest period of time and at the lowest possible cost. Concurrently, labor viewed the use of prefabricated products as debasing their traditional craft labor practices performed on the job site. Another aspect of this struggle over the use of prefabricated products was the role consumer demand played for the quick and efficient delivery of a finished product, particularly in the area of housing.

Charges of labor racketeering filed against local labor leaders represented a final challenge for St. Louis's construction labor force. The eventual outcomes of these charges varied. In some circumstances charges were dropped; other cases were declared mistrials, and in some instances, labor leaders served sentences in federal penitentiaries. For example, in December 1953, Leo F. Havey, the business representative of Local 1, Bricklayers, Stone and Marble Mason's Union, was indicted on grand jury charges of "unlawfully threatening violence in furtherance of a 'plan and purpose to obstruct, delay and effect commerce.'" Allegedly Havey prevented black bricklayers from working on a job at St. Louis's Jefferson Barracks. Within hours after the indictment, Havey resigned from his position as chairman of the St. Louis Land Clearance and Redevelopment Authority. Havey had also previously served as a member of the St. Louis Housing Authority, where it is said he repeatedly clashed with the authority's lone black member, James P. Troupe, on racial matters.[65]

Less than a year later, a federal judge declared a mistrial in a case charging three AFL leaders with labor racketeering. The three defendants were L. A. Thompson, former business agent of the Teamsters Union, Local 574, Cape Girardeau, Missouri; Carl J. (Dutch) Bianchi,

---

65. "Indicted AFL Chief Called 'Foe,'" *St. Louis Argus*, January 1, 1954, 1.

business representative of the Hoisting Engineers, Local 513; and George E. Seaton, business representative of Local 562, Steamfitters Union. Thompson and Bianchi were already serving prison sentences for previous convictions. During the summer of 1954 *Fortune* magazine ran an article wherein St. Louis was noted as "the capital of labor rackets in the construction industry." The article further noted that in the previous year one grand jury "indicted fifteen A. F. of L. construction-union leaders for extortion" and then a few months later "two other grand juries indicted eighteen more persons."[66] Regardless of the outcome, charges of labor racketeering within the building trades cast a dark shadow over organized labor and the construction industry in St. Louis throughout the 1950s and 1960s.

Collectively, challenges over wage rates, high construction costs, jurisdictional disputes, the use of prefabricated building products, and racketeering charges threatened to destabilize the labor force and industry most critical to the economic success of an urban renewal agenda. The added element of a rapidly growing and vocal black constituency seeking jobs within the central city, coupled with an expanding local and national civil rights movement, also threatened to aggravate the already shifting foundation and disorder of St. Louis's building industry. Rather than cross racial divides, the urban renewal coalition—both implicitly and explicitly—chose to compromise black workers rather than compromise the progress of urban renewal.

The size and power of the construction industry placed it at the center politically and economically of all major growth and development activities, thus ensuring the industry's role as an integral component of urban renewal. St. Louis experienced the completion of nearly one billion dollars of urban renewal work between 1945 and 1965. Such a large volume of construction activity represented tremendous economic opportunities for St. Louis's expanding black population seeking skilled jobs in the building trades. Despite these opportunities, black workers suffered extreme limitations in their search for jobs in St. Louis's white building trades. The development of black labor

---

66. "No Verdict in Labor Racket Case against 3," *St. Louis Labor Tribune*, September 23, 1954, 1; "Labor: What's behind the News and What's Ahead," *Fortune*, July 1954, 35.

coalitions, however, directly challenged the stubborn white craft union heritage of racialized exclusionary practices. This challenge of black activism threatened to bring further disorder to the city's construction industry—the industry most critical to achieving urban renewal in postwar St. Louis. But "challenge" was all black activism did. Local traditions steadfastly clung to exclusionary practices historically keeping blacks out of skilled building trades jobs. Even in this state of unprecedented economic opportunities, only conciliatory jobs appeared for St. Louis's black construction workers. Urban renewal goals could not be accomplished with labor strife in the building trades, and other matters outside of the realm of race were already creating substantial labor strife. To further exacerbate this strife by forcing white building trades workers to relinquish at least some modicum of their white privilege in the arena of building trades jobs would have required urban renewal leaders, both public and private, to compromise their aggressive urban renewal agenda. Although challenged by black activism, St. Louis's white building trades workers were not forced to relinquish their collective power over jobs.

Black activism was one thing, but sustained success also depended on political leaders' being willing to force white building trade unions to admit black workers and then guarantee an offering of actual job opportunities after union membership. Black labor's success in obtaining construction jobs depended as well on private business and commercial real estate interests' willingness to exert their power to ensure the inclusion of black labor by both organized labor and general contractors. But such a racially inclusive policy by the urban renewal coalition consisting of local government, the federal government, private business interests, and labor and management leaders in the city's construction industry required transcending the white identity of the building trades worker to include blacks. Outside the meeting rooms of the urban renewal coalition, individual members lived within the city's social climate of Jim Crow patterns of segregation and discrimination. Privilege defined by whiteness continued to prevail. Efforts by black labor to move beyond racial discrimination in the building trades occurred within a city unwilling to pass a civil rights bill, prepared to riot over the possibility of integrating public pools, and unable to realize a level of social justice wherein blacks could access acceptable housing, education, and health care. But despite this racialized climate, throughout the postwar period there were ongoing and tenacious efforts by St. Louis's black community and liberal whites to challenge racial bias and discrimination in many industries, but particularly the racial bias and discrimination exercised by St. Louis's white building trade unions. Racial divides in these unions, however, were not addressed by the urban renewal coalition so that employment equity across racial lines could be achieved in St. Louis's white construction industry during the city's urban renewal process.

The focus of this essay has been on the complex relationship between black workers and St. Louis's building industry during the city's urban renewal years. It provides, however, only a small piece of the history of this relationship, one beginning in the early twentieth century and continuing today. Some thirty years after affirmative action policies spun out of the nation's civil rights movement, the presence of black workers in St. Louis's construction industry remains negligible. Len Toenjes, president of the Associated General Contractors of St. Louis, acknowledges the dilemma, "We've had goals, quotas, percentages, numbers and so on for 35 years in the industry, and have not had the kind of progress in this area [African Americans in the building industry] that anyone would find satisfactory."[67] Racial polarization in St. Louis's building community remains a reality despite the industry's skilled worker shortage of the 1990s.

In 2000, St. Louis–based construction and design firms contributed more than three billion dollars to the St. Louis economy. Although the national trend is open-shop construction, wherein only 19.6 percent of all construction workers are unionized, St. Louis remains highly unionized. According to a September 2000 action plan for inner-city revitalization, union labor provides approximately 85 percent of the region's total dollar value of construction and "approaches 100 percent for major public sector commercial and industrial projects." Trade union membership in St. Louis currently exceeds twenty-seven thousand.[68] Within a strong unionized environment and an economically vibrant

---

67. Joe Schuster, "Targets and Training Build Minority Involvement in Construction," *St. Louis Construction News and Review,* July–August 2001, 52.

68. Peter Downs, "Construction and Design Companies Fuel St. Louis Economy," *St. Louis Construction News and Review,* May–June 2001, 1; "Building Trade Union Membership Rose in 1999; Overall Union Rolls Unchanged," *Construction Labor Report* 45, no. 2262, January 26, 2000 (Washington, D.C.: Bureau of National Affairs), 1316; ICIC Initiative for a Competitive Inner City, *St. Louis Inner City Competitive Assessment and Strategy,* September 2000, 39.

construction industry, social and economic conditions in St. Louis remain less favorable for a large part of the city's African American population. Not much has changed since the civil rights years of the 1950s and 1960s.

A 2000 Census data analysis placed St. Louis as the nation's ninth most segregated region.[69] This pattern of perpetual racial segregation manifests itself in substandard housing, education, health care, and employment patterns for most of the city's black citizens. The area with the poorest blacks living in St. Louis City has a 37 percent high school graduation rate, an 18 percent unemployment rate, and an average household income of only $18,538; 52 percent of its residents live below the poverty line. Despite efforts to integrate schools in St. Louis, students were more likely in 2001 than in 1990 to attend schools that were more segregated than integrated.[70] These contemporary conditions in the local construction industry and the broader St. Louis community suggest that the urban renewal coalition of the mid-twentieth century—local government, the federal government, private business interests, and labor and management leaders in the city's construction industry—has not yet achieved the sustained, collective commitment necessary to transcend the white identity of the building trades worker to ensure employment equity across racial lines.

69. Focus St. Louis, "Racial Equality in the St. Louis Region: A Community Call to Action," July 2001, 9. For an analysis of segregation in St. Louis, see Douglas S. Massey and Nancy A. Denton, "Hypersegregation in U.S. Metropolitan Areas: Black and Hispanic Segregation along Five Dimensions," *Demography* 26, no. 3 (August 1989): 373–91.

70. Deborah L. Shelton, "Health Status Shows Racial Divide in City, Report Says," *St. Louis Post-Dispatch*, March 22, 2001, A8; Holly K. Hacker, "Progress in Integration Eludes St. Louis City, County Schools," *St. Louis Post-Dispatch*, July 22, 2001, A1.

The Failure of Alliance/Populism in Northern Missouri

MICHAEL J. STEINER

During the middle decades of the Gilded Age a protest rose out of the fields of Texas, the Middle West, and the Great Plains that elevated to national politics the prospect of a class-based protest movement capable of transforming the established economic and political order of American life. Much has been written about the Farmers' Alliance, the Populists who followed, and the influence that their movements had on a generation of "reform" policy in America. Historians continue to wrestle, however, with the problem of why the Farmers' Alliance as a producers' movement and the Populists as a third party were not more successful in achieving their objectives, and why they saw their grand vision of a republic controlled by its laboring producers diluted by the largely conservative reforms of the Progressive Era.[1]

While the movements indeed stirred passion, hope, and belief in a

1. While the essential conservatism of progressivism is still open to some debate, a number of historians, most notably Gabriel Kolko, have quite successfully argued that the outcome of the "age of reform" was essentially conservative. Gabriel Kolko, *The Triumph of Conservatism: A Reinterpretation of American History, 1900–1916* (New York: Free Press, 1963). On the Farmers' Alliance and Populist movements, see also Lawrence Goodwyn, *The Populist Moment: A Short History of the Agrarian Revolt in America* (Oxford: Oxford University Press, 1978); Theodore Saloutos, *Populism: Reaction or Reform?* (Huntington, N.Y.: Krieger Publishing, 1978); Catherine McNicol Stock and Robert D. Johnston, eds., *The Countryside in the Age of the Modern State: Political Histories of Rural America* (Ithaca: Cornell University Press, 2001); Elizabeth Sanders, *Roots of Reform: Farmers, Workers, and the American State, 1877–1917* (Chicago: University of Chicago Press, 1999); and Robert C. McMath, *American Populism: A Social History, 1877–1898* (New York: Hill and Wang, 1993).

new order, pockets of the farmers' dominion remained stubbornly resistant to the overall movement and constantly undermined its success. A close assessment of Alliance/Populism in Missouri, and the northwestern corner of the state in particular, provides an excellent map of the varied sources of this resistance to reform by people who might have greatly benefited from it. Their reluctance lay buried most deeply in a paralyzing tension between a conservative attachment to limited government, low taxes, and notions of reform rooted in individual morality, and their desire to join the national marketplace of cash-surplus farming, machinery, and consumer goods. While farmers across Missouri were drawn to the prospect of a revised order in which their labor would be rewarded with financial prosperity and equality of esteem with those who represented the new age of industrial finance capitalism, they were largely tempered to resist the very ideas and policies that could secure the economic and political well-being of those who labored in the fields and rail yards. Offered the opportunity to benefit from the growth of the modern economy by forcing fundamental changes in the way it functioned, they made only limited strides toward a prosperity that equitably distributed the new wealth, and in the end they chose to consign their futures to the established order of political economy.

Like those in many other sectors of the American economy, farmers were torn by the dramatic changes brought by industrialization. The upheaval that came in the postbellum period created a new kind of uncertainty to which farmers were unaccustomed. At the same time, they also wanted to benefit from the new economic order. Like their urban counterparts, many farmers wanted to "get ahead" by embracing modern technology in production and consumer goods for their homes, though the transformation also met with stiff resistance from many farmers. As Stephen Hahn and others have pointed out, there were areas of strong opposition to immersion into the modern market economy among farmers, but particularly in the North and West "the 'market-focussed concept of agriculture' . . . clearly came to dominate the rural sector during the second half of the nineteenth century."[2]

2. Stephen Hahn, "The 'Unmaking' of the Southern Yeomanry: The Transformation of the Georgia Upcountry, 1860–1890," in *The Countryside in the Age of Capitalist Transformation* (Chapel Hill: University of North Carolina Press, 1985), 180.

During the decades of the 1880s and 1890s, farmers in Missouri expanded improved cropland, increased production per acre, and enlarged their investments in new implements and machinery. Those who feared the changes that would result saw their worries justified by the wild annual fluctuations in prices and production and a long-term decline in income from 1870 to 1900 that made conditions for modern farmers difficult.[3] These changes, however did not produce an immediate reaction or widespread demands for a return to traditional agriculture. Farmers, instead, continued to expand. As long as annual dips were not too extreme, the long-term decline was mitigated by a moderate decline in consumer prices for farmers, especially in the cost of machinery. One consequence was that those areas of the country that witnessed more volatile price variations (which tended to be those with less stable climatic conditions) produced a greater propensity to react.

In Missouri, the problems were mixed, both in their nature and geographic impact. Statewide, during the 1870s, the average farm size decreased; in the 1880s, it held about constant; and through the decade of the 1890s it decreased again. During these same decades, production rates for major commodities increased at nearly twice the rate of population growth (though in corn, wheat, and oats, Missouri's production per farmer drifted behind even more dramatic increases in national averages). Attempts to offset the land crunch by increasing yields per acre seem to have failed from 1870 to 1900 to bring the expected rise in incomes. Accompanying the price and production problems for Missouri farmers was a substantial increase in indebtedness, with those holding the fewest acres increasing their debt the fastest.[4]

The solution sought by many farmers, and encouraged by numerous agencies, was to increase production through improved agronomy and the acquisition of modern machinery. In Missouri, the State Horticultural Society (whose membership was 50 percent urban) and

3. Homer Clevenger, "Agrarian Politics in Missouri, 1880–1896" (Ph.D. diss., University of Missouri–Columbia, 1940), 42–45; see also F. B. Mumford, "A Century of Missouri Agriculture," *Missouri Historical Review* 15 (January 1921): 287.

4. *Twenty-fourth Annual Report of the Missouri Board of Labor Statistics and Inspection*, 1902, 66; *Twelfth Census of the United States*, 1900, "Population," I, 19; "Agriculture," II, 64–65; Clevenger, "Agrarian Politics," 41, 49–50; Mumford, "A Century of Missouri Agriculture," 287.

the State Board of Agriculture pushed for industrialization of agriculture and higher production. The theory was that the filling out of the rail network, which would open trade to the whole world, would demand the higher production and provide constant growth in standards of living for farmers. The Missouri Agricultural College at the University of Missouri likewise preached the gospel of high production and scientific industrial methods. The State Board of Agriculture took its belief in progress to small farmers through farming institutes. Starting in 1882, promoters sponsored institutes designed to inculcate farmers in industrial market farming. During the first big year of the Populists in 1892, the board sponsored eighty-one institutes in which they preached scientific methods and crop development, high investment in pedigreed livestock, and heavy spending on machinery. Local businessmen, especially bankers, in towns across the state further encouraged (and even strong-armed) farmers into listening to the forces of modernization. Concerned that small farmers were not aggressive enough as modern entrepreneurs in the pursuit of high production, the Board of Agriculture on occasion offered prize incentives for high production. Although the response of farmers often did not match the enthusiasm of university and state agents (the formally schooled meeting, perhaps, with the wary suspicion of those who learned from their fathers and experience), they did attend the meetings and showed in their actions a desire to modernize.[5]

During the last two decades of the nineteenth century, farmers in northwestern Missouri embraced modern market agriculture, bringing more land under cultivation and applying technology to produce more intensively. They showed steady increases in the number of improved acres of land in cultivation, increasing acres devoted to crop production by an average of 9 percent. While tight money kept northwest Missouri farmers leery of increased investment in equipment through the 1880s (their investment was increased by only 0.4 percent per cultivated acre), they increased their investment in machinery by a stout 28 percent during the 1890s, with farmers in several counties in-

5. David P. Thelen, *Paths of Resistance: Tradition and Dignity in Industrializing Missouri* (New York: Oxford University Press, 1986), 35–37, 40–41. In 1882 the university fired longtime dean of agriculture George Swallow, who viewed agriculture as one of the liberal arts, replacing him with J. W. Sanborn, who sought to professionalize agriculture and worked closely with large farmers. Ibid., 37–39.

vesting nearly 40 percent more on average over that decade. The added investment drove production skyward by 91 percent over the twenty-year period.[6] Prodded by either profit motive, promoters, or attempts to outrun accumulating debt, northwestern Missouri farmers adapted new methods, invested in modern equipment, and dramatically increased production throughout the Gilded Age despite stagnant incomes. Demonstrating their faith in the Industrial Age's logic of scale, farmers discovered (and continued to realize through the twentieth century) that the net result of high production typically was low prices for a market glutted with commodities. So farmers were left with incomes not noticeably higher than before they increased production, and now they were left with heavy indebtedness as well.

Also on the list of farmer woes were the railroads. Like other dimensions of the new farm economy, including mechanical equipment, the railroads were a benefit that farmers desired and needed to market their expanding production. The rails would open them up to national markets and as a result, presumably, would raise incomes. But the railroad system did not work to the benefit of the farmers in the way that they had believed. The railroads were an awkward blending of private capital and public subsidies, one that time would demonstrate to be an arrangement fraught with the peril of manipulation and corruption. Railroad promoters, in conjunction with state legislators, successfully lobbied for extensive state and local financial incentives to build the rail network. In Missouri in the 1860s the state government sold, at considerable discount, the assets the state had accumulated in public railroad development in the 1850s. Taxpayers felt betrayed. Furthermore, the railroads then pestered communities and

6. Figures are based on calculations from U.S. Census data found at the *United States Historical Census Data Browser,* Inter-University Consortium for Political and Social Research at http://fisher.lib.virginia.edu/census/; available in print at Inter-University Consortium for Political and Social Research, *Study 00003: Historical Demographic, Economic, and Social Data: U.S., 1790–1970* (Ann Arbor, Mich.: ICPSR). Statistics for northwest Missouri are based on seventeen counties: Andrew, Atchison, Buchanan, Caldwell, Carroll, Clinton, Daviess, DeKalb, Gentry, Grundy, Harrison, Holt, Livingston, Mercer, Nodaway, Ray, and Worth. The inflation rate for 1880 to 1900 averaged -0.8 percent, making the dollar nearly constant over this time period; hence the dollar averages adjusted for inflation result in identical rounded percentages. Inflation rates can be found at John McCusker, "What Was the Inflation Rate Then?" Economic History Services, 2002, URL: http://www.eh.net/hmit/inflation/.

county boards for tax and bond subsidies to complete the lines. While Missourians from the farms and cities across the state showed eagerness to join the national marketplace and sought the advantages to be gained from access to the rails, the high cost of tax-supported subsidies and the concentration of wealth in the hands of speculators soon turned taxpayers against development. As voters in numerous counties across the state worried about the growing debt and rejected bond issues for railroad development, local courts or county boards issued the bonds anyway. State laws on the matter were vague and largely supported such nondemocratic bond issues. State authorities, too, were prone to ignore any legal problems, in favor of railroad development on the backs of local taxpayers.[7] The problematic posture of Missouri farmers in between the old and the new became evident in the railroad issue. The rails would bring farmers the markets and goods they desired, but they came with the evils of corporations, government, and worst of all, taxes.

Given these conditions, and the general climate of rural Missouri in the Gilded Age, it seemed natural that Missouri farmers would join the growing national movement of farmer protest. Throughout the Midwest the first large farmer organization designed to address these problems was the Grange movement. The Grange was particularly popular in Missouri, and by 1875 Missourians had the largest membership of any state. The movement was most attractive to diversified farmers producing a variety of grains and livestock. From the beginning, the Grange emphasized solutions to unfavorable markets through cooperative economic activity and attempted to remain aloof from political activity.[8] The localized consumer and shipping cooperatives formed by the Grangers failed to meet expectations in most counties, however, and by the early 1880s the Grange was struggling to maintain support. While the Grange in Missouri faced numerous problems,

---

7. See Edwin Lopata, *Local Aid to Railroads in Missouri* (New York: Columbia Press, 1937); and Homer Clevenger, "Railroads in Missouri Politics, 1875–1887," *Missouri Historical Review* 43 (April 1949): 224–30. The anger that resulted sometimes turned violent. Near Gunn City, three local officials were murdered by a mob of over two hundred for conspiring to issue bonds against the will of local voters; see Thelen, *Paths of Resistance,* 29–35, 62–70.

8. Raymond A. Young, *Cultivating Cooperation: A History of the Missouri Farmers Association* (Columbia: University of Missouri Press, 1995), 14–15.

including the lack of dynamic leadership and the failure of its cooperatives, it educated farmers in political economy and taught valuable lessons about what did not work. Its weaknesses would be difficult to overcome, however, since the suggestion of adding stronger leadership and political activism to the Grange alienated many farmers. The solution for farmer activists was to tap into the stronger Alliance movement developing among farmers in the upper Midwest and across the South.

The Alliance movement first filtered into Missouri in the early 1880s through the Missouri Producing Men's Association, affiliated with the northern alliances. It disappeared quickly, however, when the southern Agricultural Wheel rolled in from Arkansas in 1886. By 1889 the well-organized Wheel claimed a membership of 120,000 in sixty counties, including every county south of the Missouri River. The Farmers' Alliance reached Missouri in 1887, with 20,000 members in thirty-eight counties by 1889. In that year, the two organizations consolidated their alliances under the Farmers' and Laborers' Union banner raised at a convention of their national orders in St. Louis.[9] Like the Grange, the alliances viewed their function as fraternal and economic rather than political; and like the founders of the Southern Alliance, Missouri alliancemen retained many of the lodge-hall rituals and rules of membership that characterized fraternal organizations of the period. Alliance meetings included secret handshakes, recitations, and the opportunity to blackball one another from participation, though meetings were opened to the public when deemed necessary. Gaining membership was easy and inexpensive, however, since members paid an initiation of fifty cents and annual dues of twenty cents.[10]

Growth in Alliance membership was initially quite rapid—astonishing, in fact, to observers at the time. The railroad strikes of 1886

9. Though the organization's figures may be inflated, there are no studies yet that disprove them. See Young, *Cultivating Cooperation*, 15; and Michael Steiner, "Toilers of the Cities and Tillers of the Soil: The 1889 St. Louis 'Convention of the Middle Classes,'" *Missouri Historical Review* 93 (July 1999): 397–416.

10. On the Alliance movement, and the nature of the Southern Alliance in particular, see Robert McMath, *Populist Vanguard: A History of the Southern Farmers' Alliance* (Chapel Hill: University of North Carolina Press, 1975). On the Southern Alliance in Missouri, see Clevenger, "Agrarian Politics," 87–91; and Thelen, *Paths of Resistance*, 205–6.

followed by the success of the railroads in blocking state regulation in Missouri generated hostility among farmers toward the railroads. Drought in 1887 severely damaged Missouri's farm economy, and persistently low commodities prices left farmers in financial distress and receptive to the pleas of Alliance organizers. Additionally, farmers were concerned by what might best be described as their public image. Not only were their sons and daughters abandoning the farm, but also the general view of the industrial age that farmers were backward "hicks" led them to believe they had few allies making policy. By 1890 Missouri newspapers were estimating total Alliance membership in the state at around two hundred thousand.[11] Over the next year and a half the Alliance built enthusiasm and marched into political action by throwing its lot in with the new Populist party—a coalition of labor reform groups that came to be dominated by the farmers.

The financial crisis that began to settle into Missouri in 1892 (and became a panic in 1893), coupled with further drought and pestilence through much of the state, provided an audience receptive to an increasingly radical tone. Should Farmers' Alliance and Populist leaders in Missouri capitalize on the opportunity, they would have a powerful movement on their hands. The key to their political success was their ability to offer real remedies to farmers and to distance themselves from the persistent conservatism of the two major parties.

It was with considerable optimism then, that the Alliance members and Populists approached the 1892 elections. With voting farmers outnumbering any other electoral group in the state, Populist candidates in both state and national elections had reason for optimism. But despite the unprecedented third-party showing for the Populists, their success in Missouri, particularly compared to the plains states to the west, was limited. In the presidential election, Populist candidate James B. Weaver polled only 7.6 percent of the votes in Missouri. While Democrat Grover Cleveland, whose party represented the moderate farmer reform platform, won the popular vote in the state, it was not on the basis of strong farmer support. Strong Democratic margins in

11. Gilbert Clardy, "The Rhetoric of Populism in Missouri" (master's thesis, University of Missouri–Columbia, 1972), 81. Clardy observes that speeches by organizing farmers regularly referred to this image problem; see also Clevenger, "Agrarian Politics," 96–97.

towns and cities along the Missouri River valley, and particularly Kansas City, gave strength to Democratic numbers. In rural counties north of the river, the Republican party prevailed. The Populist candidate for governor, Leverett Leonard, fared even worse than Weaver, with less than 7 percent of the vote in the state. In races for congressional representatives, the showing for the Populist party was also poor. Winning no counties, the Populists out-polled both major parties in only one county in which they were opposed by both.

Despite the broad appeal of the Populist platform among Missouri farmers, the support for Populist candidates in 1892 was disappointing to say the least. While the alliances claimed membership of 140,000 in 1889, they could only muster a little over 41,000 votes for Populist presidential candidate James Weaver in 1892. Weaver managed only 11.9 percent of the vote in northwest Missouri and a much stronger, though still disappointing 21 percent in the southwestern corner of the state. As they managed to do throughout the next five years, Democrats effectively absorbed enough of the interests of the farmers movement, without ever accepting its fundamental demands, to thwart third-party success.[12]

The Farmers' Alliance had hoped to join forces politically with the Populist party while maintaining its distinct identity, with farmers holding dual membership. The arrangement was awkward, however, as farmers were faced with the choice of sticking to the party of their fathers and addressing their particular farm interests through a moderated Alliance (something more akin to the Grange) or embracing Populism and jettisoning alliances as superfluous. The resulting lack of cohesion, along with a number of other factors, led to a downward spiral in membership. At the state meeting in Moberly in 1892, the organization had to trim its sails considerably. Membership requirements were reduced, dues were cut, and officer salaries were slashed in half. The next year saw the state alliance organization essentially collapsed: renewed economic prosperity, the rise of the Populist party, and division among Farmers' Alliance leaders on the third-party question had all but killed the Alliance movement in Missouri.[13] More

12. *Missouri Official Manual, 1893–1894,* "Elections," 8, 18–19, 42–43, 71–75; Thelen, *Paths of Resistance,* 215.

13. *Memphis Farmers' Union,* September 8, 1892; Clevenger, "Agrarian Politics," 98.

important, however, was the fact that, as a movement in political radicalism, the Missouri Farmers' Alliance was seriously hobbled from the start by a series of conditions in the state that allowed for what historian Gabriel Kolko would call the "triumph of conservatism."

The growth in the Alliance movement had been both large and fast, but from the beginning it was plagued with divisiveness over both goals and tactics. While these problems affected the national movement, they were particularly debilitating to the Alliance in Missouri, with the northwestern corner of the state showing the greatest resistance to the movement. The central problem with regard to policy objectives was the degree and method by which governments should expand the money supply. Farmers generally agreed that tight monetary policy had been one of the central sources of difficulty. The high demand for credit by modern farmers necessitated cheap money in order to insure profits. Alliance journals in Missouri devoted considerable column space to the money question (many dealing with it almost exclusively) from 1889 through the mid-1890s. By 1893 the *Hamilton Farmers' Advocate* asserted confidently that "everybody now sees the necessity of an increased currency, and we believe that demands at the polls in November will be almost universal for that much-needed reform."[14] The opponents whom inflationist farmers had to face were a combination of capitalists who wanted to protect the value of their wealth, foreign investors (whom the *Farmers' Advocate* preferred to call the "English Jew money power"), and political conservatives, from all levels of the economy, who feared breaking with the tradition of storing value in specie and government involvement in exotic monetary schemes.

In December 1889 the national Farmers' Alliance and Industrial Union adopted as a policy plank one such scheme. Known as the "subtreasury system," it proposed that government warehouses would be distributed across the country; these would issue very low-interest loans to farmers against their stored nonperishable goods. The plan would serve the dual purpose of making the money supply more elastic for farmers while also allowing them to hold their products in free storage until market prices were more favorable.[15]

14. *Hamilton (Mo.) Farmers Advocate*, May 24, 1893, 2.
15. For a full description of the subtreasury plan, see John D. Hicks, *The Populist Revolt: A History of the National Farmers' Alliance and the People's Party* (Minneapolis: University of Minnesota Press, 1931), 186–204.

The subtreasury plan, however, was not popular among all Missouri alliancemen. At the 1890 state Alliance meeting in Sedalia, farmers faced a serious split on the subtreasury question, and some state leaders were the most outspoken opponents. Leading the naysayers was U. S. Hall from Randolph County, who argued (rather dubiously) that tying their fortunes to the subtreasury scheme took farmers too deeply into politics. Hall was the leader of a group within the Alliance who believed that farmers were engaged in a free-market business and that their actions should focus on privately operated economic collectives. Hall and his supporters believed that their interests could be most effectively protected without politicking. How this could be done, of course, remained unclear and was problematic for this faction. Evidence offered by Lawrence Goodwyn regarding the national movement suggests that many farmers simply did not understand how the scheme was supposed to work.[16]

Supporters of the subtreasury were led by Leverett Leonard of Saline County, who believed, first, that the subtreasury was a good idea because the power of the federal government would finally allow a "farmer collective" to work. In attempting to formulate private collectives, especially under the Grange, farmers had found that they could not muster the strength to impact market prices or to generate the resources to extend credit amongst themselves. Supporters also countered the naysayers with the logical argument that any economic plans designed to help farmers necessitated political activism in order to get them accomplished.[17]

The thrust of the debate over the monetary issue pointed to the second major problem dividing alliancemen—the degree to which the movement should be politicized, and especially whether or not this action required the use of a third political party. While the supporters of soft money and political action at the Sedalia meeting were not yet prepared in 1890 to engage in a third party, they were quite interested in taking over the Democratic party in the state, and within another year and a half, they would be joining the Populists.

After lengthy debate at the Sedalia convention, however, the Hall faction won the day, and Hall won election as president of the Missouri

16. This was a problem that had plagued Greenbackers and their fiat philosophy a decade earlier, and the single-taxers, who followed the mystifying economic theories of Henry George. Goodwyn, *Populist Moment*, 188.

17. Young, *Cultivating Cooperation*, 2; Clardy, "Rhetoric of Populism," 83.

Farmers' and Laborers' Union.[18] But the debate had fractured the Alliance, and Hall's success was short-lived. Farmers quickly began to realize, particularly given the growing radicalism nationwide, that any action of substance would have to become political, and that they were going to have to utilize the power of the national and state governments. Action on Alliance platforms required alliancemen to attain political office. But doing so through the major parties required compromises that farmers were increasingly unwilling to make. The solution seemed to lie in the new third-party coalition of Populists.

By the middle of 1891, men who spoke fondly of a third party had already taken hold of the Missouri Farmers' Alliance through their control of the county-level chapters. Seventy-three delegates from Missouri, nearly all alliancemen, attended the convention in Cincinnati in May 1891 for the organizing of the Populist party.[19] The convention of the Missouri Farmers' Alliance in August 1891 became a battleground between the third-party men, led by the editors in the new Missouri Reform Press Association, and the conservative U. S. Hall faction. Hall intended to bolt, should the Farmers' Alliance sign on with the Populists. But alliancemen were increasingly swayed by the notion that the needs of farmers and laborers had to be met through the ballot box. The key to success was to vote as a bloc for a third party.

The ousting of Hall and the election of Leverett Leonard to the presidency of the state Alliance tested the group's ability to challenge the deeply rooted party allegiance of Missouri farmers. The Farmers' Alliance, by the end of 1891, worked hand in hand with the Populist party, and their actions in Missouri became essentially synonymous. The *McFall Mirror* cheered the move by proclaiming that "the boys are getting together. For years they have been resoluting and marching and striking together, but voting against each other. This year they are going to vote together."[20]

The "old parties" put up a strong resistance, however. Democratic newspapers warned rural readers that if they seriously pursued the Alliance platform, they would risk sacrificing the Democrats to the

18. The *California (Mo.) Newspaper* followed these proceedings carefully from December 1890 to January 1891.

19. *California (Mo.) Newspaper*, May 28, 1891.

20. Clardy, "Rhetoric of Populism," 86; *McFall (Mo.) Mirror*, October 12, 1894, 2.

opposing forces of capital concentration and urban wealth. The Democratic *Tarkio Avalanche* warned "earnest reformers that their efforts [would] be taken advantage of by their worst enemies." Republicans, they claimed, were scheming to use the third-party movement to defeat Democrats who were friendly to farmers.[21] Democrats also used the Missouri Board of Agriculture as a leveraging tool. As long as alliancemen largely operated through the Democratic party, the board allowed them to use their frequent "institutes" on technical advances in farming as a platform from which they could also educate farmers in their political economy. By early 1891, when the third-party supporters were elected to office in the Missouri Farmers' Alliance, the board indeed yanked away the soapbox, limiting presentations to agronomy and new farm technology.[22] Republicans responded with the temptingly conservative call for free-market enterprise and absence of government controls—and they relied as well on the powerful anchor of tradition.

Missourians were fiercely dedicated to the Democratic and Republican parties. Divided loyalties during the Civil War had translated in the postwar era to strong ties to pro-Union Republicanism and pro-Confederate Democracy. Nationwide, political partisanship was a popular "sport" during the Gilded Age, and Missourians were particularly loyal to their "teams." Newspapers throughout the state reflected and encouraged this partisanship. By 1892, 49 percent of the papers in Missouri were officially Democratic, 29 percent were Republican, 5 percent were Populist, and only 16 percent were neutral or independent.[23]

Alliancemen in Missouri tried to loosen the anchor of tradition by portraying the direction of the two major parties as antithetical to the heritage and traditions of rural Missouri families. The national movement encouraged state organizations to involve wives, sons, and daughters in meetings that brought communities of farm families together.[24] In theory, producer families would stand steadfast in solidarity against

21. *Tarkio (Mo.) Avalanche*, September 27, 1890, 1.
22. Clevenger, "Agrarian Politics," 81–83.
23. *Missouri Official Manual, 1893–1894*.
24. W. Scott Morgan, *History of the Wheel and Alliance and the Impending Revolution* (1891; reprint, New York: B. Franklin, 1968), 248–53; Thelen, *Paths of Resistance*, 214.

the modern commercial forces that had taken over the major parties. Since the status of American life had changed so dramatically under industrialization, conservative farmers were forced into becoming un-likely radicals and adopting a paradoxical strategy: promoting change to preserve tradition, and using those traditions to manipulate the new order to their best advantage. It was a risky strategy for increasing political activism, because the communal, social nature of the Grange—also based on tradition and heritage—had moderated that organiza-tion's activism to the degree that Grange meetings became largely social functions. Broadly speaking, the strategy proposed the self-conflicting notion of seeking change through reliance upon traditional structures.

While the fundamental problem of strategy fractured the Alliance movement, it was further weakened by a number of other problems that made the movement much tougher to sell in Missouri than in neighboring states. Northwest Missouri, in particular, proved terribly resistant to Alliance/Populism, which placed strong limitations on supporters in the southern half (especially the southwest) to influence the political parties, win offices at the state and national levels, and so-lidify a "movement culture" that would bring fundamental change for farmers. In northern Missouri, the amenable conditions of farming and landholding, and a shortage of strong leadership and convincing propaganda made even a moderately radical political movement hard to sell.

From the beginning, reformers in Missouri confronted the basic "problem" that throughout much of the state, geography was quite kind to farming, and that although periodic drought and pests might cut into annual production, farmers usually had good years. Even though long-term trends might be unfavorable—and there were some-times very bad years—farmers did not feel distressed enough to aban-don the system that was already in place. Nature was generally kinder to farmers in northwestern Missouri than elsewhere in the region, as evidenced by relatively healthy production rates. Farmers in that cor-ner of the state in particular had the great advantage of deep silt loam soil adaptable to a wide range of crops. Owing to the superior water retention of its soil, northwest Missouri was less subject to the per-iodic droughts that struck farmers in a semicircle to the west. Eco-nomically, from 1890 to 1900, northwestern Missouri farmers fared well compared to the rest of the state. By 1900, farms in seventeen northwestern counties averaged annual production of $820 a year, in contrast to the $402 averaged in counties in the southwestern corner of the state. In 1890, when Alliance organization was most robust, northwestern counties exceeded all other regions of the state in production per acre of corn, potatoes, hay, and wheat.[25]

For farmers, an even more critical measure of success was their ability to gain or hold onto ownership of the land. Across the Midwest, rates of mortgaging and tenancy increased throughout the 1880s, and farmers either lost property or were forced to borrow heavily against their land. Missouri, however, fared much better than neighboring states, and increases in the number of farm mortgages ran almost directly proportional to success of the Alliance/Populists. In Kansas, where Populists were strongest, 60.3 percent of farms were mortgaged in 1890; Nebraska followed on both counts with 54.7 percent mortgaged; Iowa was next (47 percent), then Illinois (30.8 percent), and then Missouri (25.4 percent). Tenancy rates showed a similar pattern. From 1880 to 1910 tenancy rates increased unevenly across the region: Kansas by 21 percent, Nebraska by 21 percent, Iowa by 15 percent, Illinois by 11 percent, and Missouri by 3 percent. Additionally, these rates were not evenly distributed within Missouri, and here again northwestern farmers were better off, with mortgage increase rates lower and even decreasing in some years during the period. Tenancy in the southwestern corner of the state grew at an average of 6 percent while holding steady in the northwest.[26]

Moreover, where farmers were succeeding with production, the railroads also seemed to go, much to the satisfaction of those farmers. By 1879 there were twenty-seven counties still without railroads in Missouri; all but two were south of the river. At the end of the next year, only twenty-two were without—all south of the river. A marked increase in towns substantial enough to support a market, combined with tremendous railroad growth, made access to markets considerably

25. Milton D. Raferty, *Historical Atlas of Missouri* (Norman: University of Oklahoma Press, 1982), 9–12. Data on agricultural production from the *United States Historical Census Data Browser;* and *Tarkio Avalanche,* November 30, 1889, from the *Report of the State Board of Agriculture.*

26. Data on mortgages in the *Eleventh Census of the United States, 1890,* "Farms and Homes," 306; "Real Estate and Farm Mortgages," 520–37; tenancy rates from *United States Historical Census Data Browser.*

more widespread by 1890, and this development came in favorable land in the east and the north first.[27]

In areas where nature seemed less inclined to support farming, Alliance/Populism thrived. Land beyond the ninety-sixth meridian posed natural conditions more hostile to crops and livestock. Drought, pestilence, and violent storms made farming there a much riskier proposition. Lawrence Goodwyn has pointed out, for example, that the success of the National Farmers' Alliance in the Great Plains of the Dakotas was in large part the result of a crop insurance plan, the "Hail Alliance Association," which had perhaps more success than any other single factor in drawing farmers of the Great Plains into the movement. Practical need, stemming from the harsh environment, overcame the resistance to cooperative economic organization that hindered organizers in tamer environs. John Barnhart has demonstrated that in Nebraska, interest in political activism, and especially Populism, was a function of the weather. Drought and insects were the best promoters of the movement.[28]

Given that interest in farmer activism tended to be linked to the security of environmental conditions for frontier farmers, those who turned the soil in northwestern Missouri were in conditions less fertile for discontent. While it is generally true that farming was by no means lucrative or predictable in northern Missouri, relatively speaking it was much less precarious than elsewhere in the trans-Mississippi Midwest. The task then fell upon the leaders of the movement to generate support among farmers in this region, who needed to be much more fully sold on the idea of fundamental change than was necessary elsewhere. In this endeavor they were not terribly successful. Though the Grange was a popular idea in the middle 1880s, and the Farmers' Alliance found quick support at the end of the decade, the more radical tone of Alliance/Populism by 1891 met with stronger resistance. Organizers, and the stump speakers who were their vanguard, would have to play their northwestern Missouri audience expertly in order to convince them of their imminent need.

Although the farmers' alliances and later the Populist party sent

27. Clevenger, "Agrarian Politics," 33.
28. Goodwyn, *Populist Moment*, 104–5; John D. Barnhart, "Rainfall and the Populist Party in Nebraska," *American Political Science Review* 19 (August 1925): 527–40.

their dynamic national speakers through Missouri to rouse support, those speakers often failed to serve their purpose by not playing to the peculiar interests of local audiences in Missouri. As a result, it was often up to local speakers to build a following among folks who shared common concerns. With what turned out to be the limited abilities of Missouri speakers, however, this would be an uphill struggle. Missouri, unlike other Alliance/Populist states, produced no orators of national note; no Bryan, Simpson, Watson, or Donnelly—no one who became imminently quotable, or even recognizable. The moderate tone of Missouri speakers, absent the language of class struggle, condemnation of the consumer class, and talk of bold new policies of government control, sounded too much like Democrats and Republicans to draw Missouri farmers into activism and out of the parties of their fathers.[29] In Missouri, the result for the Alliance was membership that was lukewarm, and for the Populists, disappointing election returns.

Among the state's Alliance/Populist speakers, all were farmers who had some training but very little experience in public speaking. Leverett Leonard came from a successful farm family in Saline County, and he had followed the unusual path of graduating from Dartmouth and studying law at Harvard. He decided to return to Missouri without ever having practiced law. It was his financial success as a farmer, not his social vision or rousing oratory, however, that made him a leader among Missouri farmers. Leonard was a nice man who made a poor politician—especially poor as a third-party promoter. He seemed unconvinced of his own cause and was too soft on the Democratic party, to whom most of his successful colleagues remained devoted. Leonard's 1892 campaign for governor was a poor effort. He was calm, unconvincing, and canvassed the state too unevenly.[30]

U. S. Hall had success as a leader but was often too stubborn and proud to support a sustained political movement. More importantly, he was far too conservative to press for the necessary reforms. Somewhat more engaging and energetic as a speaker than Leonard, he had

29. Clardy, "Rhetoric of Populism," 87–88.

30. For a biography of Leonard, see Floyd C. Shoemaker, *Missouri and Missourians* (Chicago: Lewis Publishing, 1943), 2:137. *Memphis Farmers' Union*, August 4, 1892, offers a critical description of Leonard's campaign.

a limited vision for the Alliance movement, one very akin to the Grange concept. His opposition to inflationary monetary policy made his conversion to Populism unlikely, and he consistently voiced opposition to a third party. Hall was a Jeffersonian agrarian who dreamed of a condition in which farmers would be so highly respected as essential to society that they would be able to command prices and freight rates. He was, in fact, more conservative than many Democrats in his outlook. Following his loss to Leonard in 1891 as president of the Missouri Farmers' and Laborers' Union, Hall refused to take the vice presidency of the organization. He had been an enthusiastic and engaging speaker, but he had not advocated substantial change in the political and economic order of Missouri. Given that, and his unwillingness to compromise, he became of little use to the Alliance/Populist movement in the state. At the ascension of Populist fervor in 1892, Hall established himself clearly as a conservative and won a seat in Congress from the second district as a conservative Democrat on a hard-money platform.[31]

Orville Jones was the best Missouri had to offer as a speaker, but unfortunately he fell far short of the more charismatic national figures. He had a habit of trying to excite his audience by adding color to his prose, like the national leaders, only to garble the syntax and scramble allusions. In one flight of metaphor, he proclaimed that "the facts show that European gold influence and its American Hessian allies have been as determined to take the legal life and destroy the United States as was Herod to take the life and destroy the infant Christ."[32] While some may have grasped his allusion to an urban Jewish/German conspiracy against Christian American farmers, more than a few practical-minded farmers must have struggled to figure out how European gold, Hessians, and King Herod were a pressing threat.

Despite their limitations, these leaders did tend to have success close to their home counties in central and southern Missouri. As a result, they seemed reluctant to advance into more unfamiliar audiences and spent very little time in the northern corners of the state. Under these conditions, it was important that the movement develop a sys-

31. Frank M. Drew, "The Present Farmers' Movement," *Political Science Quarterly* 6 (spring 1892) 304; Clardy, "Rhetoric of Populism," 125.

32. *California (Mo.) Newspaper*, November 2, 1893.

tem of training for speakers and promoters in Missouri. This approach had worked with considerable success in Kansas, but such a system never effectively evolved in Missouri, and as a result the speaking circuit lacked effectiveness. Gilbert Clardy, in his analysis of Populist rhetoric in Missouri, argues that many of the speakers who did work the state used a "progressive strategy in which the speaker assumed that the listener understood, and agreed upon the ills that they faced. In doing so they made two assumptions: one was that the farmer was necessarily unhappy with the way things were, the second was that they agreed with the speaker and every other farmer on the sources of their problems."[33] It was a risky strategy that probably did not work very well with many audiences. In this respect, Missouri's "show me" motto was something that should have been taken seriously by promoters of reform. Orville Jones used the strategy when he announced cryptically that "the Populist party is a result of individual knowledge and individual reasoning. We know how we got this good knowledge and good reasoning. We know how we must vote in future elections."[34] The reliance upon self-evident truths (and in language considerably less eloquent and moving than the oratory of Bryan) did little to energize northwestern Missouri farmers.

Another strategy was to reflect on the glory days of old when taxes were low, credit cheap, and farmers respected. Again, this was a strategy that could be easily misread. The message was essentially a conservative one—a hearkening back to when "farming was a proud profession and tables were always full and our bank accounts respectable."[35] The message was not that the system was fundamentally flawed and needed to be repaired through bold new policies, but rather that the system of old had been corrupted by new money men. Read this way, farmers might respond by cleaving to institutions of old, especially the Democratic party. The message that "we can go back" continued to reinforce the paralyzing irony of attempting to prosper in the modern economy by adhering to the past.[36]

Others underestimated the patience of farmers. One speaker told a crowd in the town of Oregon that "within the last few months we have

33. Clardy, "Rhetoric of Populism," 157–58.
34. *Memphis Farmers' Union*, January 5, 1893.
35. *Annual Report of the Board of Agriculture of the State of Missouri*, 1891, 385.
36. Clardy, "Rhetoric of Populism," 160.

noticed a decline in farm status and economy. A few weeks ago we saw
our profits go further down at the markets. This last week we have noticed fewer and fewer wagons of corn and barley heading for St. Joseph. There's no profit in selling anymore. A new party of farm
politicians can be our answer."[37] But for Missouri farmers, the events
of the last few months were not a trend substantial enough to aban-
don the political culture with which they had long been familiar. Proposals for protectionism and government ownership and talk of class
identity required much longer periods of duress.

An oratorical style weaving Christian themes and tent-meeting
passion into the message—accomplished eloquently by Bryan—was
attempted more clumsily and confusingly by Missouri speakers. Arthur Rozelle tried to persuade a friendly audience with hellfire scold-
ing, shouting at them: "you're absurd, my friends! You will again be
foolish and vote the way of the devil. Your God cries for you. Your
children cry to you. Your wife begs you. But you are blind! You don't
see God's mercy. He gave us another chance with Populism. It's God
talking to you!" His approach surely delighted Democratic and Republicans alike. The *St. Louis Republic* couldn't resist making fun of
such language, noting sarcastically that "it's a shame that so many
honest, decent citizens remain with the Republican and Democratic
Parties." The *Kansas City Star* modestly chastised Populist speakers for
their tendency to "use words and terms that confuse and insult."[38]

Whether their speeches were clumsy, cryptic, offensive, colorful,
engaging, or inspiring, Alliance/Populists faced the same problem
wherever they spoke: they could not offer Missouri farmers evidence
of a clear plan of action, or a compelling reason to embrace a new social philosophy or throw their lot in with a third party. Given this weakness, it was up to the Missouri reform press to champion the cause
and gain enthusiastic converts among farmers.

Everywhere nationally that Alliance/Populists succeeded, the reform press served a critical function in educating and proselytizing.
Papers of the reform press, labeling themselves either Alliance or Populist or both, were scattered across the state, though not evenly, with

37. *Annual Report of the Board of Agriculture of the State of Missouri*, 1891, 385.
38. *California (Mo.) Newspaper*, August 7, 1894; *St. Louis Republic*, August 30, 1894;
Kansas City Star, September 29, 1894.

more than two-thirds of the fifty-six papers published south of the Missouri River. Most were concentrated in the southwestern quarter of the state. The most influential of them was the *California Newspaper* in Moniteau County. Where the need was strongest for an engaging press, in the northwestern part of the state, the papers fell short of mark. With virtually no local activist writers, or proponents who could generate support through print, papers published in northwestern Missouri had very little editorial comment of their own. Most papers started up on modest capital and simply lifted the bulk of their editorial text from the national reform press, especially from the *Chicago Express, Wealth Makers,* the *Nonconformist,* the *Industrial Union,* the *Chicago Free-Trader,* and the *Southern Mercury.* For farmers leery of advice from the outside (especially urban "radicals"), the impact was lessened considerably. Largely, these "reform" papers were little different from any other local paper. Papers like the *Hamilton Farmers' Advocate,* the *Chilicothe Crisis,* the *McFall Mirror,* the *Princeton People's Press,* and a handful of others in the north looked little different from their "old party" counterparts. Like other local papers of the time, the front page (or more) was taken up with local gossip interspersed with comments on the weather and advertisements. For most, a page was devoted to the printed sermons of the widely popular Dr. Rev. Talmage, followed by some benign pieces on a couple of national and international events and a host of unusual crimes lifted from the national press. It was a formula that was repeated through a number of such papers. Not unlike much of today's media, stories of bludgeonings, shootings, train wrecks, and drowned children took up much more lucrative column space than political commentary.

Some papers that took on the mantle of "reform" often interpreted social ills and the need for change in ways that were little helpful to the Alliance/Populist movement. Many, like the *Rockport Missouri Agitator,* were far more concerned with the ill effects of demon rum than the inequity of the social and economic structure. Local newspapers were more inclined in the years from 1889 to 1893 to print reports from the local chapters of the W.C.T.U. than from the Grange or the Alliance. In Maryville, local farmers relied on the *Nodaway Democrat* for news about the Grange and the Alliance, but the Bi-Chloride of Gold club, a group of men (twenty-six members by November 1891) who had broken loose from the bottle, got far more attention. For the

Rockport Missouri Agitator, the problem for laborers was not rooted primarily in the social and economic order, but in the propensity for workingmen to drink. They noted that "it is a pity that so many other issues of far less consequence"—presumably including fair incomes, corruption, and safe working conditions—"have been permitted to engross the attention and exhaust the energies of the Labor associations."[39] These papers, some of which were self-described "temperance" papers, denounced the modern ills that were vexing their farmer readers, especially the railroads, but at the same time, they perpetuated old explanations for poverty (both urban and rural) rooted in the moralistic social vision of the past.

The *Agitator* denounced the Anti-Poverty Association and one of its leaders, a Dr. McGlynn, "who became suddenly notorious through the Henry George candidacy" and who had argued that poverty was a social disease that could be eradicated. The *Agitator* retorted that "poverty may be a disease in the east, but out west it is regarded as merely a symptom," the source of which was simply shiftlessness, with the paper advising "more work and less loafing as the remedy." It would become hard to find support for a major economic reform movement from a rural paper that would insist simply that "economy, industry, frugality and a good savings bank are things well understood and result in financial ease."[40]

Reform papers, including Democratic organs that had taken up the mantle of "reform" for farmers, also had a difficult time shedding the optimistic boosterism so common to small-town middle America at that time, making it difficult to tell whether there was actually any rural distress at all. The *Agitator* seemed oddly named when it observed that, unlike farmers in Europe or laborers in the city, "our native western farmers are mainly gentlemen of comparative leisure, who till their own land and carry on agricultural industries with as much ease and far less worriment of mind than our city men conduct their business." Only a week earlier, the *Agitator* had promoted a meeting in Clarinda, Iowa, of a proposed shipping cooperative for the purpose of combating the "burdensome and unwarranted tribute to

39. *Nodaway Democrat,* December 3, 1891; *Rockport Missouri Agitator,* June 30, 1887, 6.

40. *Rockport Missouri Agitator,* September 15, 1887, 4.

the mighty Caesars—the railroad corporations." The *Tarkio Avalanche* similarly undermined any sense of distress, announcing in 1890 "A Year of Unparalleled Prosperity Enjoyed by the Town," whose economic base was the farmers in surrounding Atchison County. While the paper complained of low commodities prices in the midst of bountiful harvests, it also asserted happily that "each year has shown improvement over the preceding one." With assurances that "the farmer [is] the true foundation of wealth and progress" in the successful small communities of northwestern Missouri, reformers found little help from the radical or local press in establishing the need for change.[41]

In this context it was terribly difficult for Alliance/Populism in northern Missouri to generate visions of a new and better social order. Lawrence Goodwyn has pointed out that in the national movement the "new" farmer in the Alliance no longer viewed himself in the Jeffersonian pastoral view—the humble but noble producer-entrepreneur. Instead, the Alliance farmer viewed himself as a laborer surrounded by market forces that had to be mastered.[42] If, however, as David Thelen argues, Missourians were resistant to abandoning the cultural milieu in which their fathers had settled Missouri, then the tension posed by the Alliance was considerable. It was a tug-of-war in which cultural conservatism fought against a new perception of class identity that would serve them much better as laborers in a modern economy.

Under these conditions, the leadership of the Alliance/Populist movement in Missouri proved unable to nurture a sustained social movement committed to substantial reforms. As a result of this limited class awareness, and out of their own attachment to the approaches of the past, most leaders instead sought action through holding office and participating in major-party politics—at the cost of considerable compromise.

This problem—of the "office seekers" versus the movement, which hobbled Alliance/Populism nationwide—was particularly acute in Missouri.[43] The division became most apparent when a substantial group of Populist leaders latched upon the free coinage of silver as the

41. Ibid., June 9, 1887, 6, and June 2, 1887, 2; *Tarkio Avalanche,* January 18, 1890, January 11, 1890, November 30, 1889.

42. Goodwyn, *Populist Moment*, 38–39.

43. Ibid.

cornerstone of protest politics. While the "gold-bugs" of industry and government shuddered at the thought of free silver, it was a modest proposal at best, compared to the broad concept of the subtreasury plan and the radical notions of fiat currency and nationalization of utilities. Free silver was a safe proposal, since it seemed to suggest a great change that would help loosen monetary policy, and it was simple to understand. It would, however, do nothing to redistribute wealth, guarantee farmer security in the market, or thwart the concentration of power in corporate monopolies.[44]

On the issue of railroad reform, perhaps the most potent plank for Missourians, the leaders themselves undermined any real distinction from the Democrats, since nearly all of them believed that government ownership was a bad idea. Since Democratic governor Joel Stone (1892–1895) had successfully delivered on promises of extended rail service into rural areas of Missouri still in need, Alliance/Populists were hard-pressed to offer more. For almost three decades, getting the railroad to town had been the primary objective for Missouri farmers, and debates over ownership were almost nonexistent. And the persistent mythology of the success of private enterprise in railroading carried considerable weight.[45]

Given the numerous conditions that mitigated the distress of Missouri's individual farmers and their communities, it was essential that the Alliance/Populist movement nurture a common identity among farmers as laborers that transcended regional distinctions and tradition. This sort of social class consciousness, as numerous historians of the agrarian and labor reform movement have pointed out, was critical to success. Goodwyn argues that despite the tendency for historians to view protest as a function of poverty, the "relative degrees of agricultural poverty did not play a decisive role in this process. Rather, how state third parties fared depended on the extent of mass political consciousness among farmers."[46] Evidence also suggests, however,

44. Ibid., 230–61.
45. Clardy, "Rhetoric of Populism," 96. Orville Jones was the Populist candidate for governor in 1896 when he unexpectedly withdrew his nomination and threw his support to Democrat Lon Stephens. After two decades of third-party action, Jones fell in with Populists who believed by 1896 that fusion with the Democrats on the limited monetary reform of free silver was the only hope of success. Ibid., 130–31.
46. Goodwyn, *Populist Moment*, 181, 268–69, 297–98.

that economic and environmental hardship clearly supported the movement on the Great Plains. For farmers in northern Missouri, both conditions worked against the farm labor movement, since farming remained relatively profitable (compared to other, more hard-pressed regions in the South and the Great Plains) and class consciousness never developed to a sufficient degree to sustain a movement.

There were indeed limited, and often awkward, attempts to do so in the northwestern Missouri press, though again usually through pieces lifted from the national reform press. One common approach was to blend social class identity with Christianity in attempting to defuse fears that these Marxist kinds of notions were ungodly—the producing class becomes the army of God. The *McFall Mirror* printed an article by W. T. Wallace imploring farmers to join the "commonweal army" in a battle against their "commonwoe" for the purpose of reversing the "evolution from a democracy to a plutocracy." In apocalyptic language, Wallace described the coming battle between the consumer and producer classes, "Gog and Magog finally joined in mortal antagonism." Appealing to midwestern farmers, Wallace climaxed with the technique of Christianizing the farmer/laborer cause— God's good against the plutocrats' evil: "What of the spirit of the commonwoe mob, made up of the predatory classes? Here is its creed. Get all you can and keep all you get; the devil take the other fellow. Its spirit is covetousness; its inspiration is greed; its life is selfishness; its God is gold; its heaven is hell; powder and ball are arguments. This mob is Pharaoh in government; Ishmael in commerce, and Cain for brotherhood; that is to say, Satanism diluted by sin." Among these legions of Satan are "Goggle-eyed Jews, European Shylocks and plutocratic American traitors." The Populist movement was "Christianity, communally exhibited."[47] Despite these impassioned appeals to Christian militancy in establishing the new social order, the seduction was not managed very deftly. The *Mirror* enjoyed extolling at length the success of New Zealand as an excellent example of "industrial freedom," and "successful socialism," particularly its government ownership of all public works, railroads, raw materials, and banks. The

---

47. *McFall Mirror*, June 8, 1894, 3. One can note, too, that this approach often resulted in horribly garbled references. The Jews are made into Gog and Magog—the forces that attack the Jews in the book of Revelation.

prospect of socialism to that degree being advocated in a Missouri Alliance/Populist paper, however, must have frightened more than a few farmers away.[48]

Additionally, advocates for reform found it nearly impossible to develop a clear identity for farmers as "laborers" in a way that would place them solidly within a labor movement culture. Missouri papers fumbled with a vaguely dual usage for "organized labor," sometimes including farmers and sometimes not. The distinction was most clear when farmers were making critical comment on urban labor actions that they deemed ineffective and unwarranted. When the action was political, then the farmers included themselves as "laborers." The name of the alliance organization devised in 1889, the Farmers' and Laborers' Union, also obscured the terminology to some degree—at the same time, they are both separated and linked. It was a limitation that indicated the farmers' inability to fully identify themselves as a class. The *McFall Mirror* repeated the question raised by the *Southern Mercury:* "What is the people's party anyway, but a labor party?" with a nod to agreement. But throughout the *Mirror*'s "Points for the People," "organized labor" is identified as something distinct from the farmers, and often pejoratively in reference to its methods and politics.[49]

The confusion over identity pointed toward the multiple ways in which the transformation into a modern industrial economy (with agriculture as one of its chief "industries") confounded notions of liberalism and conservatism, reform and tradition. The discovery of the allianceman was that as farming grew fully into a modern commercial enterprise, it became more pressing that he use government to regulate the national economy to his benefit. For the northwestern Missouri farmer, this created an intellectual dilemma. Although his political traditions had defined democracy in terms of small government and independence, he had to become a supporter of "big government" in much the same way as industrialists had come to see government as a potential ally and a weapon. To fend off the evils of corporations in the new economy, he had to form them himself through cooperatives and alliances. The appeal to tradition in the rhetorical strategies used by "reformers"—who adopted Christian

48. Ibid., June 22, 1894, 2.
49. See, for example, ibid., October 19, 1894, 5.

conservative visions of times past, when farmers presumably fared better without the aid of government—could easily neutralize demands for change in the minds of listeners. One Populist promoter attempted to appeal to his audience with visions of "a glorious past, when farmers made profits on their goods. We walked to town with our heads held high. Our children were happy. The government was on our side: we influenced the politics of our state. Remember those times? . . . We can have them again."[50] Those were times, of course, in which the existing parties served farmers favorably. There were no new political forces that had to be repelled. Therefore, since the parties worked before, why couldn't they work again?

Alliance/Populism and its reform agenda were far less engaging in northwestern Missouri than they might have been because those farmers had become settled and reasonably prosperous and were wary of anything remotely radical. They were pleased with their railroads, new markets, and fancy new machinery. From farms across the northwestern corner of the state came demands for consumer goods and new industrial products, rather than nationalization, fiat currency, and redistribution of wealth. While they faced periodic seasons of substandard crops and generally declining commodities prices, they were better off than many, and they remained optimistic about the structural status quo. Although economic and social change brought stress, they continued to see evil only where it had lurked before—in laziness, cities, and demon rum. Certainly election returns and membership rosters in northwestern Missouri showed enough interest in Alliance/Populism to suggest the foundation for a successful movement. But the enthusiasm was limited and too short-lived, and the leadership was too inadequate to add any muscle to the national movement for liberal reform. As a result, they became a moderating influence that contributed, instead, to the tendency nationwide to compromise with the major parties on essentially conservative agendas. While their brethren to the west had marched farther into the frontier, geographically and politically, the farmers of northwestern Missouri remained comfortably settled.

50. *Annual Report of the Board of Agriculture of the State of Missouri*, 1891, 346–47; Clardy, "Rhetoric of Populism," 162.

Survival Strategies of Farm Laborers in the Missouri Bootheel, 1900–1958

BONNIE STEPENOFF

Alex Cooper, the fourth in a family of twelve children, grew up on a hundred-acre farm in southeastern Missouri in the 1930s and 1940s. His father had two qualities essential to an African American farmer seeking upward mobility: agricultural skills and a large family. During the Depression, his father left Arkansas, where he was a sharecropper, and found a job in Missouri with the federal Works Progress Administration (WPA). Through a program of the United States Department of Agriculture (USDA), he bought a farm with no money down. The Cooper family raised cotton, corn, soybeans, oats, hay, sweet potatoes, cattle, hogs, chickens, and turkeys. Growing up, Alex Cooper and his siblings learned to pick cotton and dress poultry. His father cured meat, and his mother canned vegetables.[1]

Cooper remembered the community of about thirty farmers at Inghram Ridge in Pemiscot County. Eighteen white and twelve black families lived "across the [drainage] ditch from each other," separated by a sluggish strip of swamp water. The white families were Swedish, German, French, and Scotch-Irish, and they shared fundamentalist Christian beliefs with their black neighbors. Despite racial separation, the families developed a strong sense of community. Because she was black, Cooper's mother could not display her canned goods at the county fair, so her white neighbors exhibited them for her and brought

1. Alex Cooper interview, August 13, 1994, Bootheel Project, collection 3928, AC (audiocassette) 15, 16, Western Historical Manuscript Collection, University of Missouri–Columbia.

back the ribbons. All the families were poor, but, Cooper recalled, "Everybody was about something. Out of every black family, one member went to college." Looking back on those times, he added, "You knew what the system was, but being a person was number one." With support from his family, Cooper graduated from Lincoln University in Jefferson City and became a teacher.[2]

To survive and prosper, the Cooper family adopted various strategies, including migration, reliance on the labor of all family members, and forming personal bonds within the local community. During the Great Depression, however, hard work and family solidarity could not prevail against overwhelming economic hardship. Like other distressed groups, agricultural workers banded together and demanded assistance from the federal government. In 1939, sharecroppers camped along Highways 60 and 61 in the Missouri Bootheel, drawing national attention to the farmworkers' condition. With the help of a federal program, the Coopers purchased a farm that remained in the family throughout the twentieth century.

In *Prolegomena for a Global Labour History,* Marcel van der Linden and Jan Lucassen have distinguished between private and public strategies that laboring families have historically used to live, retain their social status, or achieve upward mobility. According to these scholars, "Co-existing alongside private strategies are *public* strategies, whereby in order to promote certain interests members of various households operate collectively with respect to third parties. Public and private strategies can occur in all manner of combinations."[3] Studying the interrelationships between private projects and public action can lead to a clearer understanding of laboring people in a variety of cultural and geographical settings, including the cotton-producing counties along the Mississippi River in southeastern Missouri.

Cotton growers migrated to the lowlands of the Bootheel in the first three decades of the twentieth century, bringing with them a labor system rooted in America's past. The sharecropping system originated in the plantation agriculture of the antebellum South. Southern historian Ulrich B. Phillips described cotton plantations as "privately owned

2. Cooper interview, July 27, 1994, and August 13, 1994, AC 15, 16, 27.
3. Marcel van der Linden and Jan Lucassen, *Prolegomena for a Global Labour History* (Amsterdam: International Institute of Social History, 1999), 13.

village estates," similar to feudal manors except that they operated within a market-driven economy. Antebellum plantations were self-contained patriarchies, dominated by white male landowners and dependent upon the unpaid labor of black slaves. After the Civil War, many former slaves returned to the plantations to work under the "share" system, through which the crop was divided between the planter and share-tenants or "croppers."[4]

As it evolved in the late nineteenth century, the cotton system created four distinct agricultural classes. At the top of the pyramid were the landholders, great and small, who depended on the labor of family members, tenant farmers, sharecroppers, and wage workers. Next to landowners in status were the tenants, who paid cash rent for the privilege of farming small or large tracts. Tenant farmers were businessmen who owned their tools and draft animals and sometimes employed croppers or day laborers. Sharecroppers worked for a portion of the crop and relied upon owners or renters to furnish mules, feed, seed, and equipment. Lowest in status were the daily wage laborers, who sold their skills as mule handlers, carpenters, and pickers to the highest bidder. Sharecropping families tended to be large and close-knit, but substantial family ties were a liability for seasonal wage workers, who migrated from one farm to another.[5]

Early in the twentieth century, lumber companies recruited rural workers to help clear the hardwood forests that still covered the Bootheel wetlands. The Wisconsin Lumber Company, a subsidiary of International Harvester, began operating in Pemiscot County around 1902.

4. Ulrich B. Phillips, *American Negro Slavery* (1918; reprint, Baton Rouge: Louisiana State University Press, 1969), 309; Rupert Vance, *Human Factors in Cotton Production: A Study in the Social Geography of the American South* (Chapel Hill: University of North Carolina Press, 1929), 54–56.

5. Cooper interview, August 13, 1994, AC 15; Ted Ownby, *American Dreams in Mississippi: Consumers, Poverty, and Culture, 1830–1998* (Chapel Hill: University of North Carolina Press, 1999), 111. For extended discussions of the socioeconomic system in the cotton South, see Charles S. Aiken, *The Cotton Plantation South since the Civil War* (Baltimore: Johns Hopkins University Press, 1998); Allison Davis, Burleigh B. Gardner, and Mary R. Gardner, *Deep South: A Social Anthropological Study of Caste and Class* (Chicago: University of Chicago Press, 1941); and Alex Lichtenstein, "Proletarians or Peasants? Sharecroppers and the Politics of Protest in the Rural South, 1880–1940," *Plantation Society in the Americas* 5 (fall 1998): 297–331.

Workers migrated from east of the Mississippi River to work in the company's sawmill in Deering. The company owned most of the town; workers rented housing from the company and shopped at the company store. According to oral testimony, the company hired both black and white workers. Although black workers traded at the company store, they lived in a separate area called Negro Town, or Colored Town. Deering's post office was located in the company store. In addition to the store, the company provided a barbershop, an icehouse, a ball diamond, and a playground.[6] In this way, the company played the role of the paternalistic white landlord.

Workers relied upon traditional agricultural skills to survive in isolated communities like Deering. Before the 1920s, the roads were so bad that it might take two hours to travel two miles. Without access to cities and markets, families raised vegetables, poultry, hogs, and cattle. People fenced in their livestock to protect it from bobcats and wolves. Other game, including wild turkeys and hogs, supplemented the family diet. Men, women, and children fished in the drainage ditches. Many homes had sewing machines, and women made clothes from any available material, including cloth feed sacks.[7]

Laboring families built racially separate communities, as required by the system of segregation. The first school for white children in Deering was in the Methodist church building. By 1916, the white community had erected a two-room grade school. According to resident Willie Garrett Baxter, "It taught all grades and you went to school until you felt like you knew all they could teach you, and then you quit." Baxter remembered that the black community had its own school. As she recalled in 1970, they had "a school, a church, a hotel, and a recreation center. They had a piano and an ice cream parlor just like we did. They did their shopping at the big general store; but otherwise stayed on the south side of the tracks. . . . After dark, you never would see a Negro in the white part of town."[8]

After logging and swamp drainage cleared the land, growing numbers of white and black farmworkers migrated to the region seeking work on the newly established cotton plantations. Indigenous white

6. Ophelia R. Wade, ed., *History of Delta C-7 School District in Deering, Missouri* (Deering, Mo.: n.p., 1976), 51–52.
7. Ibid., 51–53.
8. Ibid., 42, 48, 51.

farmworkers reacted angrily to the influx of African Americans, who were competing for jobs. In the summer of 1910, white mobs lynched black farm laborers in New Madrid and Mississippi counties. Whites, afraid for their own jobs and wages, harassed and intimidated blacks. In Caruthersville (Pemiscot County), a mob murdered a black man named A. B. Richardson and burned a black boardinghouse in the fall of 1911. Racial tension and violence probably contributed to a reduction in black population in most Bootheel counties (except Pemiscot) between 1900 and 1920. By 1915, large landowners had banded together to force local authorities to prosecute white vigilantes and protect the biracial labor force.[9]

A cotton boom in the 1920s spurred Bootheel landlords to recruit large numbers of African American families from the South to do the planting and picking. In early 1923, the *Sikeston Standard* reported that hundreds of families had recently migrated into the area. According to the paper, they were large families, well dressed, not ragged or destitute, looking for a place to settle and work the land. White tenants frequently tried to intimidate these families, warning them to leave the area and threatening them with violence. In several towns, including Pascola, Hayti, Steele, Holland, Cooter, and Denton, white residents threw stones or fired shots into black people's houses. Some African Americans left the region, but more arrived in response to offers from white planters.[10]

Sharecroppers did most of the work but received few of the rewards. While many Bootheel planters were novices, sharecroppers from Alabama and Mississippi possessed the knowledge and skills needed to plant and harvest cotton. Farm owners furnished shelter, mules, equipment, and seed.[11] Each sharecropping family tilled about thirty-five

9. David P. Thelen, *Paths of Resistance: Tradition and Democracy in Industrializing Missouri* (1986; reprint, Columbia: University of Missouri Press, 1991), 95–97, 99; U.S. Bureau of the Census, *Thirteenth Census of the United States: 1910*, vol. 2: *Population*, 1106–19, and *Fifteenth Census of the United States: 1930*, vol. 3: *Population*, pt. 1, 1341–46. For more on logging, swamp drainage, and the cotton boom in the Bootheel, see Bonnie Stepenoff, "The Last Tree Cut Down: The End of the Bootheel Frontier, 1880–1940," *Missouri Historical Review* 90 (October 1995): 61–78.

10. *Sikeston Standard*, January 19, 1923, and March 3, 1923.

11. Jim Mac Emerson, interview with David Dickey, September 9, 1986, transcript on file in University Archives and Regional History Collection, Kent Library, Southeast Missouri State University, Cape Girardeau (hereinafter abbreviated as SEMO).

acres of land. In theory, the landowner and the cropper shared the crop fifty-fifty. In practice, the planter ran a tab for seed, farm equipment, shelter, and sustenance. At picking time, he took the bill out of the cropper's share of the harvest.[12] In many cases, the sharecropper received only a fraction of what the landowner owed.

For sharecropping families, the constant message was "make do with what you have." At Christmastime, there were no store-bought toys. Men and boys used knives to whittle toys out of wood. Many communities had no schools. Alex Cooper remembered, "In many counties blacks did not have a school building, so you went to school in a church building." At those early "church schools," there were no dances, but there were debates, oration, spelling bees, and singing. With little or no cash to spend, laboring families created a vibrant social and cultural life, grounded in religious faith.[13]

Preachers rose up from among the people. For example, a prominent Bootheel preacher, Owen Whitfield, was born in Jamestown, Mississippi, in 1894, the son of sharecroppers and the descendant of slaves. Whitfield and his wife, Zella, migrated to Missouri during the cotton boom. In the words of a contemporary British journalist, the Whitfields were "ambitious, tireless workers and self-educators, and had a deep trust that God would not let their exertions be in vain." When a landowner cheated the family out of their share of the cotton, Whitfield temporarily crossed the river into Illinois, where he worked on the levee. However, the family quickly returned to Missouri and sharecropping, relying on help from their many children. By the 1930s, their older sons took over the farming, while Owen traveled around the Bootheel, ministering to other African American sharecroppers.[14]

Despite its unfairness, the sharecropping system depended upon and thus fostered certain positive values. From his early experience, Alex Cooper remembered that growing cotton gave young people a strong work ethic.[15] Because husbands, wives, and children all

---

12. Tomy Lane interview with David Dickey, August 13, 1986, SEMO.

13. Cooper interview, March 11 and July 27, 1994, AC 4, 27, 28.

14. Jean Douglas Cadle, "Cropperville: From Refuge to Community, a Study of Missouri Sharecroppers Who Found an Alternative to the Sharecropper System" (master's thesis, University of Missouri–St. Louis, 1993), 16; Cedric Belfrage, "Cotton-Patch Moses," *Harper's Magazine* (November 1948): 96–97.

15. Cooper interview, August 13, 1994, AC 15.

contributed to farm production, the system reinforced family solidarity. With access to the land, sharecroppers could retain a measure of self-sufficiency by raising their own vegetables, poultry, and livestock and by hunting and fishing. Within rural African American communities, indigenous teachers and preachers passed along oral traditions, keeping black culture alive. White communities also developed churches and schools that reinforced traditional values and brought hope to younger generations.

Unfortunately, none of these values could save families from ruin after the cotton economy collapsed at the end of the 1920s. Landowners, facing bankruptcy and foreclosure, ejected tenants in favor of seasonal workers. Even the most benignly paternalistic planters, confronting their own economic ruin, became increasingly ruthless employers of cheap temporary labor. Many landowners lost their farms. Those who survived cut labor costs by replacing sharecroppers with machinery and converting their operations into "farm factories." During the Depression, the size of farms increased, while the number of farms decreased. Between 1926 and 1936, nearly two-thirds of the sharecroppers in Southeast Missouri turned to day labor or left the cotton fields entirely.[16]

Family solidarity eroded as young people moved to distant states and cities, searching for work. Roadhouses, honky-tonks, and juke joints provided fleeting moments of solace for rambling men and women who shared a rich musical tradition but who lacked a sense of permanence or security for the future. In the small wooden churches that dotted the rural landscape, some preachers, like Whitfield, began delivering sermons of anger and protest rather than consolation and mere perseverance.

In Alabama in the late 1920s, the Share Croppers' Union (SCU) sought radical change in the social and economic system of the Cotton Belt. By 1930, this largely black organization adopted a training program to prepare workers for revolutionary action under Communist party leadership.[17] One man who joined in this effort was Marcus Alphonse (Al) Murphy. Born in Georgia in 1909, Murphy grew up in abject poverty, moved to Alabama, and finally found employment as

16. United States Farm Security Administration (FSA), "Southeast Missouri: A Laboratory for the Cotton South," December 30, 1940, 2.

17. Jeff Woods, *Black Struggle, Red Scare: Segregation and Anti-Communism in the South, 1948–1968* (Baton Rouge: Louisiana State University Press, 2004), 19.

an industrial worker in Birmingham. In 1930, he joined the Communist party and became a labor organizer. As a member of the party, he traveled widely, including to the Soviet Union. By the mid-1930s, he worked as a party organizer, lecturer, and teacher in St. Louis, when the Communist Party USA (CPUSA) brought its training program to Missouri.[18]

As dispossessed sharecroppers continued to migrate to southeastern Missouri, conditions became increasingly unstable. Population in the Bootheel counties swelled from 20 to 50 percent between 1930 and 1940. In a report entitled *Rich Land—Poor People,* published in 1938, government observers noted that laborers came and went across the Missouri state line, migrating from Tennessee and Arkansas during the picking season and returning when the season ended. Workers also moved in and out of agriculture, finding temporary employment on docks and levees when farm jobs were scarce. Periodic floods ruined crops and drove farmers out of business. Landowners came and went, often losing their farms due to foreclosure. When this happened, tenants lost their places. New owners arrived, and new tenants moved in.[19] Constant movement, swelling populations, and unstable conditions made it difficult or impossible for Missouri state authorities to enforce school attendance laws or to administer relief programs.

Following the example of planters and landowners, agricultural laborers demanded public assistance from the federal government. In 1933, Congress passed the Agricultural Adjustment Act (AAA), which promoted farm recovery by compensating farmers who reduced production. The act benefited landowners but caused even more misery for sharecroppers and day laborers. In response to rising unemployment and homelessness in the rural south, the Federal Emergency Relief Administration and the Division of Subsistence Homesteads in the Department of the Interior constructed more than one hundred planned agricultural communities, mostly in cotton-producing states.[20]

18. Joan Tinsley Feezor, "Marcus Alphonse Murphy and Communism on Trial: The Smith Act in Missouri" (master's thesis, Southeast Missouri State University, 1993), 27, 54–55, 71–74.

19. FSA, "Southeast Missouri: A Laboratory for the Cotton South," 1; Max R. White and Douglas Ensminger, *Rich Land—Poor People* (United States Department of Agriculture, Farm Security Administration, 1938), 53.

20. Dewen Grantham, *The South in Modern America* (New York: HarperCollins, 1994), 158.

After the U.S. Supreme Court struck down key elements of the AAA programs, other agencies continued to promote agricultural recovery, with mixed results. Between 1935 and 1943, the Resettlement Administration and the Farm Security Administration (FSA) of the U.S. Department of Agriculture made loans to nearly four hundred thousand southern farm families, purchased thousands of acres of nonproductive farmland, established cooperative agricultural communities, and operated camps for migrant workers. The historian Dewey Grantham has concluded that despite these efforts, New Deal programs "made hardly a dent in relieving the problem of the depressed landless farmer" in the South.[21]

New Deal bureaucrats and reporters for national newspapers traveled the back roads of the Bootheel, bringing public attention to the private pain of the sharecroppers. Sunday supplements and governmental reports published pictures of flimsy, inadequate dwellings. Most of southeast Missouri's sharecropping families lived in box-framed houses, often consisting of a single room with front door and end windows, an attic, a lean-to kitchen, and a front porch. Box-framed houses had thin walls made of vertical wooden slats. Some but not all of them had wooden stripping over the cracks to keep out the weather. More than half of the white families and nearly two-thirds of the black families lived in this kind of house. Only about 33 percent of the white families and 15 percent of the black families could afford "weatherboard houses"—frame houses with horizontal siding. Because of the wet soil, most houses had no cellars but were set on concrete blocks, slabs, or wooden piers. Dogs and chickens found shelter in the crawl spaces under the houses. Most of the farm laborers' houses had no plaster, insulation, or wallpaper.[22]

Poor housing and sanitation caused disease and death. Two-thirds of all Missouri's deaths from malaria in the 1930s occurred in the Bootheel, where swamps and drainage ditches bred mosquitoes and many houses lacked adequate screening. Deaths from typhoid fever declined in Missouri between 1926 and 1934, but the rate in the Bootheel remained much higher than in the rest of the state. The region

21. Ibid., 160.
22. Neal H. Lopinot and Brian W. Thomas, eds., *Archaeological and Architectural Resources, Route 412 Corridor Location Study, Dunklin and Pemiscot Counties, Missouri* (Springfield, Mo.: Center for Archaeological Research, Report No. 985, November 1998), 92; White and Ensminger, *Rich Land*, 40–42.

also suffered from a high incidence of pneumonia and gastrointestinal diseases. The infant mortality rate was much higher than in any other area of the state.[23]

The Mississippi River flood in the winter of 1937 created a tableau of manmade misery. In an effort to save Cairo, Illinois, and other cities downriver, the army used two thousand pounds of dynamite to blow the main levee in the New Madrid Floodway in southeastern Missouri on January 25. The army estimated that 2,500 to 3,000 refugees left the spillway in the two days before the breach. Because of inadequate warning, many failed to evacuate in time. The Highway Department had to send rescuers in motorboats. Approximately 1,500 farmers suffered property damage when nearly 140,000 acres of land overflowed. Floodwaters destroyed five hundred buildings and killed 50 percent of the livestock in the basin. At the time of the flood, there were six villages in the basin, including Bayouville, Belmont, Crosno, Dorena, Medley, and Wolf Island. Only two of these communities, Dorena and Wolf Island, survived.[24]

Refugees left the floodway in a sleet storm while floodwaters surged over the levee at their heels. Mississippi County cotton planter Thad Snow reported that although he had seen previous evacuations in rain and mud, he had never before seen one in six inches of frozen sleet. Many of the evacuees had to drive their mules through five miles of standing water in an icy wind. Many had their hands and feet frozen. On the highway that passed by his home, Snow witnessed "an unbroken line of traffic," consisting of exhausted cattle, mules, and people carrying a small amount of bedding or their children on their backs. Most of the refugees were tenants, sharecroppers, or day laborers. The Red Cross, the Salvation Army, the U.S. Army, and local citizens combined forces to care for thousands of homeless people at shelters in Cape Girardeau, East Prairie, and Charleston. Others received food and medical attention in rented rooms, with relatives, or in hospitals. Segregated tent cities housed African American refugees.[25]

23. White and Ensminger, *Rich Land,* 47–51.

24. *Cape Girardeau Southeast Missourian,* January 25, 1937; *Scott County Democrat,* March 25, 1937; Edison Shrum, "Super Floods Raging in Wide Spread Area: The *Scott County Democrat's* Account of the 1937 Mississippi–New Madrid County Jadwin Floodway Disaster," January 1994, 9.

25. Thad Snow, *From Missouri* (New York: Houghton-Mifflin, 1954), 214–22; *Charleston Enterprise-Courier,* January 28, 1937, February 4, 1937, February 11, 1937.

In an attempt to provide subsistence for dispossessed workers, the FSA established resettlement communities, or colonies, in the Bootheel. For example, in 1937, the FSA developed 6,700 acres of land at La Forge in New Madrid County. Using mass-production methods, under government supervision, local farmers built ninety-four wood frame houses in one hundred days. Typically, each house had a screened porch, a living room, a kitchen with a wood- or coal-burning stove, and two bedrooms. In contrast to the flimsy shacks of most sharecroppers, these weather-tight dwellings rested firmly on concrete piers and had screens to keep out insects. The village complex, with its white-painted houses, barns, and privies, became the hub of a biracial cooperative farming operation headed by Hans Baasch, a Danish-born New Dealer.[26] However, this project, like other experimental communities, helped only a small number of families and did not begin to solve the larger problem of farm tenancy in the region.

When government programs failed to serve their needs, some sharecroppers pinned their hopes on a revolutionary new world order. A few farmworkers attended educational programs in collective action sponsored by the SCU and the CPUSA. In April 1934, the Communist party and the union held a three-week training school for agrarian organizers at a secret location in St. Louis. Ten students (five white and five black) attended the school, taking classes in political economy, the fundamentals of communism, America's racial history, and the problems of unionizing small farmers. Al Murphy, identified in party documents as Comrade M, taught the organizational course.[27] Within a few years, he would come to the Bootheel.

By 1936, a socialist organization, the Arkansas-based Southern Tenant Farmers Union (STFU) extended its reach into southeast Missouri. In the summer of that year, John Handcox, a black organizer and songwriter, found his way to Snow's Corner, a crossroads east of Charleston in Mississippi County. Thad Snow, the white owner of a thousand-acre farm there, suffered pangs of conscience about the abuses of the sharecropping system. He had probably learned about the STFU from Owen Whitfield, a vocal union supporter. Defying social conventions

26. Stuart Chase, "From the Lower Depths," *Reader's Digest* 38 (May 1941): 109–11.

27. Communist Party U.S.A., Records of the Communist Party U.S.A., reel 287, folder 3714, Library of Congress Manuscripts Collection.

and astonishing union leader H. L. Mitchell, Snow invited Handcox to speak to the croppers on his plantation.[28]

Throughout the United States, unionism advanced dramatically in the 1930s. In Missouri, membership in the traditional organizations of the American Federation of Labor (AFL) expanded by 30 percent between 1930 and 1940. Meanwhile, the Congress of Industrial Organizations (CIO) emerged to organize steel, automobile, garment, boot and shoe, and other industrial workers throughout the state. By 1940, more than a quarter of a million Missourians had joined the AFL and another one hundred thousand belonged to the CIO. Many locals excluded black workers, although the CIO successfully integrated several unions. In urban areas, African Americans had limited occupational choices, so many remained unemployed and were therefore unserved by organized labor.[29]

Farmworkers, ignored by traditional AFL unions, began to find a place in the CIO. By 1937, the STFU represented more than thirty thousand white and black agricultural workers in seven states, but the CIO recruited a broader membership. CIO leader John L. Lewis chose Donald Henderson, a former college professor and a member of the Communist party, to organize food growers and processors into a new international union. Henderson traveled across the country, recruiting farmers, pickers, canners, and packers as members of the United Cannery, Agricultural, and Packing Workers of America (UCAPAWA).[30]

Whitfield attended the founding convention of UCAPAWA in the summer of 1937. In an article published in the *St. Louis Post-Dispatch* on August 9, 1937, Snow described an earnest conversation with Whitfield about the affiliation of the STFU with the CIO. Snow "had read that this Denver conference was coming off, and had seen only sketchy press accounts of its proceedings." He wanted to know more about it,

---

28. H. L. Mitchell, *Mean Things Happening in This Land* (Montclair, N.J.: Allenheld, Osmun, 1979), 349. For more on Thad Snow, see Bonnie Stepenoff, *Thad Snow: A Life of Social Reform in the Missouri Bootheel* (Columbia: University of Missouri Press, 2003).

29. Richard S. Kirkendall, *A History of Missouri: Volume V, 1919 to 1953* (Columbia: University of Missouri Press, 1986), 192–95.

30. Alex Lichtenstein, introduction to Howard Kester, *Revolt among the Sharecroppers* (Knoxville: University of Tennessee Press, 1997), 43–44.

and although he realized it was not "exactly cricket for a planter to listen at length to a cropper," he spoke with Whitfield.[31]

The eloquent Baptist minister emerged as the Bootheel's greatest labor leader. Snow patronizingly described him as a "dusky, bald-headed and enthusiastic cotton-cropper." Another contemporary account depicted him as a lean, "coffee-colored" man with a lined face "surmounted by an impressive bald cranium." Although he had a home-grown speaking style and a whimsical sense of humor, his message was an angry one. Instead of waiting patiently for God to help them, he told the poor farmers to help themselves. "I was just full of dynamite," he told a reporter, "From head to foot." He announced to his listeners that "anyone can tell you about Heaven and can't tell you how to get a loaf of bread here—he's a liar." He believed that God had blessed this country with enough food to feed all the hungry people. "Somebody's gettin' it," he said to the croppers. "If you ain't, that's your fault," not God's. He believed that if farmworkers banded together in a union, they could get what they needed.[32]

In 1938, Whitfield's outspoken support of the union led to his eviction from the farm where he worked. Snow would have accepted him as a tenant, but he did not ask. On the day before he and his family would have become homeless, he learned that a new, weatherboarded house was waiting for him in the FSA's La Forge project. Apparently, the man who made this possible was Snow.[33]

Although Whitfield escaped homelessness, thousands of others faced eviction in the winter of 1938–1939. Unable to accept his individual good fortune while others suffered, Whitfield conceived the idea of a mass migration to the state highways as a protest against the abuses of the sharecropping system. During a meeting at the First Baptist Church in the Sunset Addition (the black section of Sikeston), he exhorted a crowd of angry farmworkers not to suffer in silence, but to publicly demonstrate their plight. Two days later, on January 10, the *Sikeston Standard* reported that hundreds of families who had been ordered to leave their plantations after January 1 might stage a mass demonstration on Highway 61.[34]

31. Thad Snow, "Why Share-Croppers Join the CIO," *St. Louis Post-Dispatch,* August 9, 1937.
32. Ibid.; Belfrage, "Cotton-Patch Moses," 94–97.
33. Belfrage, "Cotton-Patch Moses," 99; Mitchell, *Mean Things,* 172.
34. *Sikeston Standard,* January 10, 1939. For more on the roadside demonstrations,

Newspapers all over the country picked up the story when more than one thousand people set up camps along U.S. Highway 60 between Sikeston and Charleston and U.S. Highway 61 between Sikeston and Hayti. The protesters remained resolutely peaceful, as they gathered around campfires, poured coffee for one another, and sang hymns. About 95 percent of the demonstrators were black sharecroppers. Most of the white families who chose to be part of the demonstration congregated in a large camp just south of Sikeston on Route 61. According to Snow, the sight of white families joining in a black protest shocked the people of Sikeston more than any other aspect of the protest. In his memoir *From Missouri,* he wrote that "It was incomprehensible and therefore sinister to every right-thinking observer and defender of the social order."[35]

During this public demonstration, protesters depended on basic survival skills and on the help of friends, neighbors, and kind strangers. When the demonstrators first appeared on the roadsides, they had no fuel, no food, and no shelter except for quilts and blankets draped on poles. They used shotguns to hunt for fresh meat. Each night for nearly a week, a caravan of vehicles appeared and vanished, leaving supplies at the campsites. Croppers who had not been evicted brought provisions to their friends and relatives. Middle-class people secretly supplied the band of outcasts on the roadsides. The protesters held out for a week. By the sixth day of the strike, conditions in the camp had worsened. As Snow remembered, during the first five days and nights, the weather remained mild. But on the sixth night, it snowed. Quilts and blankets provided scant shelter in wet weather, and the camps became truly unlivable when snow was followed by icy rain. But the croppers stayed out on the roadsides, trying to present a cheerful face to reporters and health officials.[36]

Groups and individuals from across the state came to the aid of the demonstrators. When Al Murphy heard about the strike, he volunteered to go to southeast Missouri. There he met his future wife, Pauline

see Louis Cantor, *A Prologue to the Protest Movement* (Durham, N.C.: Duke University Press, 1969).

35. Steve Mitchell, "Homeless, Homeless Are We," Missouri Department of Natural Resources *Preservation Issues* 3 (January/February 1993): 1; Belfrage, "Cotton-Patch Moses," 95; Arvarh Strickland, "Plight of the People in the Sharecroppers' Demonstration in Southeast Missouri," *Missouri Historical Review* 81 (July 1987): 410; Snow, *From Missouri,* 243.

36. *Sikeston Standard,* January 20, 1939; Snow, *From Missouri,* 275–76.

Hawkins Butler of Charleston. Using his Communist party connections, he helped collect money, food, and clothing for the strikers. Whitfield made many contacts in St. Louis, inspiring the creation of the St. Louis Committee for the Rehabilitation of the Sharecroppers. Teachers and students from Lincoln University raised money and sent volunteers to the Bootheel.[37]

Despite this outpouring of support, state and local officials had little patience with the demonstrators. One week after the strike began, state patrolmen, county sheriffs, and deputized citizens cleared the highways. Using trucks provided by local citizens and by the State Highway Department, officials moved thirteen hundred people between Saturday, January 14, and Monday, January 16. Some of the sharecroppers returned to their old farms. A group of New Madrid County families refused to return to their former homes. Officials transported them to a camp on a forty-acre tract of public land behind the levee about six miles east of La Forge.[38]

Forced from the highways, demonstrators crowded into temporary encampments. The swampy land behind the levee in New Madrid County became known as "Homeless Junction." Some of the dispossessed farmers took shelter in a run-down dance hall in Charleston. Walter Johnson became the leader of a group of refugees in a community centered around the Sweet Home Baptist Church near Wyatt. Some of the people there slept on pews; others camped in the churchyard. William R. Fischer took charge of a white camp near Dorena, where food was in short supply. Other families huddled in tents and shacks near Hayti and Charleston. Strike leaders set up headquarters in St. Louis, where some were reportedly "hiding out" after receiving death threats. One of them, W. P. Wells, told a reporter for the *St. Louis American* that the state police carried him back to his old farm near Matthews when they cleared the highways. Planters there seized his livestock and refused to pay him for his crops. He also said that he and his family received death threats.[39]

37. Feezor, "Marcus Alphonse Murphy," 81–85; Cadle, "Cropperville," 30; Lorenzo J. Greene, "Lincoln University's Involvement with the Sharecropper Demonstration in Southeast Missouri, 1939–1940," *Missouri Historical Review* 82 (October 1987): 40–41.

38. *Sikeston Standard,* January 17, 1939.

39. Ibid.; Mitchell, "Homeless," 9; Greene, "Lincoln University's Involvement," 27; *St. Louis American,* February 16, 1939.

Taking a public stand against injustice could be dangerous. Charles L. Blanton's editorials in the *Sikeston Standard* fanned the flames of racial hatred. Blanton called himself "the Polecat" because one of his critics had remarked that his writings smelled like a skunk (or a polecat). Enamored of southern traditions, he regarded the roadside strike as a threat to the established social order and used his column, with a picture of a skunk on the masthead, to castigate anyone who did not agree with him. On January 13, he editorialized that "The negro, Whitfield, the agitator who is one of the farmers on the La Forge project, is at the bottom of this roadside spectacle and should be dispossessed of his lease on the house and acreage."[40]

Even after the demonstrators left the roadsides, Blanton continued to rage. On January 20, he noted that the strikers were gone and warned Whitfield to stay out of the Bootheel. Lamenting the decline of the Ku Klux Klan, the newspaperman was brazen enough to suggest that "they could be revived and parade through and about La Forge." Within a few days, under the shadow of this threat, the paper reported that Whitfield was gone, but that his family remained at La Forge. One month later, his wife and eleven children, ranging in age from one month to twenty-four years, left the Bootheel.[41]

Whitfield continued traveling around the country, winning supporters for the cause. In St. Louis, he worked with activist Fannie Cook, novelist Josephine Johnson, and a variety of supporters associated with the Urban League, Eden Theological Seminary, the Fellowship of Reconciliation, and UCAPAWA. On January 22, the St. Louis Committee for the Rehabilitation of the Sharecroppers sponsored a mass meeting, attended by six hundred people, at the Amalgamated Clothing Workers Union Hall in St. Louis, to raise awareness of the sharecroppers' plight and also to raise money for relief.[42]

H. L. Mitchell and other STFU officers proposed the construction of housing for the dispossessed farmworkers on area plantations. Some sharecroppers resisted this idea, because they would still be at the mercy of landlords. In February 1939, the STFU and a delegation of Missouri croppers met with Dr. Will W. Alexander of the FSA and discussed plans for federally funded housing projects in the Bootheel.

40. Dominic J. Capeci Jr., *The Lynching of Cleo Wright* (Lexington: University Press of Kentucky, 1998), 140; *Sikeston Standard,* January 13, 1939.
41. *Sikeston Standard,* January 20, 1939, January 14, 1939, February 24, 1939.
42. Cadle, "Cropperville," 30.

The FSA developed plans for several villages to be constructed near established towns, where residents might find employment.[43]

Without government assistance, a courageous group of sharecroppers went looking for a piece of land on which to establish a privately funded settlement. Eventually they found a wooded ninety-acre tract fifteen miles southwest of Poplar Bluff on the Little Black River in Butler County. Lincoln University students raised money for a down payment on the property. With additional funds collected by the St. Louis Committee for the Rehabilitation of the Sharecroppers, the refugees purchased the land.[44] Neighbors in the county tried to prevent black people from settling there, but by the middle of June 1939, eighty black and fifteen white families moved into hastily built houses in the new community called the Sharecroppers' Camp, or "Cropperville."

By the mid-1940s, Cropperville had a church, a clinic, and a school. When local and state officials refused to provide educational facilities for residents, Whitfield mobilized the men of Cropperville to erect a school building. Private donors supplied money, lumber, and a stove. With the building in place, the local school board allotted some money for equipment. Local individuals sent books, clothes for the children, and shoes. Teachers came and went, camping out in trailers, sleeping in the school, or moving into cabins abandoned by other residents.[45]

Despite these efforts, Cropperville struggled and ultimately failed. Whitfield did some truck farming, worked part-time in a lumber mill, and raised sorghum in cooperation with his neighbors.[46] But in the hills of Butler County, unemployment was a constant problem. An observer from the American Friends Service Committee, a Quaker group that helped build the school, wrote to Fannie Cook and to the St. Louis Committee for the Rehabilitation of Sharecroppers about factionalism and tension in the community. Writing to St. Louis from the Friends Work Camp at Harviell, Clarence H. Yarrow reported in

43. Mitchell, "Homeless," 9.

44. Greene, "Lincoln University's Involvement," 40–41. William R. Fischer initially purchased the abandoned farm property with help from the Federal Land Bank in 1939; in September 1940 the Missouri Committee for the Rehabilitation of the Sharecroppers purchased the land from Fischer. The transaction is recorded in Butler County Deed Book 216, p. 242.

45. Fannie Cook, "Cropperville Gets a School," undated manuscript in the Fannie Cook Papers, box 26, folder 8, Missouri Historical Society, St. Louis (hereinafter cited as Cook Papers).

46. Belfrage, "Cotton-Patch Moses," 102.

1941 that the people there were discouraged, weary, and troubled. Facing another cold winter with insufficient fuel, no jobs, and no prospects, "They have nothing to do, but sit around and intrigue and get on each other's nerves."[47] During World War II, many able-bodied men went into military service or found employment elsewhere. By 1950, Whitfield left the community to serve as pastor of a church in Illinois.[48] As hope faded, residents drifted away, and the community fell apart.

Several public initiatives had more success. In cooperation with the state of Missouri, the federal government implemented various programs to aid farmworkers. Under the labor rehabilitation program, the FSA accepted responsibility for more than fifteen hundred families, who were on relief or eligible for relief. Landlords in the Bootheel cooperated by giving the families vacant houses, garden tracts, and pastures rent free. The FSA provided small grants to buy garden seed, tools, and other items necessary for subsistence. Many families also obtained loans to buy cows. In return for these gifts, grants, and loans, the families agreed to maintain and improve the properties on which they lived.[49]

The federal government constructed housing for workers on private land donated by landowners and on various sites purchased by the government. Construction on the Delmo (for "Delta of Missouri") Project houses began in 1940 and was completed in 1941. In all, 595 houses were built in ten racially segregated villages of thirty to eighty-five houses each. Each house had bedroom furniture, a cook stove, a coal heating stove, a dining table, and a privy. Individual properties included one-acre plots for growing food. Each village had a circular plan, with dwellings arranged in a loop around a central common area. Circle City in Stoddard County took its name from this design. The common area in each village included a well and water tower, a community building, a clinic, showers, laundry facilities, and a demonstration kitchen. Four of the villages, including North Wyatt (Wilson City), North Lilbourn, Gobler, and South Wardell, housed African Americans.[50]

47. Clarence H. Yarrow to Mrs. Fannie Cook, July 8, 1941, Cook Papers.
48. *Dictionary of Missouri Biography* (Columbia: University of Missouri Press, 1999), 793.
49. FSA, "Southeast Missouri," 5–6.
50. Ibid.; Mitchell, "Homeless," 9–10.

The Delmo Projects began as public housing but soon became privatized. After World War II, the federal government sought to divest itself of the projects. In 1945, an interracial St. Louis committee, chartered as the Delmo Housing Corporation, purchased the villages from the FSA. Setting the price of each house at eight hundred dollars, the original cost of construction, the corporation allowed residents to buy their houses for one hundred dollars down and monthly mortgage payments of from $7.50 to $10.00 per month, sometimes crediting people for "sweat equity."[51] By 1954, all the mortgages were retired, and the Delmo Corporation had a surplus of funds. With assistance from Washington University and several churches, the Delmo agency continued to serve residents of the Bootheel with social, health, and educational programs. For twenty-five years, the director of this agency was Alex Cooper.

In the 1940s and 1950s, as the New Deal era ended, organized labor faced many problems in Missouri. Throughout the nation, two great rivals, the AFL and the CIO, competed for dominance. Both these organizations concentrated their efforts on urban areas, giving scant attention to the needs of rural workers. Rising anticommunist sentiment weakened many CIO locals. The Taft-Hartley Labor Relations Act of 1947 required union officers to sign affidavits swearing that they were not communists. This resulted in purges of many unions in St. Louis and painful struggles within locals around the state.[52]

Wade Tucker, a white farmworker, encountered violent opposition when he tried to keep unionism alive in the Bootheel. Tucker had migrated to the region as a logger and won fame as a wrestler. In the 1920s, he raided bootleggers and moonshiners as sheriff of New Madrid County. Defeated for office in the 1930s, he returned to work as a tenant farmer. Although he did not participate in the roadside strike, he became involved in labor militancy in the spring of 1939. He traveled around the Bootheel, speaking to crowds of farmers as an organizer for the Associated Farm Laborers, Sharecroppers, and Tenant Farmers of Southeast Missouri (AFLST), a rival of the STFU. While the STFU organized workers against landowners, the AFLST tried to organize cotton farmers against ginners (cotton processors and dealers).[53]

51. Alex Cooper, telephone interview with the author, June 1, 2001.
52. Kirkendall, *History of Missouri*, 5:341–43.
53. *Sikeston Standard*, May 12, 1939, and May 23, 1939.

Facing virulent antiunionism, Tucker fought an uphill battle against farm mechanization. By 1940, tractors were rapidly replacing mule-drawn plows, and mechanical cotton-pickers would soon revolutionize work in the fields.[54] Union leaders like Tucker were powerless to stop this trend. As a matter of fact, Charles Blanton urged planters to mechanize their operations in response to Tucker's activities. A May 19, 1939, editorial encouraged producers to attend a demonstration of a cotton chopper at the Van Ausdall Brothers' farm two miles west of Caruthersville. The editorial suggested that mechanization might be an antidote to labor troubles: "If Wade Tucker succeeds in organizing the farm labor in Southeast Missouri and places them on eight hour shifts at $2 per day, this cotton chopper will do the work and no strikes."[55]

Tucker's career ended abruptly. In July 1940, he made a speech from his automobile at Peach Orchard, in Pemiscot County, Missouri. After he finished and was shaking hands with the crowd, an angry man confronted him. Tucker responded with a joke, and the man shot him twice in the abdomen. At the hospital in Poplar Bluff, Tucker suffered through two operations and a bout with pneumonia, but he survived. Neighbors rallied around him, and friends helped him get a job as a supervisor for the FSA.[56]

While African Americans fought for and won some improvements in civil rights during and after World War II, the Bootheel descended to the depths of racial violence. Early in 1941, the trade unionist and civil rights leader A. Philip Randolph organized the March on Washington Movement, protesting discrimination in the armed services and defense industries. The *St. Louis Argus*, a black newspaper, supported the movement. Randolph called off the march after President Roosevelt established the Committee on Fair Employment Practices, a civil rights agency at the federal level. Demands for equality resonated at this time, because America was entering a war against Nazi Germany, a nation that carried racism to its most horrible extreme.[57] In

54. Aiken, *Cotton Plantation South*, 100; Williams Maxwell, interviewed by Ray C. Brassieur, "From Two Mules to Twelve-Row Equipment: An Oral History Interview with Maxwell Williams, Bootheel Farm Manager," *Missouri Historical Review* 91 (1996): 85.

55. *Sikeston Standard*, May 19, 1939.

56. *St. Louis Post-Dispatch*, July 12, 1941.

57. Kirkendall, *History of Missouri*, 5:247–49.

this changing racial context, an infamous act of violence drew national attention to the Bootheel.

Shortly after midnight on Sunday, January 25, 1942, in the Sunset Addition of Sikeston, citizens and lawmen rushed to the aid of a white woman who was bleeding from stab wounds. Police officers apprehended a black man named Cleo Wright, who lashed out at them with a knife. Later that morning, word spread that Wright had confessed to the crime. A mob gathered around City Hall. County Prosecutor David L. Blanton, the son of *Sikeston Standard* editor Charles Blanton, tried to defuse the situation, but he could not stop the crowd from grabbing Wright, kicking him, dragging him through the Sunset Addition, dousing him with gasoline, and burning him to death.[58]

After the lynching, Charles Blanton, the Polecat, tried to defend race relations in the Bootheel. His son, the prosecutor, could not prevail upon him to maintain a dignified silence. In his newspaper columns, he lashed out at anyone who criticized this vigilante action, making odious insinuations about black men climbing into white women's beds. The death of Wright inspired widespread outrage, prompted an investigation by the attorney general of the United States, and helped focus federal attention on racism and the violence it spawned.[59]

Racial animosity, farm mechanization, and competition from migrant laborers drove sharecroppers from the Bootheel. Because of labor shortages during World War II, the U.S. government sanctioned the importation of seasonal farm laborers from Mexico. H. L. Mitchell and the STFU protested against this practice without success. The government mandated minimum wage rates and housing standards for the Mexican laborers, but not for American farmworkers. Despite these regulations, Bootheel landowners relied more and more on Mexican laborers, who worked for a season and then went back across the border.[60]

Anticommunism, already strong in the 1940s, became a national obsession in the 1950s. Prodded by the inflammatory rhetoric of Senator Joseph McCarthy, Americans began rooting out communists and alleged communists from all walks of life. The Bootheel's Al Murphy

---

58. Capeci, *Lynching of Cleo Wright*, 13–23.

59. Ibid., 50–51, 155.

60. Jeannie M. Whayne, *A New Plantation South: Land, Labor, and Federal Favor in Twentieth-Century Arkansas* (Charlottesville: University Press of Virginia, 1996), 227; Jim Mac Emerson, interview with David Dickey, September 9, 1986, SEMO.

became a target of this crusade. After participating in the roadside demonstrations, Murphy returned to St. Louis and remained active in the Communist party for several years. In 1940, he ran for lieutenant governor of Missouri on the Communist ticket. An energetic, articulate man, he took part in struggles against segregation, unfair labor practices, and police brutality. In 1948 he campaigned in Mississippi County for the Progressive party.[61] During the Korean War, he protested against American militarism. By the early 1950s, he had settled down in Charleston with his wife, who taught in rural schools in the Bootheel. Murphy supported himself with various jobs, working part-time as a carpenter and farmhand. In March 1952, he and his wife began construction of a white frame ranch-style house on a country road. Reportedly, he accepted a position with an automotive firm in Cairo, Illinois, across the river from Charleston.[62]

On September 17, 1952, FBI agents arrested Murphy at his home in Charleston. The U.S. government charged him with violating the Smith Act, a 1940 law making it a crime to join an organization that taught, advocated, or encouraged overthrowing the government by force. Murphy's alleged crime was teaching classes in communism. The Smith Act resulted from American fears of totalitarianism in the years before World War II. During the McCarthy era, FBI agents and federal prosecutors invoked the Smith Act in order to round up communists and so-called radicals from coast to coast.[63]

Two years later, Murphy and four other defendants from the St. Louis area endured prosecution in court for violating the Smith Act and for agitating to overthrow the government. During the five-month trial, prosecutors provided no evidence that Murphy had ever participated in or advocated violent revolution. Nevertheless, the jury convicted him and all the other defendants, who were released on bail pending an appeal. In 1957, after the McCarthy hysteria subsided, all five defendants were granted a new trial, and in the fall of 1958, the

---

61. *St. Louis Argus,* September 19, 1952; *Charleston Enterprise-Courier,* September 18, 1952.

62. *Charleston Enterprise-Courier,* September 18, 1952; Feezor, "Marcus Alphonse Murphy," 96–99.

63. Feezor, "Marcus Alphonse Murphy," 1–7; Robert J. Donovan, *Tumultuous Years: The Presidency of Harry S. Truman, 1949–1953* (New York: W. W. Norton, 1982), 25.

charges were dropped. Murphy continued to live in Charleston, working at odd jobs.[64]

When public strategies failed them, sharecroppers resumed their private struggles to earn a living and maintain a sense of pride. Family solidarity suffered as, one by one, young people left home in search of nonfarm employment. Private patronage failed them as landowners mechanized and shifted to a wage-labor system, employing seasonal workers who never became integrated into the local communities. Former sharecroppers who remained in the Bootheel depended on occasional farmwork, nonfarm employment, or public assistance. The rest migrated from the region in search of a new way of life.

Hard work and individual effort did not provide sustenance for Bootheel farmworkers in the first half of the twentieth century. During the Great Depression, workers joined collective organizations, demonstrated their grievances, and demanded attention from the federal government. Protesters faced personal danger and political persecution. The New Deal was a decidedly mixed blessing, but a few innovative programs had lasting benefits. Sharecroppers who became farm owners at Inghram Ridge built a future for their children. The Delmo housing projects outlasted federal involvement and fostered community spirit.

Despite setbacks, people gained knowledge from private struggle and public action. As a young man, Alex Cooper taught in rural black schools for about twelve years. These segregated schools had poor facilities, outside toilets, and minimal equipment. In the early 1950s at a Friday afternoon gripe session, one of his students said to him, "We are the worst school in the whole county. How can we be proud?" Cooper replied, "I'm going to teach you all that I know. And I know a lot." Years later, that student also became a teacher.[65]

64. Feezor, "Marcus Alphonse Murphy," 159. Thad Snow put up the money for Murphy's bail. The *St. Louis Globe-Democrat*, January 1, 1953, confirms that Murphy's bail was set at ten thousand dollars. Thad Snow's estate was admitted to probate after he died on January 15, 1955, and it was settled on May 18, 1956, while Murphy's case was still pending. In 1958, after Murphy's case ended, the executor of Snow's estate collected additional assets in the amount of ten thousand dollars. Documentation of the settlement of the estate can be found in the abstract of Snow's property on file at the Mississippi County Abstracting Company in Charleston, Missouri.

65. Cooper interview, Bootheel Project, March 11, 1994, AC 4.

Constance Runcie and the Runcie Club of St. Joseph

JANICE BRANDON-FALCONE

In June 1871 the small city of St. Joseph, Missouri, welcomed the arrival of a new clergyman, his wife, and their three children, along with an unmarried sister. The bustling city of twenty thousand souls nestled on the hills that overlooked the Missouri River at the western edge of the state. James Runcie arrived to take up the position of pastor at Christ Episcopal Church, a position he would hold until his death eighteen years later. His wife, Constance Fauntleroy Runcie, sized up the city and its western feel as having distinct possibilities. At thirty-five years of age, she arrived with a new baby and two older children, aged six and eight. "I like the people right well," she wrote her cousin, suggesting the diction of the Ohio River town of Madison, Indiana, which they had just left. "The society is mixed here—English, Irish and all parts of the Union. . . . It was a hard pull to leave Madison . . . [but] we thought it best to make the move as Mr. Runcie's health was so poor."[1]

It was a city bursting with the energy of impending growth in 1871. With the Civil War over and a transcontinental railroad laid, the country was poised to develop the West, and St. Joseph was poised to thrive on that development. In the fifteen years after the Runcies' arrival, the city's population would quadruple. Wholesale houses in dry goods and groceries expanded to supply the retailers of the new western

---

1. Letter to Della Mann Owen, June 20, 1871, Kenneth D. Owen Papers, New Harmony, Indiana, a private, closed collection, hereinafter cited as K. D. Owen Papers, New Harmony, Indiana.

towns. Steamboats plied the river, and trains steamed into and out of town several dozen times a day. The city was larger in 1871 than both its neighbors on the river, Kansas City and Omaha. It was a city whose ambitions matched that of the new pastor's wife. A year after her arrival, Constance Runcie, an aspiring composer and music lover, gleefully witnessed the construction of an opera house that would host concerts, lectures, and plays. Meanwhile, St. Joseph also retained a wild and woolly reputation. Within a year of the opera house construction, Runcie also read in the newspaper a notice of a reward set for a thousand dollars for the capture of the outlaw brothers Frank and Jesse James. Jesse James would later be killed in St. Joseph in 1882.[2]

Constance Runcie paid little attention to bandits. She longed for culture and possessed her own burning ambitions, which chafed under the constraints of motherhood, running a house, and being wife to the rector. "Were I a man, I would struggle to the front," she later complained to her daughter Ellinor in a letter. "I must do what others can do better than I [make beds] and waste the gift to a great extent which was . . . so sweetly given me." As a young mother with small children, she could continue to write music because her sister-in-law assumed the management of the household, which she admitted in a letter to her sister: "I don't pretend to keep house. Miss Anne is the presiding genius and it is very little sewing I do either." She saw herself as a frustrated artist and berated her abilities as a housekeeper and even as a parent, confessing to her cousin by marriage, Della Mann Owen, "I am such a poor mother, a fraud of a mother . . . and I cannot endure to sew."[3]

Although Constance Runcie would never break away from the duties of motherhood or running a house, she would nevertheless develop a forum for her musical and literary efforts. In 1894, she founded a women's club in St. Joseph, naming it for herself. The Runcie Club

2. Sheridan Logan, *Old Saint Jo, Gateway to the West, 1799–1932* (St. Joseph, Mo.: John Sublett Logan Foundation, 1979).

3. Letter to Ellinor, February 14, 1892, Runcie Papers, Missouri Western State College Archives, St. Joseph, Missouri (hereinafter cited as Runcie Papers); Letter to Ellinor Davidson [daughter], February 22, 1875, George Davidson Collection, University of California at Berkeley, hereinafter cited as Davidson Collection; Letter to Della Mann Owen, March 16, 1883, K. D. Owen Papers, Mary Owen Collection, box 1, Runcie Correspondence, New Harmony, Indiana.

would remain active for more than a hundred years, long past her death in 1911. This organization would serve Runcie well as a vehicle for her ambitions and as a way to earn money as a widow, while she avoided the then-negative image of working outside the home. The club would also serve the women of the town who dutifully accepted the leadership, even the tyranny, of Runcie, as they used membership in her club to assert their claims to take part in public activities. However, they also accepted Runcie's directing their expansion toward socially acceptable activities.

There was a continuity in Constance Runcie's club building, as well as in the self-confident ego that left its mark on the club long after she died. She had created two other clubs at critical junctures in her life. A brief look at the first club she created, in New Harmony, Indiana, will demonstrate the strong character of Runcie as well as outline the contributions that women's clubs provided toward community building. Then, a detailed examination of the Runcie Club of St. Joseph will establish the parameters of the club's activities. Runcie imprinted her personality on her club as she led women into more public arenas. These public activities never fully challenged the status quo of social and economic power, but participation in them did serve to reinforce club members' social relations and the status of those who occupied higher levels of urban society. If Runcie's club served Constance Runcie, it also became a means of empowerment and leadership training for the ladies of the club. However confident they became under her tutelage, the clubwomen enhanced their position in society without questioning existing social relations. The Runcie Club was not so concerned with social change as it was with social cohesion.

Constance Fauntleroy Runcie came to her understanding of cultural leadership and the duty of social contribution in a very natural way: she was born into it. Born in 1836 into the leading family of the town of New Harmony, Indiana, she possessed from an early age a sense of the unique contributions of her family to regional and national life. Her grandfather was Robert Owen, the English textile industrialist who had built a model factory town in New Lanark, Scotland, married the factory owner's daughter, and begun a series of social experiments that resulted in communal health care, eradication of child labor in his mills, a cooperative grocery store that helped create the cooperative movement in England and elsewhere, and a free system of education.[4] So proud was Constance of her Owen connections, she often called herself Constance Owen Runcie, dispensing her maiden name of Fauntleroy and using her mother's maiden name.

Robert Owen decided the United States was the ideal place in which to experiment with model communities and utopian socialism. In 1825, Owen purchased the entire town of New Harmony, Indiana, from a group of religious communitarians who wanted to move back to Pennsylvania. His planned community attracted educators, naturalists, and several who held ideas about labor rights, ending slavery, and women's rights.[5] It also, however, attracted many who wanted the benefits of collectivism without performing the work required to attain such benefits, and in two years, Owen's experiment had failed. He returned to England to carry out his social experiments there, but he left behind the town he bought as well as his four still-living sons— Robert Dale, William, Richard, and David Dale. Owen's sons went into politics, geologic studies, and surveying; their influence was felt in the establishment of the Smithsonian Institution, in the movement to liberalize divorce and property laws for women, in the antislavery movement, in the development of the science of geology, and in the promotion of an intelligentsia in what was, in antebellum America, the West. A few years later, their one surviving sister, Jane, who sailed down the Ohio River and up the Wabash to New Harmony with her harp and several boxes of clothing, china, and books, joined them. A few years after her arrival, in 1835, she married Robert Henry Fauntleroy, a Virginia-born surveyor who worked with one of her brothers, and she settled into her own family life. Widowed unexpectedly at age forty-three (her husband died of cholera contracted on a surveying expedition in 1849), she faced the challenge of providing for her four

4. More information on Owen's life and thought can be found in several biographies. Among them are G. D. H. Cole, *The Life of Robert Owen* (New York: Archon Books, 1966); Oakley Johnson, *Robert Owen in the United States* (New York: Humanities Press, 1970); Lloyd Jones, *The Life, Times, and Labours of Robert Owen* (New York: AMS Press, 1971); Frank Podmore, *Robert Owen: A Biography* (New York: Kelley Publishing, 1968).

5. Johnson, *Robert Owen*. Among the reformers who were drawn to New Harmony were educators Marie Fretageot and William Phiquepal, naturalists Thomas Saye and Charles Lesueur, labor activist William Maclure, and Frances Write, a radical thinker and leader in the women's rights, abolition, and education-reform movements.

children in the sheltering proximity of her brothers and their families.[6]

Into this lively milieu of Owen brothers and sister Jane, came the next generation; Constance was one of the eldest children among her cousins. Constance Fauntleroy was Jane's oldest child. She came of age in the small town of New Harmony with a large extended family, most of whom were intellectually curious and relished literature, music, and science. "By the time I reached twelve years of age," Constance remembered later, "I already knew and loved the works of Shakespeare, Milton, Scott, Addison, and the music of Beethoven, Mozart, Handel, and Haydn." Describing a typical evening of her childhood, she might have overemphasized the heady environment but remembered much stimulation: "It was here that Robert Dale . . . would give us a Shakespearean evening, that David Dale would lecture on geology and chemistry, Richard Owen on natural history, and my father [would] superintend the musical rendition of one of his own compositions."[7]

In addition, she spent five of her late teenage years in Europe with this extended family after her uncle Robert Dale Owen was appointed the ambassador to Italy (then the Kingdom of the Two Sicilies). When she returned home to the sleepy Indiana town in her early twenties, she had acquired a rich background in languages and music, along with a firm concept of herself as a person of culture and breeding with great promise (she felt) as a poet and a musician. She burned with an ambition that grew in sharp contrast to her rather conventional ideas about women and family life. It was difficult to leave European cities and culture and return to the sleepy town on the Wabash River. In dealing with the "stifling"—as she later called it—atmosphere of New Harmony, the young Constance took an action that she would later repeat at other important crossroads in her life: she organized a women's club.

This first club, the Minerva Society, established in 1859 when Constance was twenty-three, was primarily a literary club for young

6. See Richard W. Leopold, *Robert Dale Owen: A Biography* (Cambridge: Harvard University Press, 1940); and Jane Dale Owen Fauntleroy, "Records of a Beloved Life, for My Children," courtesy of the New Harmony State Historic Site, part of the Indiana State Museum System; Private Correspondence, box 15, the Library of the Workingman's Institute (hereinafter cited as WMI) New Harmony, Indiana.

7. Constance Fauntleroy Runcie, *Divinely Led, or Robert Owen's Granddaughter* (New York, 1880), 7–8, 10

unmarried women (later, as members married, they remained in the club) and, as such, provided a safe, nonpublic place where they could present to one another essays, poetry, and stories they had written. Constance was excited to have a forum for her work. "I have made up my mind to become very learned," she had written six years earlier. "I wish to become some celebrated personage whom all the world will hear of."[8] By the time she formed her first club, she was confiding to her sister that a visitor from New York had collected some of her poems with the promise to publish them.[9]

It was a heady experience for many of the other young women, who had less experience in social exchange or with speaking in public. For several of the members of the Minerva Society, reared as they were in what historian Barbara Welter has dubbed the "cult of domesticity," standing in front of a group to read their own work proved stressful. Club records relate how one seventeen-year-old member fainted shortly after she had read her essay to the club.[10] Constance had no such misgivings about speaking before a group, as she was accustomed to a free exchange of opinions with her uncles, cousins, and their visitors from Washington and Europe. Short pieces of anonymous poetry from the club began appearing in the local paper.

Her experiences with the Minerva Society would provide her with ideas for club building and confidence in the future, but the organization itself did not last long. The impending Civil War, the deaths of Constance's mother, brother, and an uncle all in the span of a year, and the courtship of a young Episcopal clergyman led Constance Fauntleroy away from her youthful club venture and into marriage in April 1861. Ten years later—after the Civil War, after another attempt at a women's club, and after the births of three babies—Constance and James Runcie moved to St. Joseph.[11]

8. Letter to Aunt Caro, Original Collection, box 25, correspondence, July 1853, K. D. Owen Papers, New Harmony, Indiana.

9. Letter to Ellinor, July 12, 1859, Davidson Collection.

10. Della Mann Owen, "Memories for Daughters of Minerva, 1920," Minerva Society Papers, Workingman's Institute Library (WMI), New Harmony, Indiana. All of the primary source information on the Minerva Society is made available through the courtesy of the New Harmony State Historic Site, part of the Indiana State Museum System, found in the Workingman's Institute Library; and the Archives of the Workingman's Institute Library, New Harmony, Indiana.

11. The Bronte Club of Madison, Indiana, was another club organized by Con-

Constance Runcie enjoyed living in St. Joseph. For the first fifteen years, she led a busy life running a household that included four active children (the fourth child was born in 1874), an unmarried sister-in-law, and a husband busy with ministerial duties. In addition, she experienced the renewal of a cultural and creative life. Not since the days of her youth had she enjoyed access to lectures and concerts as she found in Kansas City and St. Joseph. Periodically, she published her own musical compositions and poetry and enjoyed a small measure of fame in the publication of an autobiography that focused on the contrast of her religious conversion as a young woman and her grandfather Robert Owen's freethinking ways.[12] She trekked to Kansas City and tried to convince musicians to perform her work. She traveled to Boston to visit music and book publishers. She entertained visitors such as the journalist and poet Eugene Field and his wife, Julia, who was from St. Joseph, and she created and promoted her role as culture maven in church and community. She saw herself as belonging as much to a social elite of four hundred as did the female patrons of the Gilded Age back east. Her husband, the Reverend James Runcie, a mild-mannered and much-loved churchman who admired his wife's many artistic endeavors, invited his unmarried sister, Anne, to live with the family and help run the household. This arrangement provided Constance with the leisure for her explorations in the areas of art and music.

The security, leisure, and social status Runcie enjoyed in St. Joseph might have carried her easily through the rest of her life in smug comfort had it not been for one development. In the spring of 1889, when she was fifty-three, her husband died, leaving Runcie with an economic dilemma.

At a time when Runcie felt herself to be at the height of her powers for cultural achievement, she faced an uncertain future: How was she to educate her eighteen-year-old daughter, Ellinor? How was she to bring her fifteen-year-old son, Percy, to some respectable position in life? How was she to find a new place to live, since the family had to move from the rectory? And how could she provide for herself and aging sister-in-law, Anne? She had inherited an estate from James

---

stance during the early years of her marriage from 1861 to 1871 while her husband was rector at a church in Madison.

12. Runcie, *Divinely Led.*

worth about fifteen hundred dollars and had inherited from her family of origin a farm in southern Indiana, which she sold for five thousand dollars. The church took up a special collection for her. With this money, she decided to build a house for herself. Keeping the future in mind, and convinced that she had much to give her adopted town of St. Joseph, as well as to the rest of the nation, she refused to accept a widowhood of diffident and genteel impoverishment.

With her inheritance, she sent her daughter off to a preparatory boarding school in Massachusetts in hopes that she would attend one of the new women's colleges. She also sent her son to another school in New Hampshire. She managed to persuade the church to let her remain in the rectory while she built a house for herself east of downtown. It was a house of unusual design for the nineteenth century. The downstairs was built as one great room, divided only by a double-sided fireplace in the center. It was a room ideally suited for entertaining large groups, hosting lectures, offering classes, sponsoring a small concert, or supporting a regular gathering of twenty-five to a hundred women—exactly the kind of activities Runcie planned.[13]

For a woman of Runcie's social standing in 1889, working outside the home was nearly out of the question. Her two adult children lived nearby, but neither was capable of supporting her; her small successes at publishing songs and poetry were not nearly profitable enough to live on. She needed some sort of income, and to suit her social position, it needed to come from somewhere that looked as little as possible like a job. Gathering groups in her home was a solution to this dilemma; she could gain some income without violating the social and economic proscriptions against women working outside the home. Furthermore, she might make her influence felt past her role as the pastor's wife and widow.

At that time, there were numerous women across the country involved in public activity who escaped censure by using the home as a base of operation. At the same time as Rev. Runcie's death, for example, Jane Addams was opening Hull House, which would serve as both her home as well as an entrance into the public arena. Appropriately,

13. Janice Brandon-Falcone, "Biography as Prism: The Life of C. F. Runcie" (Ph.D. diss., Saint Louis University, 1990), chapter 6.

upon her arrival in Chicago, Addams was immediately invited to join the prestigious Chicago Women's Club. [14]

Teaching was one of the few respectable avenues of earning a living, but teaching was not limited to a contract with a school district. Any number of people held public lectures, concerts, and theatrical offerings. A friend of Runcie's from St. Joseph, Mrs. Richard Proctor, provided for herself after her husband's death by giving public lectures using her own ideas and her dead husband's professorial notes. She appeared in Omaha, Kansas City, and Chicago, and she even ventured as far as London in her public venue. The boundary between what had earlier been sharply defined as private and public space was by then becoming blurred, and Constance Runcie was part of the hidden army of women who increasingly traversed that boundary. "One does not have to teach full time," advised a manual for female entrepreneurs of the time; "classes and lessons have multiplied so of late years that a qualified instructor seldom experiences any difficulty. . . . A lady with influential recommendations . . . can usually find occupation." [15]

Constance Runcie had been giving music lessons for quite a few years, but she seized upon an idea in 1891 that would utilize her new home, allow her to engage in holding a class, and supplement her income at the same time. She organized a "ladies class . . . for intellectual advancement among women" for two hours every Tuesday afternoon in her home, for twelve weeks, for the price of one dollar per lecture. About thirty-five women signed up for the class. The lectures ranged freely over a wide variety of topics, including the "silver bill," Henrik Ibsen's work, and the lives of celebrated women. "Oh! It is just splendid!" one woman exclaimed to Runcie after her lecture on the free coinage of silver. "I don't understand one word of it, but I do enjoy it so much." [16]

14. See Jane Addams, *Twenty Years at Hull House,* ed. Victoria Bissell Brown (New York, Boston: Bedford/St. Martin's, 1999); and Allen F. Davis, *American Heroine: The Life and Legend of Jane Addams* (New York: Oxford University Press, 1973).

15. Ellen Rodman Church, *Money-Making for Ladies* (New York, 1882), 77. Advice books such as Church's listed numerous schemes for making money and discussed teaching as "the Last of the three legitimate occupations for *ladies* in what might be called the Dark Ages of women's work." On the other hand, holding classes, as Runcie proposed to do, was an occupation that carried some status as well as remuneration of "fifty cents to a dollar an hour" (ibid.).

16. Constance Runcie to Ellinor Runcie, November 21, 1891, Runcie Papers.

Over the next several years, as the country sank more deeply into economic depression, Constance Runcie engaged in a variety of enterprises for the community. She staged a musical benefit for herself in which all of her own music was performed and some of her poetry was recited. Months later, she obtained a teaching position for her daughter at the local high school when Ellinor returned from Europe. In 1893 she began another series of lectures, this time charging much less than she had for the original series two years earlier.[17] The lectures, held in the church basement, proved a preview of an organization yet to come: the Runcie Club.

In 1894, Constance Runcie began to create her new club. Recalling her earlier successes in organizing women's clubs, she now invited the women of St. Joseph's middle and upper classes to an organizational meeting for the formation of a club. The club she envisioned would generate dues sufficient to provide her an income; it would also support her long-held musical and literary ambitions. In return, she would provide the women of St. Joseph with an intellectual outlet, a sort of continuing education, and a source of self-esteem. It would prove to be a good exchange. The exchange was beneficial not only to Runcie and the ladies of the club, but also to St. Joseph.

Constance enjoyed the idea of cultural uplift for the women of St. Joseph in much the same way that Jane Addams advocated cultural uplift in the immigrant neighborhood of Chicago, though Runcie's intended audience was not immigrant women, but rather the middle- and upper-class women of St. Joseph. Cultural uplift benefited the community; it was part of Runcie's sense of duty as inherited from her Owen relatives and embellished by her husband's religious sense of duty. It was in keeping with a larger cultural sense of duty alluded to by those in eastern intellectual circles, who saw their work as embedded with a mission to society, part of the sense of obligation drawn from the genteel tradition. Certainly Runcie possessed an acute sense of mission to lift up the lowly and use highbrow culture as a means to imbue noble purpose, character, and values in a society racing feverishly in the direction of economic development. Her focus, however, was not to challenge her sense of status and position, nor anyone else's, but to make them equal to their social position. She wrote her

17. *St. Joseph Herald*, May 28, 1893, November 5, 1893.

daughter in Europe, complaining of the shallow parties that everyone attended:

> Thank goodness I am not one of the dear "400" in this respect [card playing]. I behold my friends, nervous, pale, exhausted yet prancing into every amusement offered. Their bodies—intellects—souls all perishing for proper treatment. . . . They are my friends only because I must have love and not because I admire this craze for cards and dancing. Of course this interferes with any real desire to improve their minds . . . in this way [card playing] only do their husbands meet them on their own ground. . . . Moral or spiritual influence is felt to be an irksome restraint—all is . . . nervous jollity—no real elegance or elevating atmosphere.[18]

At the organizational meeting, Runcie presented the women gathered there with a constitution and bylaws she had already drawn up. The forty women who enrolled in the club at that meeting voted to name their group the Runcie Club, and, not surprisingly, Constance Runcie was elected president. Her first lecture to the club was entitled, "Higher Education of Women." For Runcie, and many of the women who followed her, the act of self-improvement would lead to the overall improvement of society.[19]

Within six weeks, the Runcie Club boasted ninety-five members, mostly from important and well-to-do families of St. Joseph, who were willing to pay dues of one dollar per month, whether they attended the weekly meetings or not. Constance Runcie had finally found the means to provide herself with an income at the same time as she provided herself with an audience for her music (and ideas) and the opportunity to engage in what she considered cultural missionary work. "I am so sorry you cannot come this week to hear my music and my poetry," she wrote to one young woman. "Do come next week and let me do you some good."[20]

18. Constance Runcie to Ellinor Runcie, February 14, 1892, Runcie Papers.

19. It is interesting to note that one of the first debates that the Minerva Society held in 1859 concerned the higher education of women. Evidently, Constance felt sure of herself on this topic.

20. Note to "Fairy," March 17, 1908, Runcie Papers. In the early years of the club, except for Constance Runcie herself and her daughter, Ellinor, the women did not

The Runcie Club maintained a yearly schedule of meetings from mid-fall through spring. In the early years it chose a country on which to focus its study for the club year, and Runcie herself assigned the members essays to write about the literature, culture, history, drama, and architecture of the featured country; the first year, they studied Greece.

The Runcie Club was in many respects similar to hundreds of other women's clubs being formed around the country in the late nineteenth century. Although each club possessed a certain uniqueness, all were devoted to the extended education of women and to fostering social networks. Clubs were not only a network connecting members with one another; they also imparted status in the local community and, in time, in the broader community of clubs across the nation. In 1892, the General Federation of Women's Clubs (GFWC), a newly created national organization, had begun holding biennial meetings in a variety of cities around the country.[21]

As clubs evolved and women acquired a confidence that sprang from their programs of self-improvement, they increasingly turned their attention outwards, seeking to improve the community around them as well as themselves. The Runcie Club was at first an exception in this regard, as Constance Runcie's personal stamp so heavily influenced the club and she tried to avoid political questions in favor of cultural ones. In December 1894, she went to New York, where she visited the Sorosis Club, an early, large, and influential women's club that supported a political agenda including suffrage, labor laws, and laws protecting women and children. On her return to St. Joseph, she reported that the New York club, "with its political tendencies," was "losing prestige." "Our Club aspires to improvements only, disdaining women's rights, political leagues, etc.," she proclaimed.[22] Dependent as she was on the money her club brought in, she could ill afford to risk adopting divisive political positions.

---

risk the presentation of their own original work, though one member grew so interested in Indian ethnography that she pursued her study independently and eventually published a book on the subject. Minutes, November 17, 1896, Runcie Club Papers, YWCA, St. Joseph, Missouri (hereinafter cited as Runcie Club Papers).

21. Karen J. Blair, *The Clubwoman as Feminist: True Womanhood Redefined, 1868–1914* (New York: Holmes and Meier Publishers, 1980).

22. Minutes, December 31, 1894, Runcie Club Papers.

In this regard, too, the Runcie Club differed from other women's clubs across the nation because it provided an income for its organizer. "I suppose Ellie has told you of my Club," Runcie wrote her brother-in-law in California. "It pays me well and is a good thing for the place."[23] In later years, when membership fluctuated, she could not always claim that the club "paid her well," but generally she could count on its activities to provide a supplemental living for her.

By 1898 the Runcie Club joined the GFWC. By that time, the club had moved far enough along the road of self-culture to be willing to engage in community-building activities in concert with the General Federation's focus on civic improvement. Like their counterparts across the nation, the clubwomen of St. Joseph began to engage in civic-improvement projects that were in keeping with the accepted idea of "municipal housekeeping." For example, the women supported the creation of "traveling libraries" that brought books to smaller towns surrounding St. Joseph. They lobbied the state legislature to appropriate money for this project. They underwrote many of the activities of the St. Joseph Public Library: sponsoring public lectures there, purchasing and donating art reproductions for the library to loan, and donating a number of books to the library. This practice was customary in towns and cities, which made use of Andrew Carnegie's foundation that built libraries across the nation in the early years of the twentieth century. The Carnegie Foundation granted funds for the construction of a library building; the people in the community (largely women) stocked the library. "Four-fifths of the public libraries . . . were originally the project of some woman's club," boasted a historian of the General Federation of Women's Clubs.[24]

By the fall of 1898, the clubwomen began to support more public ventures other than the sponsorship of cultural venues such as concerts or receptions for the poet Eugene Field, who had lived in St. Joseph and returned occasionally to visit his wife's family. They began to endorse the creation of a home economics course for the high school and vigorously worked to enact a ban on public expectoration.[25] In April 1899, they financed the visit and lecture of the Chicago sculptor

23. Constance Runcie to George Davidson, November 18, 1894, Davidson Collection.

24. Mildred White Wells, *Unity in Diversity: The History of the General Federation of Women's Clubs* (Washington, D.C.: General Federation of Women's Clubs, 1953), 171.

25. Runcie Club Minutes, December 6, 1898, Runcie Club Papers.

Lorado Taft. Runcie hosted a reception in his honor at her home to which the club was invited. It proved so successful they sponsored the sculptor's appearance for three winters in a row. The more they worked on civic improvement, the more they were mentioned in the daily papers; their leadership skills were honed on nondivisive projects.

Several women used the network of the club to open a free kindergarten for the poor children of St. Joseph. The burgeoning kindergarten movement in the United States borrowed much from the vision of Friedrich Froebel and other European pedagogues who saw kindergarten not only as a professional opportunity for women, but also as a training ground among all classes for the creation of independent and socially active citizens. In much the same way that earlier generations had vaunted public education for democracy, the kindergarten movement sought to fit the children of all social classes for citizenship.

Joining the state and national federations of clubs brought the St. Joseph women into contact with other women and other club projects and encouraged them to assume a more public role for the club, although they still avoided controversial political positions—and still do to the present day. (Today the Runcie Club hosts professional women as well as upper-class matrons.)

Despite her unwillingness to address controversial political concerns such as suffrage, Runcie began to funnel her earlier passion for music and literature into a vision for the club and its work in St. Joseph. In one essay, she praised the work of women's clubs around the nation:

> Splendid results are being attained by Women's Clubs all over the civilized world. Woman has thrown her influence upon the side of reform. I omit details of her achievements, although it is of the deepest interest to read what she is doing to better conditions in every section of the country . . . to raise higher standards of morality—protect children, preserve archaeological ruins of lost races, purify neighborhoods, stem intemperance and obtain juster laws for women and children . . . with her face set against intemperance, gambling, impurity and evil . . . against sweat shops, child slavery, the cigarette habit and unjust laws.[26]

26. Constance Runcie, *Woman: An Essay* (St. Joseph, Mo.: Lon Hardman Printing, n.d.).

The club expanded its public endorsements and activities in keeping with the national federated group, which publicly supported such measures as child labor laws, the Pure Food and Drug Bill, a minimum wage bill, and protective legislation for women. On the local level, the St. Joseph women supported the establishment of an "industrial normal school" in Missouri. The art lectures by Lorado Taft not only paid for themselves but also generated a small profit for the club. About the same time, in 1901, the women became more energized after they hosted the state federation of women's clubs and learned about the endeavors of their peers around the state. They enthusiastically discussed "St. Joseph's principal needs, cleaner streets, and a better system for disposal of garbage . . . improvement of our city parks, of the riverfront." The women published the proceedings of their discussion in the newspaper and continued their discussion of civic improvements the following week. "Club seems in earnest," Runcie confided in her private journal.[27] The women of the club had begun to accept their role as municipal housekeepers. When Jane Addams visited St. Joseph in the fall of 1902, they entertained her and hosted a reception to honor her work in Chicago as well as her membership in the Chicago Women's Club.

The club began to change with the new century, but St. Joseph had also begun to change. From 1902 on, the club began to work in areas of civic improvement as well as to endorse specific legislative bills at the state level to make cigarettes illegal, establish traveling libraries in the state, create child labor laws, pure food laws, and to create free kindergartens and manual training schools. As the club was drawn under the influence of the agenda of the national federation, it adopted positions that reflected the goals of the progressive movement in general. On the community level, some club activities supported the notion that St. Joseph needed more than improvement of wealthy women's minds: the club voted a donation to a newly created "Rescue Home for Women"; the club also hosted a fund-raising event for a local orphanage, joined other groups to encourage retail stores to close by six o'clock on Saturday night, engaged a traveling art exhibit, developed a sewing guild to make clothes for the local orphanage, created their own committee on forestry, which raised money to plant trees in the

27. Runcie Club Minutes, March 26, 1901, and March 11, 1902, Runcie Club Papers; President's private journal, March 11 and 18, 1902, Runcie Club Papers.

town, established a committee to foster tuberculosis education in town, continued to press the local school system for a domestic science class, created an ongoing Library committee, and worked on city-beautification projects. A Civic Improvement League formed early in 1904, and the Runcie Club sent three delegates. In February 1904, Runcie read an article to the club on the activities of clubwomen in other states that "plainly showed how the women were reaching out, with increased energy, striving to 'benefit all classes of people, morally, mentally and physically.'" The club's social focus was typical of many similar organizations, whether in small towns or big cities such as St. Louis and Chicago.[28] The change in focus signified social and economic changes the city would have to face.

By 1900, St. Joseph had a population of 102,000, but it was on the edge of a decline. In another ten years, the population would drop to 77,400. At the century's beginning, though, the city was still building impressive new bank buildings, a public library in 1902, a city auditorium in 1906, and the elegant Robidoux Hotel in 1908—named for the fur trader who had founded the town. By 1910, St. Joseph boasted its own skyscraper, an office building of twelve stories. Such building projects belied the economic change that undermined St. Joseph's central business activity—the wholesale supply houses. Chain stores were developing nationwide and bought directly from factories, no longer requiring the services of the "middleman" of wholesale supply houses. The incredible transportation network of rails crisscrossing the West allowed factories to ship small quantities directly to stores at the same price it paid to ship large quantities to the wholesale houses. Mail-

28. Minutes, February 16, 1904, Runcie Club Papers. In examining the life of a literary culture club in Osage, Iowa, Christine Pawley finds that membership in the club led members not only to become culturally educated but also "to develop a political awareness, and establish themselves as leaders in the continuing process of transforming Osage from a frontier settlement into a permanent community." The lobbying efforts of this club are strikingly similar to the Runcie Club. On the state level, the Osage women lobbied for widows' pensions, teachers' pensions, pure food laws, water conservation, flag protection, playgrounds, and parks, as well as woman suffrage and factory safety standards. On the local level, they lobbied against animal cruelty, smoking, and spitting, lobbied for playground space, and donated books and art to the library. Christine Pawley, "Not Wholly Self-Culture: The Shakespeare Women's Club, Osage, Iowa, 1892–1920," *Annals of Iowa* 56, nos. 1 and 2 (winter/ spring 1997): 41.

order catalogs also eliminated the need for those businesses that had allowed St. Joseph to thrive and prosper. Kansas City surpassed St. Joseph in size and in certain key industries such as meatpacking. St. Joseph found that one of its central functions was disappearing. By 1915, the city had to face a decline that continued steadily until long after the Depression of the 1930s.[29]

By 1915, the character of the Runcie Club had also begun to change, beginning even before the death of Mrs. Runcie in 1911. The new century would gradually grow to ridicule the "bluestockings" that Mrs. Runcie represented and parodied her ambitions of elevating rich people's values beyond the consumer values adopted by the twentieth century. Her daughters' lives reflected a bit of the old century as well as the new. Her married, oldest daughter, Blessing, continued to live in St. Joseph, served the club in minor capacities through much of her life, and supported her husband's political activities as a two-term mayor of the city. Her unmarried, younger daughter, Ellinor, also continued on in the club, but she imparted to it a new identity: the professional working woman. Ellinor Runcie worked as a teacher at the elite Barstow School in Kansas City but often returned to St. Joseph and to the club as well. As St. Joseph changed and faced new economic realities, so did the women of the club, but their entry into the workforce hardly threatened their social position, nor did it challenge class relations in general.

Through its programs of public outreach, the Runcie Club offered its members an opportunity to better their community; through its own internal networking, it offered them a safe haven where discussions of history, art, and current events would not be met with patronizing smiles by husbands or with smirks by those who were not the clubwomen's "social equals." The club encouraged a strong sense of sisterhood among its members as the women honed their speaking and writing skills and developed the confidence to speak before groups and defend their ideas. Even in its first year, Constance Runcie summed up the club's value when she congratulated the women on "the intellectual and moral influence which the Runcie Club has exercised in St. Joseph."[30]

29. Logan, *Old Saint Jo,* 180–82.
30. Minutes, May 21, 1895, Runcie Club Papers.

The sense of sisterhood extended itself as the years passed and they joined ranks with other St. Joseph clubs, the Missouri State Federation of Women's Clubs, and the national organization, the GFWC. Initially diffident about the efficacy of these out-of-town organizations, Runcie Club members came to see that much could be accomplished by working in unison on a larger scale. If the club itself offered safety in its exclusivity and its private home meetings, federations offered empowerment on the city, state, and national level. In 1908, by Runcie's report, the General Federation represented eight hundred thousand women. By 1912, the year after Constance Runcie died, the GFWC, with almost one million members, was endorsing women's suffrage as a vehicle of municipal housekeeping.

Eighteen months before her death at age seventy-five in May 1911, Constance Runcie, in assessing her life's work, did not write of her children; her music, poetry, or essays; or her church work, all of which had occupied much of her time. Instead, she wrote frankly of the club as her gift to St. Joseph. When she thought of that club and of the women with whom she had worked for seventeen years, she wrote, "for it is I [who] . . . taught these women how to think . . . and how to speak with womanly self-poise."[31] She was proud that she was a woman and was convinced that she had offered something special to other women; they, in turn, she said, had something special to offer to the wider society; she might have called it an "elevation of spirit," the upholding of special values apart from the business sector of getting and spending.

The most enduring legacy of Constance Runcie is the empowerment she passed on to the ladies of her club. After her death, the club had to face the question of its continued existence. Runcie had been the president for the life of the club, and her death raised the possibility of the club's end as well. Instead, the women decided to continue the club by electing new presidents and new committees to carry on without Runcie. Obviously the club was not merely a self-serving vehicle for Runcie's ego or economy. The women got a high return on their dollar-a-month investment. They had acquired enough organizational skills through the years and enough confidence in their con-

31. Constance Runcie to George Davidson, November 9, 1909, Davidson Collection.

tributions to run the club themselves. The ladies of the club would continue to promote cultural education and charitable activities well into the twentieth century.

The clubwomen were not unique in these efforts, of course. There were other clubs in St. Joseph besides the Runcie Club, and their histories ought to be explored as well. There were (and are today) hundreds of women's clubs in Missouri whose efforts at civic improvement and civic reforms offer continuing examples of community building and strengthening. Researchers examining other clubs have observed much the same patterns of development as described here. The Runcie Club has some particular uniqueness—led as it was by the vision and strong personality of one woman, who gained at least partially in terms of economic support—but in many respects it is a very typical club in its moderate measures and types of activities. Runcie led St. Joseph women in the assertion that they as a group had something to offer toward making the western city a vibrant community. Women's clubs as a whole succeeded in what the historian Sara Evans describes as "carving out a public space located between the private sphere of the home and public life of formal institutions of government."[32]

The life and club work of Constance F. Runcie can be viewed as something of a paradox: She asserted her right to a public sphere even as she rejected such proposals as suffrage, but she also mediated that assertiveness for other women into safe, culturally sanctioned, community-building activities that never challenged the traditional social or economic order. She preferred the black women's clubs to be separate from the General Federation. She preferred the social obligations of class-based patronage, such as rescuing fallen women or caring for orphans, to the headier challenges offered by the Progressive Era of government regulation. Her club opened the way to the empowerment of women, but seldom, if ever, challenged the social and economic system that placed them in positions of leadership and security.

As society changed, however, so did the Runcie Club. To this day, the Runcie Club continues to do its work in St. Joseph. Although it no

---

32. Sara M. Evans, *Born for Liberty: A History of Women in America* (New York: Free Press, 1989).

longer meets in private homes and is a much larger club than it once was, much of its focus remains the same. The club still sponsors cultural activities for the city and offers programs of interest for its members. However, like Runcie's unmarried daughter, many of its members are professional women with their own businesses or careers in such fields as medicine, social work, law, or education. The Runcie Club no longer offers a singular avenue to status and power; women have found other ways of achieving that. The club no longer needs to meet behind the protection of a home meeting place, nor are its leaders as uncertain of their civic contributions as were the original women. A hundred years ago, for Constance Runcie and the women she enticed, manipulated, flattered, and bullied into joining her organization, the Runcie Club provided a unique opportunity to develop a sense of self-worth and to make a substantial contribution to the life of the community.

Women, Identity, and Reform in Missouri's Lead Belt, 1900–1923

ROBERT FAUST

Flat River, Missouri, must have seemed much the worse for wear to Mr. and Mrs. O. M. Bilhartz when they arrived there with from Illinois in 1906. Flat River, a young mining town in St. Francois County's old lead belt, was new, rough, and dirty. Free-roaming pigs delighted in the potholes of Flat River's streets. Downtown stores looked bare and uninviting, apparently to the delight of no one. Typhoid and tuberculosis wracked the community, the former periodically, the latter chronically. The few dilapidated local schools were overcrowded and unsanitary.

O. M. Bilhartz came to Flat River to take over as general manager of the Doe Run Lead Company and to keep that business profitable in a world of labor troubles and unpredictable markets. His wife also had a vision, and by 1907 she had gathered a group of like-minded women around her. In short, the women's goal, as founders of the Mothers' and Patrons' Club, was to clean up Flat River and to make it a place where they and their children could feel safe and comfortable. As women did in mining towns throughout the United States, Bilhartz and her colleagues entered a predominantly male-oriented environment and made part of it their own. This included not only improving the aesthetics of a grimy mining town, but also acting as the ambassadors of social, cultural, and spiritual uplift. Between tea parties and piano recitals, the Mothers' and Patrons' Club evolved into a private charity and health-care service, and when private action proved inadequate, it was among the leaders in demanding greater participation on the part of local government and industry in addressing social and environmental issues. Like Progressive Era women throughout the United States, the middle-class reformers in the lead belt "domesticated" politics, incorporating issues such as school hygiene, health maintenance, town beautification, care for the indigent, and other forms of social welfare into the realm of public and political discourse.[1]

This, of course, is not a new interpretation of women's activism at the turn of the twentieth century. Many historians have commented on the primary role that women played in Progressivism. Yet there is a unique quality to lead-belt progressivism. Women reformers' connection to a wider social and political movement, a wider "environmental" movement, the Progressive movement, did not diminish their focus on local issues or change the fact that they lived and worked in conditions fairly different from those of most of the nation's progressives. Whatever influence industry might have had on city government in places like Boston, New York, Chicago, or St. Louis, progressives in these cities could and did draw on fairly wide bases of support and created politically and socially diverse alliances. But what could be done when the town itself was company property, when the local economy rested on the fortunes of one industry? Far removed from the cosmopolitan areas that have received the most attention from historians, the Mothers' and Patrons' Club found itself dealing with the externalities of an industry to which they owed their influence and relative affluence. In Flat River, only lead mining mattered, and—directly or indirectly—it involved everyone. Challenging the power of the community's principal employer, landlord, and social service provider could prove futile, unpopular, or even dangerous.[2]

1. See Paula Baker, "The Domestication of Politics: Women and American Political Society, 1780–1920," *American Historical Review* 89 (June 1984); reprinted in *Unequal Sisters: A Multicultural Reader in U.S. Women's History*, ed. Ellen C. Dubois and Vicki L. Ruiz. Although an older essay, Baker's classic work on how women passed on voluntary work to governments and influenced politics through nonelectoral means strongly correlates to the activities of middle-class women reformers in the lead belt.

2. A fascinating albeit perhaps extreme example of what could happen to women who challenged corporate authority and local economic progress in Missouri can be found in Gregg Andrews, *Insane Sisters: Or, the Price Paid for Challenging a Company Town* (Columbia: University of Missouri Press, 1999). In this instance, Andrews asserts that two women who stood in the path of corporate expansion in northeast Missouri faced harassment from the courts and lost their property; one of them was declared to be mentally unbalanced and institutionalized. I have not found anything

In spite of these constraints, the women reformers of Flat River accomplished, albeit in a limited way, what women throughout the nation had succeeded in doing: the bridging of the "separate spheres" of male-dominated, public institutions, on one hand, and the domestic concerns of wives and mothers, on the other. Although not as completely as reformers might have hoped, political, mercantile, and industry elites in Flat River became more responsive to the needs of women and children, the poor and the sick, and indeed all those who shared water, air, and space with the new order. By "domesticating" politics as activists, consumers, and eventually as voters, women at both the national and local levels carved out a more comprehensive role for themselves in industrial America and industrializing Missouri. Lead-belt progressives justified one scholar's observation that many Missourians used grassroots activism and politics "to reassert traditional community, moral, and public control over private and economic activity that was moving far beyond any popular control."[3]

In a rollicking, rapidly growing mining town like Flat River at the turn of the century, the reform-minded had plenty to think about. French settlers, farmers, and slaves had been mining lead in the eastern Ozarks since the 1700s, but railroads, outside investment, and new technologies made large-scale, underground mining feasible by the 1880s and 1890s. Whether they began as small farming settlements or were built from scratch by mining companies to accommodate new miners, towns such as Flat River, Bonne Terre, Desloge, and Rivermines became boomtowns by about 1900. One local newspaper triumphantly proclaimed the lead belt a "Yukon at St. Louis' very door." Still, for all of the wealth created by lead mining, this practice entailed a number of social and environmental costs. The goal here is not to simplistically indict industrial America for a lack of social and environmental responsibility—that has been done elsewhere. More to the point, those who moved to Missouri's lead belt to take part in the industrialization of this quiet corner of the Ozarks were ultimately willing to accept certain unwelcome externalities in exchange for steady

---

of quite this magnitude in the lead belt, although working-class women regularly sued the mining companies for damage done to property and family members.

3. David P. Thelen, *Paths of Resistance: Tradition and Dignity in Industrializing Missouri* (New York: Oxford University Press, 1986), 219.

work. The price of a better standard of living included not only the dangers inherent to mineral mining but also water pollution, over-crowded schools, tuberculosis, and even an influx of foreigners.

Yet industrialization did not distribute the costs and benefits evenly. As was the case throughout Gilded Age America, these costs created "differential burdens" for those who lived in the mining communities.[4] Not all lead-belt residents had to contend with the same problems or to the same degree. Since all members of the mining communities did not then experience industrialization in the same way, their responses to it varied in accordance with their ideological, material, gender, and ethnic backgrounds.

Consider the problem of water pollution. Naturally, polluted water adversely affected all members of a community. But the willingness or ability of those in the mining district to address this issue differed in terms of both action and rhetoric. To men of the middle-class Pro-gressive and Commercial clubs, water pollution was but one challenge in a struggle for political autonomy and economic opportunity. Pol-luted water, they reasoned, was a threat to further population growth and economic development beyond mining. These men considered clean water a fundamental right that the lead companies could not deny, regardless of their economic importance.[5] Middle-class men worked to incorporate the company towns and establish community govern-ment independent of industry control. The lack of clean, reliable drink-ing water was a political problem that could best be solved by wresting political control of Flat River away from the lead industry. As a con-flict between two male-dominated institutions—business and would-be local government—men dominated the fight for control over local utilities.

This is not to say that middle-class women did not concern them-

4. The phrase "differential burdens" comes from Angela Gugliotta, "Class, Gender, and Coal Smoke: Gender Ideology and Environmental Injustice in Pittsburgh, 1868–1914," *Environmental History* 5, no. 2 (April 2000). Gugliotta refers to the "differen-tial burdens" of labor and women when dealing with pollution, but I think the phrase also can be applied when comparing men and women, and women of differ-ent socioeconomic backgrounds.

5. "Progressive Club Discusses Water Works," *Lead Belt News*, March 2, 1917. The role of middle-class men, as well as the activism of miners and their families, receives greater attention elsewhere in my research.

selves with water quality. Rather, these women couched their opposition to pollution and their demands for change in different terms. Whereas some reform-minded men wanted to take power away from the lead industry, middle-class women in St. Francois County appeared more determined to co-opt that power. Instead of punishing a sometimes recalcitrant industry, the women of the Mothers' and Patrons' Club wanted the industry to live up to its social and environmental, as well as economic, obligations. Lacking direct political power to instigate change, middle-class women attempted to create an informal partnership with the mining companies. They served as a de facto private charity network subsidized by the industry to improve conditions in the schools, jails, hospitals, and homes of the lead belt. When club members deemed that this voluntary approach was insufficient, they lent their voices to demands for more comprehensive public services generously supported by corporate taxes. The Mothers' and Patrons' Club significantly helped to redefine the roles and responsibilities of women, the lead industry, and local government in ameliorating the worst abuses of industrial capitalism. Primary and secondary sources suggest that this strategy was not unusual and almost certainly increased the scope and effectiveness of Progressive Era activism.[6] The Mother's and Patron's Club of Flat River, Missouri, did not exist within a vacuum but drew on the work of public health, education, and social service reformers in other parts of the state and nation.

It is here, between acceptance of the new order and opposition to its dehumanizing qualities, that the progressive women of the lead belt at times attempted both accommodation and resistance. This duality is reflected in the name these women initially and later chose for their organization. As "patrons," middle-class reformers used their personal connections and economic status to act on behalf of those who had not or could not fully embrace aesthetic beauty, public health,

---

6. For more on how men and women approached similar problems through different means as a reflection of both political reality and gendered social ideology, see Kathryn Kish Sklar, "Two Political Cultures in the Progressive Era: The National Consumers' League and the American Association for Labor Legislation," in *U.S. History as Women's History: New Feminist Essays,* ed. Linda K. Kerber, Alice Kessler-Harris, and Kathryn Kish Sklar (Chapel Hill: University of North Carolina Press, 1995).

or the need for a good education. This elite position need not be viewed cynically: after all, club members had taken upon themselves the task of reforming the very system underlying their influence and relative affluence. Bilhartz, we must recall, was the wife of an industry executive. The husbands of other clubwomen included engineers, clerks, and foremen in the mines. And other members' husbands occupied important professional positions within Flat River: doctors, dentists, teachers, and small businessmen. To one degree or another, all of these depended on mining for their livelihood.

While their records never explicitly comment on this paradox, women reformers in Missouri's lead belt undoubtedly realized that they were treading a fine line between class privilege and social responsibility. Being middle-class patrons clearly helped to define the scope of their efforts. Mrs. Bilhartz's stated desire to create a more hospitable and humane community is certainly sincere, but she was no Mother Jones.[7] By softening industrial capitalism, Progressive Era reformers—in Missouri and elsewhere—helped to insure its dominance over people's lives. Kathryn Kish Sklar writes,

> The central dilemma of Progressive Era social justice activism revolved around the need for reformers to embrace many of the values and modes of operation associated with machine production at the same time that they sought to humanize that production. While reformers sought to preserve human agency and other qualities of human individuality from the relentless forces of industrialization, they also had to cooperate with those forces.[8]

Like progressives elsewhere, women of the lead belt attempted to balance their vision of an equitable *and* affluent society.

And yet the close personal and economic ties that many women

---

7. One of the more interesting challenges for this researcher has been to discover more about Mrs. Bilhartz. Not knowing where she was born or where she died, and since available public records only refer to her as "Mrs.," I am left with the embarrassing situation of not even knowing the first name of this important character in my work. Neither she nor her husband appear in the 1910 Census schedule for St. Francois County, though it is known that she lived in Rivermines, Missouri, just outside Flat River. She and her husband moved to Illinois after 1915.

8. Sklar, "Two Political Cultures," 37.

had to the mining companies did not preclude the Mothers' and Patrons' Club from becoming a critic of both industry and the lack of local, public services. After all, they were mothers as well as patrons and clearly possessed of an ideology that went beyond economic affiliation. To make changes in the new industrial order, to bring about a more efficient, humane sense of shared responsibility among both business and community leaders, club members expanded the scope of civic reform to include particularly "female" virtues: caring for the sick and indigent, looking after at-risk women and children, educating the young, and maintaining healthy social, home, and natural environments. In short, because they were middle class, and because they were women, the members of the Mothers' and Patrons' Club had the unique opportunity to serve as a bridge or conduit between various elements of the lead-belt community. Because they were women, and because they were middle class, they possessed both the motivation and the means to address the social and environmental impact of industrial growth heretofore ignored by men.[9]

While the literature on the Progressive Era includes relatively few studies of reform in small, company towns, the history of mining in the American West offers at least a few, but important, examples. Scholars like Paula Petrik and Mary Murphy argue that women on the mining frontier (Helena and Butte, Montana, respectively) consistently expanded their independence in an effort to provide better lives for themselves and their families. Murphy's assessment might apply to the lead belt of Missouri when she states, "The development of voluntary associations in western mining camps and western cities was originally an accommodation to life on the frontier as well as an expression of a national phenomenon. . . . This vast network eased the strangeness of new places that an extraordinarily mobile work force confronted."[10] There were, of course, significant differences between

9. The distinct issues facing working-class men and women receive greater treatment in other portions of my research. What is known about their lives and their response to industrialization comes primarily from newspaper accounts of union activities and circuit court records. These sources help to illuminate the fact that working-class women and men pursued different forms of civic activism in ways quite different from middle-class people.

10. Mary Murphy, *Mining Cultures: Men, Women, and Leisure in Butte, 1914–1941* (Urbana: University of Illinois Press, 1997), 137. See also Paula Petrik, *No Step Back-*

these communities and those in Missouri. Helena and Butte became bustling urban centers, while at its peak, Flat River's population stayed somewhat under ten thousand. And with St. Louis scarcely seventy miles away, people in eastern Missouri did not have to rely on lead-belt towns as sole centers of economic activity, political power, or cosmopolitan delights. Flat River was one small town—albeit a busy one—in a region dominated by small towns and settled farmlands. Whatever cultural isolation they may have felt, women in the lead belt did not face the same geographic isolation experienced by many of those in the West.

What all of these women did share, however, was immersion into the inherently "male" society of mineral mining. Mining attracted large numbers of single men. Even when married men brought their families to a mining town, more often than not creature comforts, so-cial services, and civic aesthetics proved secondary to the activities of extracting and processing ore. It would seem that the initial, nearly complete lack of a woman's culture in these mining communities was itself an incentive and a call to action. Having no separate sphere in which to exist, mining town mothers and patrons emphatically demon-strated their willingness to occupy male space and shape corporate policy. Contemplating the role of women in progressive politics is essential in understanding how turn-of-the-century Americans re-defined democracy and constructed new ideologies for social and en-vironmental justice. Perhaps nowhere did progressive women prove more resilient and flexible than in those Missouri mining towns mostly populated by men and owned by industry.

The crusade of middle-class women in Flat River began in 1907 not on behalf of workers, the environment, or even women, but on behalf of mules. Not long after moving to the Flat River district, Bilhartz began visiting local schools, urging the children to take up the cause of animal kindness. These early visits to local schools probably gave Bilhartz her first real sense of conditions in the lead belt, and here she linked the campaign for St. Francois County's equine inhabitants to a

---

ward: Women and Family on the Rocky Mountain Mining Frontier, Helena, Montana, 1865–1900 (Helena: Montana Historical Society Press, 1987); and Anita Ernst Wat-son, Jean E. Ford, and Linda White, "The Advantage of Ladies' Society: The Public Sphere of Women on the Comstock," in *Comstock Women: The Making of a Mining Community* (Reno: University of Nevada Press), 1998.

broader vision of social responsibility. Bilhartz later wrote, "I firmly believe that if young children are taught kindness not alone to animals but everything that lives they in later years will never become criminals."[11] Ersatz criminology aside, the notion that a society could be reformed through its children was popular among many Progressives, and Missouri was no exception.

On March 3, 1907, Bilhartz invited a number of women to her home with the purpose of starting an organization that would seek "social and civic" improvements. Calling themselves the Mothers' and Patrons' Club of Flat River, these women also resolved to improve conditions in the county jail, county infirmary, and company hospitals, and to provide aid in a general way to the "indigent and sick," particularly those suffering from tuberculosis.[12] Under Bilhartz's leadership, however, the club also spent much of its time and resources emphasizing cultural refinement. According to Bilhartz, the Mothers' and Patrons' Club was as much a social organization as it was a citizen action group, "for there was little entertainment in Flat River in those early days, and I do think they [the members] all enjoyed the work, the lectures, and the entertainments." As patrons, these women occupied a somewhat more elevated position within the new industrial hierarchy, and they sought to use that position both to make industry more humane and to make the lives of the working class more pleasant. As mothers, they made themselves nurturers of the young community, fostering compassion for animals, concern for the poor, and attempting to make Flat River not simply a functional community, but a comfortable one as well.[13]

Women all across the country drew on their personal and class connections to men in their communities, but frequently the agenda they

11. Letter, Mrs. O. M. Bilhartz to the Flat River Woman's Club, April 2, 1937. This letter is part of a microfilmed collection, R70, the Minutes of the Mothers' and Patrons' Club of Flat River, Missouri, Western Historical Manuscripts Collection–Rolla. This collection, along with R206, contains the minutes of this organization from 1907 to 1953. These records make up the bulk of the sources employed for this research on middle-class women reformers in Missouri's lead belt.

12. Collection R70 Information Sheet.

13. Letter, Bilhartz to Flat River Woman's Club. For a discussion on how women came together for the purpose of reform in other parts of the country, see Sarah Deutsch, "Learning to Talk More Like a Man: Boston Women's Class Bridging Organizations, 1870–1940," *American Historical Review* 97, no. 2 (April 1992): 385.

set was their own. Whether or not a majority of women in Flat River or other mining towns shared the expectations and motivations of these middle-class women is not known. Other women's groups in the lead belt did not leave behind detailed records. But clearly, some women in this region shared with other women around the country common assumptions about the nature of reform and their role within that process.[14]

Perhaps the title of "patron" reflected an elitist tendency, or perhaps it was simply a strategy for getting more accomplished. There is little doubt, however, that these women allied themselves with elite men in the community to further the influence of the Mothers' and Patrons' Club. Granted, some of these alliances were personal and predated the activities of the club, but women reformers nonetheless used these connections with some success. In October 1907, the club began holding its meetings in a building that had been constructed by the Doe Run Lead Company (managed by Bilhartz's husband). Later, a local bank invited the club to use its upstairs rooms at no charge. Again with the assistance of Bilhartz's husband, the club sponsored a charity baseball game in 1908, followed by a concert performed by the Bonne Terre Band. Doe Run underwrote both concert and ball game.[15]

This seemingly one-way relationship, in which women went to elite men for help, did not last long, however; soon, local political and business leaders realized that the support of a group like the Mothers' and Patrons' Club could be instrumental in their own efforts. Up for reelection in 1910, Congressman Politte Elvins, a once and future attorney for the Federal Lead Company, spoke to the club on the "Inadequacy of Missouri Laws for the Protection of Children." Local merchants even recognized the role of the Mothers' and Patrons' Club in the local economy. As late as 1923, in an effort to expand commercial possibilities and diversify the local economy somewhat, the Flat River Commercial Club asked the women's club to find a young lady who would be "suitable to canvass the town in the interest of a shirt factory."[16] Prominent local men sought the help of the Mothers' and

14. A sense of the identity of these women comes from their words and deeds as recorded in the organization's minutes. More detailed information for at least some of the club members can be gleaned from the 1900, 1910, and 1920 census schedules for St. Francois County.

15. Minutes of the Mothers' and Patrons' Club, October 11, 1907, and May 13, 1908.

16. Minutes, November 11, 1910, and January 2, 1923.

Patrons' Club in much the same way that the clubwomen looked for help among sympathetic men. Among the commercial interests in the district, this may have reflected the growing power of women as consumers in the late nineteenth and early twentieth centuries, and certainly by 1923, women would have been courted as voters.

Yet—and this may be the key to understanding the interactions of male and female progressives in the lead belt—women found it difficult to achieve their goals without male cooperation. The historian Sarah Deutsch writes, "The desire to expand, given the economic structure of [cities], warred with the desire for self-reliance. It required [women] to find what historians of imperialism have called 'indigenous collaborators'—in this case, elite men—whom they believed they could turn to their own uses."[17] In short, women reformers in Flat River came to rely both on themselves and sympathetic (or politically and economically savvy) men to pursue their goals of a cleaner, safer community.

So what kind of women joined the Mothers' and Patrons' Club? Along with the minutes of the club's meetings, census records tell us something about these women, but nothing provides a clear picture of who these women were and why only some women joined. One difficulty in using census records to find and describe these women has to do with the demographic fluidity of the region. The population of the Flat River district grew rapidly between 1890 and 1920, and for the most part, few people in Flat River were natives to the area. This was true not only of miners and their families, but also of the middle managers and merchants who were attracted to the region by business opportunities. This rapid demographic change may indeed be reflected in the membership roles of the Mothers' and Patrons' Club. The club's minutes show that while a core of ten or so women appear to have remained active in the club for long spans, the names on the membership rolls changed pretty frequently. Between 1912 and 1914, seventy-four different names appear on the annual membership rolls, but at no time did the membership in any of those years exceed thirty-three individuals.[18]

17. Deutsch, "Learning to Talk," 391.
18. U.S. Census Schedules for Flat River, Missouri, 1900, 1910, and 1920. These records are available, among other places, at the State Historical Society, Columbia, Missouri, and at the State Records Center in Jefferson City. Finding individuals in the census schedules required using the Soundex System. Much of the information in the following paragraphs is derived from these censuses.

Still, some general observations concerning the membership in the first two decades of the 1900s can be made. Nearly all of these women were between the ages of twenty-five and forty-five, and most of them had at least one child at home. Ama Higgins, thirty-nine, had five children at home. Six of these women had a live-in servant or cook. Five of the six known servants were native born, white, and in their late teens or early twenties. Two women listed boarders in their households, in each case an unmarried female schoolteacher.

All of these women's families bore some kind of connection, either directly or indirectly, to the lead industry. Bilhartz, of course, moved to the Flat River district because her husband became general manager of the Doe Run Lead Company. A number of other members' husbands worked in the mining industry, but they do not seem to have done the hardest, most dangerous, lowest-paying work. Stella Thompson's husband, John, was a foreman in one of the mines, and they had a cook living in their home. Martha Mosier's husband was also a foreman, and Addie Lawrence's was an engineer. While a number of club members' husbands would be thought of as "blue collar," they were skilled workers or had crews of men working under them, and thus they enjoyed higher wages and status than less-skilled laborers. John Bennett, a mine electrician and husband of a Mothers' and Patrons' Club member, also raised livestock.

Some of the women who joined the Mothers' and Patrons' Club depended less directly on the mining industry, but they still benefited from industrial expansion in the region. Moses Topping, whose wife, Amanda, was an original member of the club, managed the local phone company. The husbands of Lucy Norwine, Louisa Higgins, and Ida Carr identified themselves as merchants. Emma Johns's husband, William, was a local school principal and an advocate of civic reform. Other husbands included a dentist, a manager of a "picture show," a newspaper agent, and a drugstore owner. It is not certain where all of these people came from (many did list Missouri as their place of birth), but it is fairly clear that the majority of them were newer members of the community.

The club's list of women who had been or were members was probably a publicity measure (the list later appeared in a local newspaper). Membership rolls from other years do not indicate that the club's dues-paying membership exceeded thirty-five women at any one time, and it was frequently much lower.

The Mothers' and Patrons' Club placed considerable emphasis on networking even though they expended most of their efforts on strictly local issues. In 1908, the club hosted women from clubs in St. Louis to talk about organizing strategies, energizing the community, and establishing links to other women reformers. A Mrs. Crocher of St. Louis emphasized the importance of maintaining a strong nucleus around which the Mothers' and Patrons' Club might build.[19]

Just as significantly, women from other parts of the county strongly encouraged the Mothers' and Patrons' Club not only to carry out their local reform efforts, but also to become active in the Missouri Federation of Women's Clubs. Women in Farmington, Bonne Terre, and Desloge had established women's clubs of their own by 1908 and were already engaged in various kinds of "civic improvements." Between 1907 and 1909, 486 women in clubs in Bonne Terre, Farmington, and Desloge joined the Missouri Federation of Women's Clubs and became actively "engaged in study and self-culture work."[20]

The Missouri Federation of Women's Clubs was itself part of the national General Federation of Women's Clubs, founded in 1890. By 1900, over 150,000 women, representing 595 clubs in thirty states, belonged to the national organization. Recent scholarship on the national organization describes a connection, both in ideology and strategy, between women leaders at the national and local levels: "The founders envisioned an agency for the cultural, intellectual and philanthropic interests of individual clubs, and also as a national body of social workers to promote the general welfare by assisting the poor, fighting famine and disease, raising the educational and cultural level, and working for reform." This was, in short, the purpose of the Mothers' and Patrons' Club. Like the national umbrella organization, many local women's clubs evolved to place less emphasis on personal improvement and more on altruism.[21]

This transition, from self-culture to social welfare work, is illustrated in the changing title of the organization. In 1913, the group

19. Minutes, February 1, 1908.

20. Minutes, May 5, 1909, Missouri Federation of Women's Clubs, *Record Book,* Collection 1172, Western Historical Manuscripts Collection–Columbia.

21. Lorine Goodwin, "The Pure Food, Drink, and Drug Crusaders" (Ph.D. diss., University of Missouri–Columbia, 1996), 246, 247. See also Karen Blair, *The Clubwoman as Feminist: True Womanhood Redefined, 1868–1914* (New York: Holmes and Meier Publishers, 1980).

changed its name to the Lead Belt Woman's Club. If the designation of "mothers and patrons" reflected a fairly specific understanding of gender and class responsibilities, what did this name change represent? Did it reflect changing membership, changing goals, or both? The minutes of the club offer no explanation for the name change. The group would change its name again in 1923 to the Flat River Woman's Club, which it kept until the 1950s. Again, it is not known for certain why this second name change occurred, unless it was the recognition that many of the smaller communities surrounding Flat River had by the 1920s established their own women's organizations. Having helped to organize women throughout the lead belt, the women of Flat River could then begin to focus more specifically on their town.

The first name change arguably reflects the evolving character of this organization. First, in 1913 Bilhartz resigned as president of the club. Under Bilhartz's guidance, the club focused on what might be termed aesthetic improvements or self-culture work. Along with cleaning up schools, the club attempted to beautify the town, created interest in animal kindness and nature study, and directed much of its energy to helping its own members become better mothers and homemakers through the sharing of magazine articles, entertaining each other at tea parties, and providing musical numbers, short plays, and literary readings. While certainly not insignificant, these activities reflected a more limited vision of what this club's role in the community might be. Time and experience would help to expand this vision.

The second development coinciding with the name change to Lead Belt Woman's Club in 1913 was the club's decision to join the Missouri Federation of Women's Clubs. In this respect, the Flat River women trailed women of nearby communities who already had been members of the Federation for four or five years.[22] Again, does the unwillingness or inability of the club to join the state organization at an earlier date reflect the attitudes or leadership philosophy of Bilhartz and some of the club's original members?

Available records do not conclusively answer these questions, yet the change of self-identification to a "woman's club" may indeed be significant. As one historian argues, club work during the Progressive Era became a type of feminism, for "whether dedicated to social reform or self-improvement, women's clubs had in common their power

22. See Minutes of the Missouri Federation of Women's Clubs.

to afford women a more complete, and therefore a more authentic, self expression."[23] Perhaps as these women became involved in a larger network of women's clubs, it was no longer satisfactory to be only "mothers and patrons." Instead, these reformers may have been seeking to create a broader identity as women rather than simply as mothers and were no longer willing to couch the language of reform primarily within the construct of motherhood. Social dislocation, pollution, public health breakdowns, and political inequality impacted all women in the lead belt, regardless of whether or not they had children.

The changing of the titles of this organization arguably reveals a transition from self-study to social welfare activism and, conceivably, to a feminist identity. This shift gradually altered not only the gendered expectations of womanhood and a woman's obligations to her community, but in turn altered the community's responsibility toward women and their families. It was this growing emphasis on social welfare work that helped to shed light on the inadequacies of local government and corporate paternalism in addressing issues of environmental and social justice.

Aside from its initial goal of imbuing the children of miners with a greater appreciation for animal welfare, the first real cause of the Mothers' and Patrons' Club was educational reform, both in terms of subject matter and the learning environment. The club members wanted to discover which of the local schools were in greatest need of improvements in the areas of cleanliness, obtaining classroom supplies, and providing safe playground equipment. A Mrs. Parker observed the Taylortown school, in a newer section of town on the north side of Flat River, surveying it "not only as a Mother and a Patron, but as a Teacher as well."[24] After a report that the Red Top school in nearby Elvins "might be somewhat improved," club minutes indicate that "ladies" from Elvins used their influence with the Doe Run Company to see if the school could not be improved. Upon revisiting the Taylortown school in October, the club found it to be much neater.[25]

Unfortunately, the Mothers' and Patrons' Club does not provide

23. See Blair, *Clubwoman as Feminist*, xii.

24. Minutes of the Mothers' and Patrons' Club, May 10, 1907.

25. Minutes, November 8, 1907, and April 24, 1908. The Sanborn Fire Insurance maps for Flat River have been especially useful in figuring out the exact location of the various local schools in Flat River. Sanborn Map Company, New York, 1908, 1915, 1927, located in Special Collections, Ellis Library, Columbia, Missouri.

much in the way of detailed descriptions of local schools, only the
general assessment that children suffered from a lack of a hygienic
learning space, clean blackboards, and an unenlightened curriculum.
The rapid increase in Flat River's population at the turn of the century
also meant an increase in the number of children needing public
schools. In only three years, between 1900 and 1903, the number of
students enrolled in Flat River public schools more than doubled,
from 560 to 1196. In 1903, there were only twelve teachers employed
in the Flat River schools, creating a student-to-teacher ratio of more
than 99 to 1.[26] In 1904, the Flat River district had a two-room school
building at Elvins (Red Top), a two-room building in the East Ward
(East Flat River), a two-room structure in the North Ward (Taylortown), and a four-room building in the middle of Flat River. But when
fire destroyed the four-room building in 1904—lacking a fire escape,
students reportedly had to jump from second-story windows—only
six schoolrooms remained in Flat River to serve about one thousand
students.[27]

The need for new schools demonstrated both the critical role that
the mining companies played (or were expected to play) in adminis-
trating these communities and the ability of the Mothers' and Patrons'
Club to identify and address issues of local concern. Because the Doe
Run and National Lead companies owned virtually all of the surface
property in the Flat River district, they constructed many of the public buildings, including the schools, or at least they made land available for these purposes. After the 1904 fire, Doe Run donated a new
parcel of land in the center of Flat River that eventually became the
Central School and Flat River High School. Overcrowding in both the
North and East Wards of Flat River led to the construction of two new
schools in 1907 and 1909. Also in 1907, Mrs. Bilhartz's husband over-
saw the completion of the Domestic Science Building next to the Flat

26. See *Report of the Public Schools of the State of Missouri*, State Records Center, Jefferson City (Jefferson City: Tribune Publishing Company, 1900–1926).

27. Dave Darnell, *Desloge, Missouri, and Surrounding Area* (Marceline, Mo.: Walsworth, 1990). This is one of the many local histories that provide some interesting
accounts albeit with a limited number of credited sources or analysis. The description and number of schools given in Darnell's brief account, however, seem to coin-
cide with the information available from the Sanborn Fire Insurance Maps and the
state's public school reports.

River High School. The Doe Run Company paid the entire cost of construction and operating expenses for the first year. The Mothers' and Patrons' Club then held its meetings there in 1908 after being invited to do so by Doe Run. In 1916, the club secured, at no cost, from the Federal Lead Company five acres of land for another new school. This spurt in school construction coincided with the hiring of more teachers, which by 1920 brought the student-to-teacher ratio down to 50 to 1.[28]

Overcrowding was not the only problem that plagued local education. The club took a special interest in how home life affected a child's ability to learn. At their third meeting, the members invited local high school teachers, all husbands of club members, to comment on the importance of home life in school performance. Mrs. Bilhartz read a paper on "The Home in Its Relation to the School." Ensuing meetings included many such papers and discussions of magazine articles arguing that a good educational system starts at home. The Mothers' and Patrons' Club became an important local voice supporting not only more classrooms, but a greater public awareness of and emphasis on the cultural, moral, physical, and psychological development of local schoolchildren. For instance, along with visiting schools and conducting impromptu seminars on bodily and classroom cleanliness, clubwomen encouraged teachers to spend at least twenty minutes per week discussing "humane work."[29]

This issue of humane work, or concern for animal welfare, coincided with a growing interest, locally and throughout the state, in what was termed "nature study." When local school officials, along with members of the women's club, revised the rules and regulations of Flat River's public schools in 1911, they expected teachers to devote considerable time to nature study, including lectures, reading, and even fieldwork. Interest in this new curriculum was statewide by the turn of the century. Teachers from several Missouri school districts incorporated everything from classroom work to hiking and field observation. Some teachers even employed old folk tales and religious stories.[30]

28. Ibid.; *Report of the Public Schools* (1920).
29. Minutes, April 12, 1907, November 8, 1907, and April 24, 1908.
30. "Comment on Nature Study," *Report of the Public Schools* (1901): 11–12.

This course of study within the context of a modernizing, industrializing state seems to contradict other Progressive educational reforms—or at least the manner in which some historians have interpreted those reforms. Missouri's 1901 *Report of the Public Schools* noted: "As important as is the practical knowledge of facts learned in the study of nature its aim is still higher. It is a means of securing personal, individual investigation, a means of developing all of the powers of child mind and of training children to see and think and express for themselves."[31] In other words, nature study and its emphasis on direct observation, patience, attention to detail, and empathy for things non-human prepared students for instruction in other areas and encouraged them to develop awareness not only of their own needs but for those of a wider community.

And yet the same Flat River Education Committee that argued for nature study as a means to encourage students "to think and express for themselves" also initiated changes that curbed the free-spirited nature of local children. Under the direction of William Johns, a local teacher and husband of a club member, and with the help of the Mothers' and Patrons' Club, the committee offered guidelines for changing the behavior of both teachers and students. The Education Committee prohibited teachers from using corporal punishment on children. On the other hand, the new regulations disallowed activities such as smoking, chewing, or spitting tobacco, gambling, swearing, fighting, "molesting parties passing by the school," loitering at the post office, "unlawfully riding locomotives," and climbing onto any vehicle "without the consent of the driver." With the organization of a Flat River Playground Association in 1908, even recess between classes became "directed recreation."[32]

Clearly, the Mothers' and Patrons' Club recognized no inconsistency in promoting the child's need for developing analytical skills and a belief in an orderly, well-trained, progressive society. Again with reference to David Thelen, some historians have interpreted Progressive Era educational reform as another step in the process by which industrial capitalism co-opted individuals. Thelen argues that an at-

---

31. Ibid., 12.
32. Flat River Public Schools, *Course of Study and Rules and Regulations* (Columbia: State Historical Society of Missouri, 1911), 83–84; Minutes, April 24, 1908.

tack on gambling, smoking, hopping trains, and loitering was an attack on the recreation, and thus the values, of working-class or rural
Missourians. Children in the new schools of a more refined Flat River
ultimately were expected "to be obedient to the requests and direc-
tions of the teacher, and to the rules and regulations of the school.
They shall conduct themselves in a quiet and orderly manner."[33] This
is an interesting and important argument, though by no means convincing. The likelihood that Flat River's educational reforms fit into
the broader industrial discipline does not negate the real improvements in the local schools, particularly in rapidly growing communities like Flat River.

Flat River's education reformers believed that they had succeeded
in creating a school system with facilities "second to none in the state
considering the size of the city." One of the town's proudest achievements was the fourteen-thousand-dollar Domestic Science Building
completed in 1908. There, girls and young women could not only take
advanced courses in cooking, sewing, and household management, but
also study music, art, and social entertaining.[34] The Domestic Science
Building—paid for by industry and subsequently supported by local
taxpayers—elevated the status of at least some women in Flat River by
turning potentially mundane activities into subjects of study. It was
both a real and symbolic acknowledgment of the importance of female space in a community hitherto controlled by male-dominated
institutions.

It would seem, then, that educational reform in Flat River could not
be reduced to a plot to turn young men and women into industrial or
domestic drones. Industrial discipline may have been an element in the
new schools of Flat River, but it was tempered by an accentuation on social empathy and self-improvement. School reformers, many of them
clubwomen, affected the climate of learning in Flat River not only in
campaigning to have more schools built or to have nature study included in class work, but in demonstrating the effectiveness of citizen
activism. This is not the sort of lesson one would wish to teach if the
objective was to break down all resistance to industrial dominance.

33. *Course of Study*, 82. David Thelen addresses the motivations behind Progressive Era educational reform in Missouri in much greater detail in *Paths of Resistance*.
34. *Course of Study*, 93, 115–16.

By 1920, in spite of some lingering problems in East Flat River, a local paper proclaimed the schools of Flat River to be "splendidly equipped," with new equipment for vocational training and home economics, hot lunches, and fresh milk provided at cost by the St. Joseph Lead Company's dairy. While the number of students enrolled in the Flat River schools increased by about 48 percent between 1903 and 1920, the number of teachers hired increased by over 70 percent, with a total of thirty-eight men and women working in seven schools. Communities like Flat River benefited from mining companies' willingness to at times donate money, land, and buildings to local school districts, frequently at the urging of organizations like the Mothers' and Patrons' Club. In 1920, a local newspaper declared "the Flat River schools are now better equipped than the state university at Columbia."[35]

The Mothers' and Patrons' Club extended its volunteer spirit beyond the school-improvement campaign to other local issues. In 1911, the club formed a committee to oversee visits to the county insane asylum (which would later become a state hospital for the mentally ill) and purchased a number of rocking chairs for the patients. The club also worked to improve conditions in the county jail in the late 1910s. In 1923, the *Lead Belt News* published an article comparing jail conditions in St. Francois and surrounding counties. Although an undercover reporter from St. Louis criticized jails in Jefferson and Iron counties, that same source praised the St. Francois county jail for its cleanliness and humane treatment of the inmates. One prisoner even purportedly wrote to the paper that "the county Court and many civic organizations has to its credit that those of our citizens who have fallen by the wayside in the battle for existence, have been given at least the ordinary comforts of life."[36]

The club also sought to improve the aesthetic standards of its community. The idea of civic improvements such as landscaping, tree planting, and occasionally cleaning the streets "provoked a lively discussion and everybody clamored for a clean and spotless Flat River, but how to get it! After discussing a number of plans—wise and otherwise—it was decided to make an appeal direct to the people." A num-

---

35. *Report of the Public Schools* (1903–1920); *Flat River Lead Belt News,* September 10, 1920.

36. Cited in *Flat River Lead Belt News,* January 5, 1923.

ber of clubwomen went door-to-door, passing out handbills that asked each family "to clean and to try to keep clean as nearly as possible their own premises and street."[37]

Along these lines, the clubwomen went back into the schools handing out packets of flower seeds and espousing the need for tree planting along Flat River's streets. The Mothers' and Patrons' Club sent a delegation around to local businessmen in 1909 urging them to plant trees in front of their establishments and to hang out colorful but tasteful awnings. In 1910, Mrs. Bilhartz called on the general manager of the Federal Lead Company, Henry Guess, to ask if his company would help to pay for a new, safer footbridge over the Big River. Grumbling to another businessman that he did not really think the company had any such responsibility, he donated about two hundred dollars anyway.[38]

Although the Mothers' and Patrons' Club never adopted an official policy on conservation, it promoted nature study in the public schools and devoted a number of meetings to conservation-related themes. In 1910, clubwomen addressed such themes as "Nature and Some Practical Points of Same," "The Cost of a Feather," "Birds and Ladies Hats," and "The Economic Value of Birds."[39] About this time, women across the country were growing concerned about the overhunting of birds for the sake of ladies' hats; on a national level, their concern gave much energy to the emerging conservation movement.

Although the clubwomen showed interest in what we would today call an environmental ethic, much of their effort was centered on city beautification and concern over water pollution, which were in many ways more political and economic reforms. Clean water, according to the *Lead Belt News*, was a right to demand on the part of Flat River residents.[40] To address this problem, Flat River men led a campaign to establish city government independent of corporate control. Toward

37. Minutes, May 10, 1907.

38. Minutes, January 14, 1909; Henry Guess, Flat River, to Robert Sellers, Bonne Terre, January 24, 1910, Federal Lead Company Letter Books, Collection R520, Western Historical Manuscripts Collection–Rolla, 166.

39. Minutes, April 1, 1910.

40. "Progressive Club Discusses Water Works," *Lead Belt News*, March 2, 1917. Emphasis on town beautification may have been linked to the nationwide "City Beautiful" movement, although no direct links or references have been discovered.

that end, Flat River and other lead-belt towns experienced intermittent campaigns by local people to incorporate these communities under Missouri law and establish publicly elected town councils. Environmental reform in this sense was indeed political and economic reform, and that was an area still dominated by men. In terms of rhetoric and public activism, women approached environmental change through town beautification, educational awareness, and public health. This is not to say that women were only concerned with some problems and men with others, but it is clear that men and women progressives in the lead belt divided their labor.

Perhaps this was a conscious strategy to rally more public support by simultaneously bringing the message of reform into both public and private spheres. On both the national and local levels, progressives would cross and sometimes remake the social boundaries that separated men's and women's interests. However, most of women's early efforts to bring about change, the reform of education and beautification of the town concentrated on changing the behaviors of others so that individuals would each feel a greater personal responsibility for improving Flat River. What could clubwomen do when townspeople proved unwilling or unable to significantly alter their habits or living conditions?

This dilemma ultimately led to two very important developments. First, clubwomen became much more personally active in addressing the social needs of their community. Rather than just trying to persuade people to be more generous to the poor, clubwomen took it upon themselves to look after the poor, using their own money and labor. This burgeoning of social welfare activities (as opposed to self-improvement) led to a second strategy of lead-belt reform. As these women became more deeply committed to assisting the sick, widowed, orphaned, and poor, many of them became convinced that purely voluntary social work could not meet the demands of the Flat River district. If social and environmental issues could not be completely addressed by changing the behavior of the public, and if the club-women themselves lacked the personal and financial means to assist everyone in need, then the next step was to call on greater involvement from local government and industry. This approach had met with some success in improving educational opportunities in Flat River. Now the club wanted to use this approach in dealing with other concerns.

The growing movement to empower local government in part stemmed not only from the age-old problem of poverty, but from the recurring threat of communicable disease. Although tuberculosis and typhoid affected poorer people at higher rates, these diseases could pose a public health threat to all members of a community. It was in addressing the problems of public health that the limits of voluntary social welfare work became most notable. In July 1922, Dr. Linn Thurman reported that seven wells in and around Potosi, Missouri, partially accounted for the typhoid outbreak of that summer. The town council of Potosi did little but ask the State Health Office to send another investigator. With a potential epidemic on their hands and local government dragging its feet, the Potosi Civic League, a women's group similar to the one in Flat River, paid for several estimates on having deeper wells dug by a private contractor.[41]

This pattern—a lack of reliable public services and the thinly concealed frustration of women with local political and business leaders—exemplified the spirit of reform by the early 1920s in both Potosi and Flat River. In Potosi, the situation with the water supply, along with poor public schools, led a number of women in the Potosi Civic League to propose direct involvement in local politics by running women for the school board. While there was "much opposition" to this proposal within the league, President Rebecca White told a communitywide meeting that women should not "narrow down to just house-hold affairs, but should broaden out, knowing conditions around us." The commentary in a Potosi newspaper by a contributor known only as "Old Ike" noted that, "We [the public] appreciated the meeting, the ladies are coming to the front, and are able to take care of their own interest on polite question[s] on the floor of any meeting that may interfere with [their] rights."[42] However condescending, Old Ike recognized the changing nature of politics in Missouri.

Like the women in Potosi, those in Flat River became frustrated with half-hearted county efforts to alleviate some of their environmental and social concerns, and they too came to demand greater accountability on the part of local government and business. Clubwomen in

41. Minutes of the Potosi Civic League, Collection R187, Western Historical Manuscripts Collection–Rolla, July 24, 1922.

42. Potosi Civic League Minutes, May 9, 1923. The microfilmed minutes of the Potosi Civic League contain a number of microfilmed newspaper clippings that leave out the title and date of the publication.

Flat River had been making occasional donations of food, clothing, and a little money to the city's sick and indigent for years. When a child of Clem Black's needed an operation in St. Louis, the club gave his family money from its various funds, but only after "investigating the case . . . and finding the family quite worthy of help."[43] Limited private resources, and perhaps a little middle-class elitism, determined that assistance would be conditional.

The growing concern for the poor and sick included support for women who lacked other means of social protection, which then led the Lead Belt Woman's Club to turn to the St. Francois County Court for help. As early as 1914, the court had been making regular payments to the clubwomen out of the public Pauper and Insane Fund. The monthly payments came to about fifty dollars, but when combined with the work done for free by the clubwomen, the county court was probably getting a bargain: in the Lead Belt Woman's Club, it had a reasonably well-run and motivated private relief agency. This may have initially slowed county involvement in alleviating poverty and playing a larger role in public health, in that these women were willing to do for a small fee what a public-health bureaucracy would charge considerably more to accomplish.[44] And yet this minimal financial investment by the county and the growing time and labor investment of women only solidified the women's belief in the need for greater public awareness and support. In fact, the Lead Belt Woman's Club became so concerned with its duties as a welfare agency that it established a private Employment Bureau and hired a "social welfare worker" in the early 1920s.[45] Until that time, women did the work of visiting the poor and sick, distributing food and clothing, and investigating the conditions of local residents themselves.

The club also petitioned the county court to obtain a "Mother's Pension" for several poor women in Flat River.[46] It is not certain who these women were. Mining accidents injured and sometimes killed a dozen or so men every year, frequently leaving women to either provide for the family or seek damages in the circuit court against the lead companies. Records indicate that if the women won damages at

43. Minutes of the Mothers' and Patrons' Club, September 2, 1927.
44. *County Court Records,* St. Francois County, Missouri (1914–1930).
45. Minutes, March 14, 1919, and January 13, 1922.
46. Minutes, April 9, 1920.

all, the awards may not have covered the lost salaries of the miners. The point is that the inherently dangerous occupation of mining sometimes left women and their families without immediate support. Neither circuit court records nor the club's minutes clearly indicate if the "mothers" and "stranded women" on whose behalf the women's club petitioned were in fact widows of miners. Yet however these women came to their plight, the Lead Belt Woman's Club believed that their assistance was a matter of social responsibility, not just private charity.

No other issue inspired as much discussion concerning the role of the public, county government, and industry leadership in public health management as the tuberculosis epidemic in St. Francois County. In 1911, the tuberculosis rate in St. Francois County was 218 cases per 1,000 people, almost twice as high as the average for the rest of the state. Actual deaths from tuberculosis in that year alone totaled 77 people. Between 1913 and 1920, the rate of tuberculosis infection remained about twice as high as that in the rest of the state. Combating tuberculosis was one of the original projects of the Mothers' and Patrons' Club, which in 1908 offered to show to the entire town an "illustrated lecture" on causes and prevention methods of tuberculosis.[47] This objective proved to be a daunting task for a volunteer-based organization.

In May 1912, Bilhartz proposed that the club pay for a nurse to visit those infected and ordered to stay in their homes (although the county did not strictly enforce quarantines). In February 1913, the club finally hired a Miss Watson from Hannibal to serve in this capacity. Soon after, club members suggested that they join Watson on her rounds. Only two or three clubwomen actually accompanied Watson. In any event, in December 1913 alone, Watson and her assistants went on 138 calls, gave fifty baths, gave twenty-four shampoos, discovered two new cases of tuberculosis, and sent one case to the hospital for surgical aid, expenses paid by the club.[48]

Watson only stayed about one year in Flat River, after which the visits to the homes of the sick declined sharply. The club tried to revive the idea in 1917, again providing baths and sanitary services for the sick and even helping the undertaker to fumigate the homes of the deceased. This effort, too, dwindled. The last attempt to combat tuberculosis

47. *Lead Belt News* (January 19, 1923); Minutes, April 24, 1908.
48. Minutes, December 5, 1913, and January 6, 1914.

through principally volunteer means came in 1921, when the club attempted to hire another nurse with about twelve hundred dollars donated by three mining companies.[49]

In the end, the reliance on volunteer work and occasional donations did not make a serious dent in the tuberculosis problem. Like other reformers at the local, state, and national levels, clubwomen in Flat River realized that successful, comprehensive reform required cooperation with government and business, whether that cooperation was grudging or voluntary. Beginning in the late 1910s, the Lead Belt Woman's Club joined in the public debate for setting up a taxpayer- and industry-supported county health service. The club also voiced its support for the incorporation of Flat River, which would have allowed townspeople to more directly control utilities, enforce quarantines, and increase public involvement in public health issues. Outside of proclamations in favor of greater political independence in the company towns, the women's club generally left the incorporation movement in the hands of middle-class men.[50]

This is not to say that the Lead Belt Woman's Club viewed its private, voluntary efforts as a failure; indeed, the clubwomen carried on private relief efforts for tuberculosis sufferers late into the 1920s. The call for a county health service and incorporation signified the perceived need to expand the campaign for a healthier community to the next level. With the resignation of the club's second president, Mary Keith, in 1921, Secretary Elsie Moore wrote that since 1907, the progressive women of Flat River had made their town a "better and safer" place in which to live. Over the years, they had "reawakened those ties which had brought to our minds a realization of duty as co-laborers for a common good."[51] They had collaborated with each other, with other women's organizations, with business and industry leaders, and with progressive-minded men. In the 1920s, the clubwomen wanted to reinforce that cooperation by institutionalizing it in the form of greater government involvement in social reform and public health.

49. Minutes, January 12, 1917, and January 14, 1921.

50. The movement to incorporate the lead company towns is itself an important part of the reform efforts in the lead belt during the Progressive Era, but its details fall somewhat outside the scope of this essay.

51. Minutes, December 9, 1921.

Having encountered limits to volunteer activism, by the early 1920s the women's club turned its attention to the creation of a county health service subsidized by the lead industry. Local reformers believed that a better-funded county health service could provide basic medical needs to the poor, educate the public about communicable diseases, promote better health and hygiene for poor children, and ensure that quarantines of the sick could be maintained. Many of these reformers, including those in the woman's club, argued that the lead industry should pay part of this expense. Although the woman's club never adopted an openly hostile stance toward the industry, its involvement with more vocal critics of the industry during this debate is in some contrast to the much cozier relationship the club had earlier in its existence with, for example, the Doe Run Lead Company. This may reflect a change in club leadership, or simply continued exasperation with slow-moving change.

For the women's club, a county health service would be a welcome resource in its own efforts to control tuberculosis and a number of other health problems. In 1921, smallpox swept through Flat River and St. Francois County, with 108 cases being reported. The spread of the disease was blamed in no small part on the inability of local government to act quickly and efficiently. According to an editorialist for the Lead Belt News, "In the unincorporated towns in the Lead Belt it is always difficult to maintain an adequate quarantine owing to a lack of officials to enforce it."[52] Advocates of a public health department argued that it would provide the local government with the machinery necessary to declare and enforce quarantines.

The women's club even conducted its own research to shed light on the need for a health department. In April 1920, the Flat River Woman's Club launched a "Campaign for Child Hygiene." Volunteers weighed 1,097 children in and around Flat River, and found 687 of them to be underweight. Along with this work, the club petitioned the school system to hire a visiting nurse and organized a mass meeting of Flat River residents to build support for a county health service.[53] Whether in terms of monitoring the health of schoolchildren or maintaining adequate quarantines, women in the lead belt became active proponents

52. *Lead Belt News*, January 14, 1921.
53. Minutes, April 9, 1920.

in demanding that nutrition, disease control, and care for the sick become part of public and company policy.

Toward that end, the Flat River Woman's Club also recruited support from outside the lead belt. Dr. Edith Long of the U.S. Public Health Service spoke to the group in 1920, and the following year, Mary Coleman of Columbia University spoke on child welfare legislation and preventable diseases. Adding to the rising tide of at least middle-class sentiment, the club sponsored Dr. Thomas Parron, of the Missouri State Board of Health, who lectured on the need for a county health center at a public meeting in Flat River.[54]

With heavy financial support from the St. Joseph Lead Company, the county finally established a public health department in 1922. The Flat River Woman's Club now worked alongside the health department to care for shut-ins, and it even continued to use its own funds in special cases. In 1926, the club sent thirteen children to St. Louis for better medical treatment.[55] Nevertheless, women and other reformers in the lead belt considered the creation of a county health department to be one of their more important achievements.

It is perhaps not surprising, then, that as public (and male-dominated) institutions began to display greater involvement in what had been considered women's issues, the distinct place of women in social reform became a little less discernible from the activities of men.[56] Women certainly remained active in public life in the lead belt. But when the issues that women had long supported became intertwined with institutions that men had long controlled, either the perceived need or the opportunity for women to continue to direct the public discussion over these concerns diminished. The Flat River Woman's Club officially existed until 1953, but after the mid-1920s, with many of its original goals at least partially met, the activism of this organization gradually waned.

Perhaps the general decline of progressivism after World War I, and almost certainly during the Great Depression, presented challenges too great for the Flat River Woman's Club, and indeed for virtually all

54. *Lead Belt News,* January 21, 1921; Minutes, April 9, 1920, and November 12, 1922.

55. Minutes of the Flat River Woman's Club, Collection R206, Western Historical Manuscripts Collection–Rolla, February 3, 1925, and February 17, 1926.

56. See Sarah Deutsch, *Women and the City: Gender, Space, and Power in Boston, 1870–1940* (London: Oxford University Press, 2000).

private charitable organizations. During those years, corporate paternalism offered many in the lead belt the best chance for relief. In 1937, a writer for *Fortune* magazine visited St. Francois County and described what he thought was the ideal American corporation. The St. Joseph Lead Company kept most of its mines open during the worst years of the Depression along with building a hospital, natatorium, and library in Bonne Terre, Missouri. The "Benevolent St. Joe" halved production but managed to give most miners a few hours of work each week.[57] Other mining companies responded similarly, or St. Joseph Lead Company purchased them. The economic disaster of the 1930s left many in southeast Missouri almost completely dependent on the lead industry. Paradoxically, perhaps, the lead industry took on the sort of role in social welfare that many reformers had long demanded. Yet in doing so, it acquired an even stronger hold on the pocketbooks and the loyalties of the lead-belt residents. This was not necessarily a bad thing, but this greater degree of dependence on benevolent capitalism almost certainly reduced the moral authority of those who remained critical of industry's opposition to town incorporation and seemed to have quieted complaints about the quality of water and public health.

Women reformers in Flat River, Missouri, shared similar class and gender ideologies with other Progressive Era women around the country. But the conditions of life in a company-owned mining town provided unique challenges. Reforming the very institutions that allowed them to be middle-class, feminizing a political and social environment dominated by men, enhancing appreciation for beauty and self-improvement on the part of those who worked hardest to create dignified lives in the industrial hierarchy: the Mothers and Patrons of Flat River used these goals to define for themselves personal and political democracy in their pursuit of a more progressive community. These coworkers for the common good demonized neither industry nor the working class nor immigrants nor single mothers, but they expected that, like themselves, all members of their community would initially share in the social responsibilities and then ultimately the rewards of industrializing Missouri. At least in part, the world they inhabited was of their making.

57. "The Benevolent St. Joe," *Fortune* (April 1937): 92–99.

Prostitution and Reform in Kansas City, 1880–1930

AMBER R. CLIFFORD

As home to native farmers and immigrant meatpackers, cowboys and congressmen, future presidents and prostitutes, Kansas City combined rural sensibility and urban modernity. Because Kansas City was an "eastern" city within a rural "western" world, it became a city of experimentation and adventure for rural and urban citizens alike. Integral to Kansas City at the turn of the century was a growing number of working-class women whose contributions to the success of Kansas City's growth have been ignored and forgotten. Kansas City's elite saw these women, who lived in a class where sexuality and labor were as much public as private, as immoral and unacceptable. Consequently, the stories of working-class Kansas City women were discarded in favor of histories of city bosses and cowboy culture. This essay discusses Kansas City's prostitutes, a subject previously treated by researchers and local historians as taboo. Using prostitutes as an example, this research begins to rebuild the story of women, work, and sexuality buried by decades of moral indignation.

While the ignorance of prostitution in local and regional history is a problem, it is not the only thing lacking in the history of prostitution. Although this study is intended to fill a gap in regional history, it is also aimed at addressing debates and breaches in the written history of prostitution. One of these debates is the choice of subject—are prostitutes the subject of oppression, or the object of legal protections for mainstream Americans? Perhaps the best-known work on the history of American prostitution, and central to this debate, is Ruth Rosen's *The Lost Sisterhood: Prostitution in America,*

1900–1918.[1] Rosen's feminist work concentrated on the Progressive crackdown on prostitution, and the ways in which prostitutes formed a "sisterhood" to fight Victorian sexuality. Rosen's work gave subjectification to the women who worked as prostitutes in the early twentieth century, and it provided an important critique of the effect of Victorian social and moral standards on working-class female prostitutes.

Other historians of prostitution, however, have critiqued Rosen's work (and the work of other feminist scholars) as lacking an analysis of the sociological and criminological aspects of prostitution. Thomas Mackey's *Red Lights Out* is an example of the rancor in this debate. Mackey's work focused specifically on the legal definition and prosecution of American prostitution from 1870 to 1917. "No adequate, convincing, conceptual framework of prostitution exists," wrote Mackey, "and, in this study, prostitution is viewed only from the world of the legal bar, or legal definitions, distinctions, and determinations." It is Mackey's critique of feminist analysis (which I would suggest is a framework) and Rosen's work, however, that demonstrates the subject-object debate among historians of prostitution. According to Mackey: "Having produced a work that tears apart American society and structure by the feminist-marxist-socialist numbers, Rosen leaves her readers without guidance about what to do to correct all these terrible problems."[2] Mackey's work situates prostitutes themselves as the "terrible problems," leaving little doubt that the legal prosecution of prostitution is both just and necessary. Rosen, who situated prostitutes as the casualty of Victorian sexuality, questioned the legal and moral underpinnings of antivice movements in the Progressive Era. This study suggests that Rosen was likely correct. While brothel prostitution and red-light districting decreased in Kansas City after 1917, by no means was prostitution eradicated. Instead, prostitution was driven further underground, much to the detriment of sex workers. Unlike Rosen, however, this study uses the legal definition and prosecution of

1. Ruth Rosen, *The Lost Sisterhood: Prostitution in America, 1900–1918* (Baltimore: Johns Hopkins Press, 1982).
2. Thomas C. Mackey, *Red Lights Out: A Legal History of Prostitution, Disorderly Houses, and Vice Districts, 1870–1917,* American Legal and Constitutional History: A Garland Series of Outstanding Dissertations, ed. Harold Hyman (New York: Garland, 1987), 9, 14.

prostitution as evidence of the oppressive nature of antiprostitution reform.

Another major debate among historians of prostitution is region itself. Admittedly, this study of Kansas City is a regional one. Kansas City, however, is a city that I suggest defied the conventional concept of "region" by embodying both the rural sensibility of the western frontier and the modernized development of eastern American cities. The study of Kansas City is, therefore, one of rural western and urban eastern regionalism. A large number of works on the history of prostitution focus on cities such as New York and Chicago, where large and traditional vice districts were easily identifiable. Studies of prostitution in cities where such delineation was not always as clear, such as cities in the Midwest and West, are more difficult. At the same time, while studies of prostitution in the American West have focused on women's experiences as frontier sex workers, they have not dealt significantly with the work of women in western cities at the turn of the century. Anne Butler's *Daughters of Joy, Sisters of Misery,* widely recognized as the seminal work on western American prostitution, focused only on "the contributions prostitutes made to frontier institutional development, and the final rewards for prostitutes who participated in the experience."[3] Kansas City existed in both an urban and a rural, a Western and an Eastern region, and such a clash of regional sensibilities is not prevalent in histories of prostitution.

A final intention of this work is to expose and explore a major breach in the history of prostitution: the effect of antiprostitution reform *after* the end of Prohibition. Traditionally, studies of prostitution end with the beginning of World War I and the passage of national prohibition. The works of Rosen and Mackey end at 1917, while Joel Best's recent work *Controlling Vice: Regulating Brothel Prostitution in St. Paul* ends much earlier, in 1883. Why do historians of prostitution close their studies with the end of a broadly defined Progressive Era? I believe the answer to that lies in the antivice reforms of the Progressive Era themselves. After World War I, the popular belief was that prostitution was eradicated, displaced, or for some reason no longer a concern. Once the concentrated red-light districts were "closed," the public view of prostitution went underground along with the work.

3. Anne M. Butler, *Daughters of Joy, Sisters of Misery: Prostitutes in the American West, 1865–90* (Urbana: University of Illinois Press, 1985), xviii.

Historians are evidently following that trend, rather than investigating the long-term effects of antivice reform in American cities. As Joel Best explained:

> There are relatively few studies of twentieth-century prostitution following the implementation of prohibition; however, the evidence from the major cities suggests that prohibition's critics were at least partially correct. Instead of eliminating vice, reform dispersed it into more neighborhoods, while increasing official corruption and, in some cities, the influence of organized crime. Yet these new problems did not cause as much public outrage as the Progressives had mustered against tolerating vice. Public awareness of prostitution as a major social problem fell throughout most of the twentieth century; prohibition did not have as many vocal critics as the policies it replaced.[4]

While this study of prostitution in Kansas City does not completely agree with Best's conclusions, it does provide a different view of the effects of reform in American cities. Prostitution and its reform did not end in 1917, and neither should the work of historians of prostitution.

As is the case with other American cities, the history of Kansas City's working-class women was shaped by the Victorian social values of the city's nineteenth-century elite. Victorian morality, an English system that flourished in America before World War I, elevated the nuclear family and female "purity" as society's ideal. A woman's role was as wife and mother, and proper women prized modesty over emotion. Victorian men were free to work outside the home and congregate with their friends in the homosocial (single-sex) atmospheres of saloons, but women were taught to build a refuge in the home.[5] In fact, the arbiters of Victorian morality considered female sexuality an emotional illness that was either abnormal or nonexistent.[6] Consequently, Victorian wives and mothers sheltered their sexuality

---

4. Joel Best, *Controlling Vice: Regulating Brothel Prostitution in St. Paul, 1865–1883* (Columbus: Ohio State University Press, 1998), 113.

5. Harriet Sigerman, "An Unfinished Battle, 1848–1865," in *No Small Courage: A History of Women in the United States,* ed. Nancy F. Cott (New York: Oxford University Press, 2000), 266.

6. Carol Z. Stearns and Peter N. Stearns, "A Traditional View of Victorian Sexuality," in *Major Problems in American Women's History,* ed. Mary Beth Norton (Lexington, Mass.: D. C. Heath, 1989), 250.

to protect the home, while their husbands "sowed their wild oats" in saloons and brothels.

However, as working-class neighborhoods such as Kansas City's West Bottoms grew with the railroad, it became increasingly difficult for the city's elite to keep female sexuality hidden. Working-class women required access to saloons and other institutions of the "men's sphere" in order to survive. Saloons and brothels often also served as the only source of clean water, cooked food, and warm shelter for working-class women and their children. These laboring families found Victorian morality oppressive.[7] In an effort to provide for themselves, working-class Kansas Citians began building nickelodeons, burlesque theaters, and red-light districts to provide both employment and entertainment. Working-class ideas about sexuality, which included prostitution, invaded Victorian society through popular culture that (either fictionally or in reality) sold female sexuality as a commodity.

Though little information about Kansas City's red-light district survives, some details exist about the major brothels and madams of the city's pre–World War I period. As a railroad hub, Kansas City inevitably developed a large and thriving red-light district controlled primarily by three women. Once the city's cribs and brothels became subject to municipal and state laws, the women of the "resorts" became targets for antivice Victorian reformers. The resulting clash with the Victorian elite did not destroy working-class women's labor or sexuality. In fact, the events in Kansas City between 1880 and 1930 show that Victorian upper-class moralists simply reasserted their control over sexuality by appropriating working-class city spaces and defining public sexual expression as "abnormal" according to regional values and laws. Kansas City's elite adopted the aspects of working-class sexuality they could reshape to their liking; they successfully outlawed everything else.

Kansas City's urban elite was part of a national movement against the public display of working-class sexuality. With the advent of the Progressive Era in the 1900s, both evangelists and urban reformers considered mass amusements emblematic of declining morality and rising working-class anarchy.[8] Americans increasingly connected

7. John Higham, "The Reorientation of American Culture in the 1890s," in *The Origins of Modern Consciousness,* ed. John Weiss (Detroit: Wayne State University Press, 1965), 31.

8. Lewis A. Erenberg, *Steppin' Out: Nightlife and the Transformation of American Culture, 1890–1930* (Westport, Conn.: Greenwood Press, 1981), 63.

working-class leisure and immorality, especially with unregulated amusements. The biggest concern about leisure spaces was moral health, especially when it came to women and young people.[9] Urban reformers criticized mass amusements as a threat to public health—a danger that required both regulation and reform. Kansas Citians interested in amusement reform also discussed the danger of women seeking pleasure in the public sphere. According to one reformer, working-class women in amusement spaces were a source of social danger. In his investigation of working-class girls, the reformer wrote that he feared the cultural effect of "girls who were idling along, seeking some diversion, some amusement, girls who were loitering on the edge of that precipice over which so many fall to destruction."[10] Urban reformers often connected the immorality of theaters, movie houses, and amusement parks with prostitution and "fallen women." Consequently, following the adoption of state laws and city ordinances governing most working-class leisure activities, all that remained for Kansas City's urban reformers to attack were the red-light districts.

There were several reasons why urban reformers did not attack prostitution initially. First, defenders of Victorian American culture could see and criticize amusement parks and theaters because they were open to public view. Mass amusement advertisements appeared in newspapers and in public places in Kansas City, where upper-class reformers encountered them. Second, because prostitution was illegal, the red-light districts of American cities supposedly did not exist. They were a part of an urban subculture that was out of sight to most people. Consequently, mainstream Americans had little contact with the red-light culture, and those who did have knowledge of the red-light districts certainly never discussed their experiences in polite company. The blatant sexuality of red-light districts also slowed the bourgeois response. Open sexual expression was still suppressed in mainstream American culture.[11] Though mass amusements challenged

9. Alan Havig, "Mass Commercial Amusements in Kansas City before World War I," *Missouri Historical Review* 75 (April 1981): 341.

10. Recreation Department, *Annual Report of the Recreation Department of the Board of Public Welfare of Kansas City, Missouri, April 18, 1911–April 15, 1912* (Kansas City: Cline Printing, 1912), 242–43.

11. For a discussion of subcultural invisibility as it pertained to other sexual minorities such as gays and lesbians, see Alan Sinfield, *Out on Stage: Lesbian and Gay Theatre in the Twentieth Century* (New Haven: Yale University Press, 2000), 26.

the prevailing gender roles and moral codes at the turn of the century, sexuality remained a taboo subject. In urban red-light districts, sexuality was recognized as a special context. In addition, powerful women with political connections often controlled the establishments in red-light districts.

According to the theory of social construction, gender identity and behavior were understood only in the context of the time. Kansas City's elite, and their counterparts in other American cities between 1880 and 1920, believed that sexuality was inherently male-driven and acceptable only as a man's activity. Women were seen as reproductive, not sexual. The diffusion of female sexual behavior from the wedding bed into mass amusements and social visibility resulted in a legal and moral "general policing of the gender order" in that period.[12]

The regulation and eradication of gender expressiveness in public amusements such as the red-light district affected both men and women, while keeping the dominant upper and middle classes in power in America. According to historian Christine Stansell, the relationship between working women and the American upper classes was based on class divisions as much as gender divisions. The class distinctions between urban white women and their working-class counterparts were a major factor in the marginalization of working-class women. This marginalization of working-class women included the control of working-class gender behavior in public spaces such as red-light districts. As historian Richard Butsch wrote in his study of American leisure *For Fun and Profit:* "Thus, hegemony in leisure may be assessed by the degree to which practitioners of leisure are not the producers of

12. George Chauncey, *Gay New York: Gender, Urban Culture, and the Making of the Gay Male World, 1890–1940* (New York: Basic Books, 1994), 28. The concept of gender is a continuing source of debate among scholars. Rather than discussing difference in biological terms (male vs. female), the term *gender* is used to discuss differences in behavior, social relationships, and cultural acceptability (man vs. woman). The benchmark work for definitions of gender behavior is Michel Foucault, *The History of Sexuality: An Introduction,* vol. 1 (New York: Random House, 1978). Sources for further investigation of gender in American history and culture include Gerda Lerner, *The Creation of Patriarchy* (New York: Oxford University Press, 1986); and Myra Marx Ferree, Judith Lorber, and Beth B. Hess, eds., *Revisioning Gender* (Thousand Oaks, Calif.: Sage, 1999). For an explanation of gender identity cross-culturally, see Sherry Ortner and Harriet Whitehead, eds., *Sexual Meanings: The Cultural Construction of Gender and Sexuality* (Cambridge: Cambridge University Press, 1981).

their own leisure, the degree to which they are constrained by the conventions of the practice or limited by their access to the means of 'producing' that leisure activity."[13]

For working-class women, prostitution was much more complicated than reformers imagined. The transformation of American industry in the 1880s meant that working-class families could not survive on a single income. Rosen has pointed out that single and widowed women could either remarry, work in industry or domestic service, or become prostitutes. As the historian Kathy Peiss has explained, working-class women received mixed messages about sexual behavior because the expectation was that sexuality would be confined to the dependent conditions of marriage. Therefore, while many working-class women sought work as prostitutes, many others fought against prostitution and sought instead the legitimacy and respectability that came with marriage.[14]

Yet just as the demand for prostitutes increased in the late nineteenth century, women sought some autonomy and economic security in the home by becoming part-time prostitutes known as "crib girls." Upper-class women initially tolerated the rise of prostitution. According to Victorian moral codes, prostitutes protected American wives from the male sex drive. Though working-class women used prostitution as a source of income, moralistic reformers also explained prostitution as a product of inherently immoral working-class society. Of course, upper-class women had little or no experience in red-light districts. Residents in red-light districts had their own commercial subculture with values and morals that outsiders hardly understood.[15]

Until the 1900s, gender issues attracted scant attention among Kansas City's movers and shakers. As in other American cities, upper- and middle-class notions of proper Victorian morality and behavior prevailed. Kansas Citians were concerned with maintaining moral

13. See Christine Stansell, *City of Women: Sex and Class in New York, 1789–1860* (Urbana: University of Illinois Press, 1987); Richard Butsch, "Introduction: Leisure and Hegemony in America," in Richard Butsch, ed., *For Fun and Profit: The Transformation of Leisure into Consumption* (Philadelphia: Temple University Press, 1990), 8.

14. Rosen, *Lost Sisterhood*, 3; Kathy Peiss, *Cheap Amusements: Working Women and Leisure in Turn-of-the-Century New York* (Philadelphia: Temple University Press, 1986), 110.

15. Rosen, *Lost Sisterhood*, 4, 5, 6, xiv.

standards among the city's working classes tempted by commercial amusements and attractions. Their definitions of morality conformed to dominant Victorian definitions of gender behavior—the public man and the private, morally superior woman. In fact, until Progressive reformers began their campaign in Kansas City in the 1900s, only one city ordinance dealt with gender behavior. City Ordinance No. 291, which defined lewd behavior, was applied to everything from club entertainment to prostitution until the 1910s. The ordinance stated:

> No person shall be or appear in or upon any street, avenue, alley, park, public place or place open to public view, in a state of nudity, or any dress not belonging to his or her sex, or in any indecent or lewd dress, or shall make any indecent exposure of his or her person, or be guilty of an unseemly obscene or filthy act, or any lewd, indecent, immoral or insulting conduct, language or behavior; or shall exhibit, circulate, contribute, sell, offer or expose for sale, or give or deliver to another, or cause the same to be done, any lewd, indecent or obscene book, picture, pamphlet, card, print, paper writing, mold, cast, figure or any other thing, or shall exhibit or perform, or cause or allow to be exhibited or performed, in or upon any house, building, lot or premises owned or occupied by him, or under his management or control, any lewd, indecent, or immoral play or other representation.[16]

Although this law existed, it was seldom enforced. Numerous clubs, theaters, saloons, and brothels in Kansas City violated Ordinance No. 291. Kansas City civic leaders declined to close every saloon and brothel in town lest they offend workers and visiting businessmen.

An organized assault on the red-light districts developed, however, in the 1900s. Increasingly, reformers embraced movements to "purify" American life by ridding its cities of commercialized vice. With accusations of the white enslavement of working-class girls, anti-prostitution movements appeared in tandem with park and movie house reform campaigns.[17] Along with their attacks on red-light districts, reformers

16. Board of Public Welfare, *Fifth Annual Report of the Board of Public Welfare of Kansas City, Missouri, April 21, 1913–April 20, 1914* (Kansas City: Cline Printing, 1914), 53.

17. John C. Burnham, "The Progressive Era Revolution in American Attitudes toward Sex," *Journal of American History* 59 (March 1973): 887.

exhibited a sudden urge to "counterbalance the home" with various other establishments. Their efforts produced a series of seemingly disconnected reforms, such as a 1914 regulation requiring Kansas City skating rinks to attain official permits.[18] Civic reformers demanded public licensing of dancing and drinking establishments and the creation of censorship boards to control vice.[19] However, these were all mass amusements, and urban reformers came to view the red-light districts as a true form of evil. Located in the waterfront or tenement districts of a city, the bohemian red-light districts exemplified a more obvious threat to the purity of women and acceptable gender behavior. "The intimacy, vitality, and exuberance of these districts were deemed too inherently unladylike," wrote historian Lewis Erenberg, who also observed that "In a society dedicated to progress and purity, sex was a troublesome matter."[20]

While Kansas City leaders certainly agreed with the avoidance of sexuality, they also depended on a public display of sexuality for good business. Kansas City was an important city in the 1880s, but it had not lost its Wild West character. The city had a reputation for permissive behavior and was frequented by cattlemen and farmers who visited it on weekends in search of entertainment.[21] The city directory of 1878 listed eighty saloons—four times the number of city schools, libraries, and hospitals combined.[22] "Machismo was marketable, and bawdiness meant big business," wrote one historian of 1880s Kansas City; "the city that limped out of the Civil War had become a cocksure, burgeoning town literally drunk with success."[23]

Although the elite depended on working-class people to keep the city's bawdy reputation alive, working-class city dwellers were kept separated from the benefits of such big business. Kansas City's neighborhoods were clearly stratified. Wealthy residents lived primarily in

18. Havig, "Mass Commercial Amusements," 338.

19. James R. McGovern, "The American Women's Pre–World War I Freedom in Manners and Morals," *Journal of American History* 55, no. 2 (September 1968): 331.

20. Erenberg, *Steppin' Out*, 21; on the particular threat of red-light districts on women's purity and gender behavior, see Sinfield, *Out on Stage*, 50.

21. Nathan W. Pearson Jr., *Goin to Kansas City*, Music in American Life Series (Urbana: University of Illinois Press, 1987), 78.

22. Rick Montgomery and Shirl Kasper, *Kansas City: An American Story*, ed. Monroe Dodd (Kansas City: Kansas City Star Books, 1999), 85.

23. Ibid.

Quality Hill, a cliffside area on the east side of the city away from live-stock barns and the railroad. Quality Hill overlooked the city's working-class neighborhoods, known as the West Bottoms and the North End. The West Bottoms, located between Quality Hill and the Kansas state line along the southern edge of the Missouri River, became the center of industry in Kansas City.[24] Home to meatpacking houses, railroad yards, and factories, the West Bottoms was also home to most work-ing-class Kansas Citians, who lived in overcrowded tenements.[25] Dis-ease and muddy streets in the flood-prone area compounded the poor living conditions. Because the West Bottoms was the city's industrial center, its tenements primarily housed newly arrived European immi-grant packinghouse workers along with most of the city's African American population.[26]

The city's other principal working-class neighborhood, known as the North End, was located just north and east of the West Bottoms. Called the "dingy North End," the neighborhood was the center of Kansas City's red-light district.[27] What the North End lacked in indus-try, it made up for in gambling halls and brothels. Most red-light activ-ity took place in the North End's Knob Hill section, where one-third of Kansas City's police force was concentrated from 1870 to 1875.[28]

The key to Kansas City's phenomenal growth was the railroad. Railroads were the corner of the city's economic system. As a railroad terminus Kansas City had national importance. The city's livestock and meatpacking industries attracted businessmen and investors as well as a large transient workforce. Railroads brought seventy thou-sand people to Kansas City in 1869, the first year the Hannibal Bridge was open. The number of livestock brokered yearly in Kansas City rose from approximately one hundred thousand in 1870 to almost one million by 1880.[29] Cattle brokers and meatpackers, who depended

24. Lyle W. Dorsett, *The Pendergast Machine* (New York: Oxford University Press, 1968), 4.

25. Ibid., 5.

26. Montgomery and Kasper, *Kansas City,* 102, 130.

27. Dorsett, *Pendergast Machine,* 5.

28. A. Theodore Brown and Lyle W. Dorsett, *K.C.: A History of Kansas City, Missouri,* vol. 2 of the Western Urban History Series (Boulder, Colo.: Pruett Pub-lishing, 1978), 45.

29. Brown and Dorsett, *K.C.,* 50–51.

on the railroads, soon controlled Kansas City government and business. The Kansas City Livestock Exchange was founded in 1871 and was governed by a group of local railroad tycoons. When the Plankinton and Armour meatpacking plants made Kansas City their base of operations in the 1880s, the West Bottoms became the nation's leading packing district.[30]

Red-light districts were so named because of the red lights of railroad lanterns. During the development of Kansas City railroads, train brakemen carried red signal lanterns to brothels during stops. By hanging the lantern on the brothel or crib door, the brakemen were easily located in an emergency.[31] Prostitutes adopted the red railroad lanterns as a symbol, hanging them on their doorways when they were open for business.[32] Kansas City's red-light district was easy to find. "Crib girls," as prostitutes were called in the 1880s, lived near the levee in houses close to saloons or railroad tracks. Saloons were vital to life in red-light districts. Saloon owners frequently promoted or managed prostitution.[33] Owners built saloons near brothels to attract business and sometimes housed crib girls upstairs over their saloon. Kansas City's machine boss Tom Pendergast had interests in prostitution and saloons, in a manner similar to that of systems in other cities. For instance, Pendergast owned at least two hotels where the availability of prostitution was an open secret. Pendergast simply took a cut of the prostitution income payments to the city police. Pendergast also protected other venues such as the all-nude Chesterfield Club in exchange for the club owner's agreement to purchase Pendergast liquor. In an effort to hide prostitution from Victorian sensibility, city police allowed red-light districts to thrive without publicly mentioning their existence. Saloon owners and madams paid police in return for such protection.[34] One Kansas City madam recalled her morning routine in the 1890s: "I always had plenty to do, getting the police and city hall cut of the night's take put in envelopes, inspecting the laundry with the housekeeper, the cleaning bills, replacing busted chairs, lamps,

30. Montgomery and Kasper, *Kansas City,* 107, 111.
31. Rosen, *Lost Sisterhood,* 105.
32. Fred L. Lee, "Annie Chambers' High-Toned Brothel," *Kansas City Geneaologist* 38 (fall 1998): 83.
33. Rosen, *Lost Sisterhood,* 44.
34. Dorsett, *Pendergast Machine,* 68, 4.

linens."[35] Kansas City's police essentially helped create the red-light district, and they punished saloon owners and madams only when they failed to make protection payments.[36]

Kansas City's red-light district was bounded by Second Street on the north, Main Street to the east, Sixth Street on the south, and May Street on the west. Those crib girls who were managed by a "madam" lived in female boarding houses called "resorts." By 1905, most resorts were located in the 200 block of West Fourth Street.[37] There were literally hundreds of resorts and cribs in the red-light district. Single women who simply put red lanterns on their doors ran some cribs. Other women worked in high-class resorts run by powerful and wealthy Kansas City women. The red-light district created four hundred thousand dollars in Kansas City revenues each year.[38] There were 128 brothels listed on Kansas City police fines lists in 1910 alone: ninety-nine Caucasian and twenty-two African American, and seven with unlisted owners. The red-light district also revealed the city's continuing links to rural and western America. A 1910 survey of prostitutes found that about 33 percent of Kansas City prostitutes were born in small towns, while only 3 percent were foreign born.[39]

As Kansas City expanded south, the red-light district moved south along Main Street. Some of the better-known resorts and cribs on Main were Clara's Crib at 1801 Main, and the Hotel Ester at 2035 Broadway. A crib at 1711 Walnut was called "The Irish Village"; it catered mostly to Irish and German immigrants. Itinerant printer John Edward Hicks mentioned visiting several resorts or cribs in his memoirs. Hicks referred to the "high-priced beauties of Annie Chambers" and the "twenty-five cent crones at Lone Cottonwood." Hicks's tour of the red-light district on one drunken evening took him to many cribs and resorts now forgotten. Hicks listed a series of what he termed "boarding houses": Mollie Paupaw's on West Fourth, Em

---

35. Nell Kimball, *Nell Kimball: Her Life as an American Madam by Herself* (New York: Macmillan, 1970), 9.

36. Rosen, *Lost Sisterhood*, 5.

37. Lee, "Annie Chambers' Brothel," 83.

38. Rosen, *Lost Sisterhood*, 71.

39. Fred R. Johnson, "The Social Evil in Kansas City," in *Second Annual Report of the Board of Public Welfare of Kansas City, Missouri, April 19, 1910–April 18, 1911* (Kansas City: Fratcher Printing, 1911), 127, 138.

Williams's on Third, Bessie Stevenson's on Broadway, Mollie O'Brien's at First and Main, "and the tent kept by the notorious Becky Ragan at the foot of Main Street." Hicks also reported a sensational story he overheard about madam Jennie Armstrong, "who kept a 'small place of sin' at Fifth and Bluff and got arrested for beating one of her three painted mermaids with the business end of a stovelifter."[40] These sensational stories only added to the growing Victorian fear of the dangers of open female sexuality in Kansas City.

The most notorious and popular resorts in Kansas City were located in adjacent buildings in the 200 block of west Third and Fourth streets. The madams of these three resorts ran busy brothels that bore their names: Annie Chambers, Madame Lovejoy, and Eva Prince. One Kansas City reporter called these "the three most notorious houses of the kind in the 'red-light district.'" The reporter also referred to the three resort owners as "the queens of the red-light" and mentioned that the "Salvation Army workers thereabout used to call them 'gilded palaces of sin.'"[41] Eva Prince's resort was located at 204 and 206 West Fourth Street. The Prince resort shared a wall with Madame Lovejoy's twenty-four rooms at 200 and 202 West Fourth Street. The most famous of all these resorts was the house of Annie Chambers, a building at the southwest corner of Third and Wyandotte streets, just north of Lovejoy's.[42]

By 1900, reformers, who began to use the medical discourse of sexologists, classified prostitutes as sexual deviants. The moral classification of prostitution led to "social purity" crusades intended to reform sexuality. Reformers described prostitution as the result of working-class urban culture. In their efforts to convince urban women that prostitution is a "social evil," reformers created a market for published memoirs of prostitutes. Although little is known about the lives of Kansas City's madams and crib girls, one firsthand account was published by social purity reformers in 1919. *Madeleine: An Autobiography* was the memoir of a prostitute who worked in the cribs of the American Midwest. According to historian Ruth Rosen, *Madeleine*

40. John Edward Hicks, *Adventures of a Tramp Printer, 1880–1890* (Kansas City: MidAmerica Press, 1950), 29–30.

41. A. B. McDonald, "Gift to Union Mission of Old North Side Resort," *Kansas City Star*, February 18, 1934, A5.

42. Lee, "Annie Chambers' Brothel," 84.

was one of the few substantiated memoirs whose publication was sponsored by reformers.[43]

Madeleine worked in Kansas City in the late nineteenth century as a crib girl in Laura Lovejoy's brothel on West Fourth Street. Lovejoy's was known as the "Old Ladies Home" because the clientele was mostly local older men. When she was seventeen, Madeleine arrived at Lovejoy's after leaving Chicago because of illness. Although Madeleine had worked in brothels before, Madam Lovejoy insisted on interviewing her about her life and family. Madeleine was then given "working clothes" and sent to the parlor to entertain a "regular."[44] She worked at Lovejoy's for over a year before moving west. Madeleine described red-light life in Kansas City:

> Red-light segregation was a name only, not a fact. . . . Vice flourished in all parts of the city; wine rooms were wide open for anyone having the price of a drink; private houses and assignation houses abounded—and the roadhouses ran full blast for twenty-four hours a day.[45]

Annie Chambers is probably the most famous madam in Kansas City history. She was born Leannah Kearns in Kansas, and she was married as a young girl to a man named Loveall. The Lovealls came to Kansas City in 1869, where they settled north of the Missouri River. However, when her husband died, Leannah was forced to earn a living. She opened a resort in the Loveall home north of the river and welcomed Kansas City visitors who came across the river by ferry.[46] She then changed her name to Annie Chambers and moved her resort to Kansas City in 1871. The resort house at Third and Wyandotte was built with Chambers's own money and was completed according to her instructions. From the beginning, the Chambers house was a brothel.[47] The Chambers brothel, with stained-glass walls and a tiled

43. Rosen, *Lost Sisterhood,* 13, xiii, 11, 78.
44. Madeleine, *Madeleine: An Autobiography* (New York: Harper and Brothers, 1919), 65, 63.
45. Ibid., 70.
46. Lee, "Annie Chambers' Brothel," 83.
47. Fred L. Lee, "Gone but Not Forgotten: Annie Chambers, Kansas City Madam, Dead at Age Ninety-Two," *Kansas City Geneaologist* 38, no. 2 (fall 1998): 88.

entrance bearing Annie Chambers's name, operated daily until 1913. During a conversation with a missionary couple in 1924, Chambers defended her resort as the only place where her girls could count on being safe and in control. As Chambers told the young couple: "People think women of my sort are hard-hearted, but we have hearts, too, and sometimes they melt in sorrows. But we hide it from the world, for our business requires us to put on a gay front."[48]

Reformers for social purity gained support in both public and government sectors after 1900. The growth of sexual reform was largely attributed to violence in the red-light districts. A lurid axe murder took place in Kansas City in 1880 when a rejected brothel customer murdered another customer in a crib at Nineteenth Street and Broadway.[49] In a report on New York's Tenderloin district, a Kansas City reporter wrote of "girls who wearied of the monotony of rural life . . . and are frequently found by detective skill in the dens of infamy."[50] To combat crime associated with prostitution, reformers and their government supporters classified prostitution as a crime. Special courts, police units, and correctional facilities were created especially for prostitutes.[51] The Kansas City Florence Crittenton Mission opened in the red-light district to rescue "fallen women." Social workers from Crittenton visited local saloons and dance halls to increase support for the mission.[52]

Kansas City's Board of Public Welfare, the agency charged with managing correctional facilities, launched an investigation in the red-light district in 1910. Kansas City was one of forty-three cities that conducted formal vice investigations between 1900 and 1917.[53] Kansas City police were required to enforce new antivice laws. Consequently, 957 brothel owners and 471 prostitutes were arrested in 1911 alone.[54] The Board of Public Welfare appointed reformer Kate E.

48. MacDonald, "Gift to Union Mission."

49. "A Bloody Tragedy," *Kansas City Times*, February 3, 1880, 5.

50. "Gotham Dance Houses," *Kansas City Times*, January 30, 1880, 2.

51. Rosen, *Lost Sisterhood*, 19.

52. Sally M. Miller, *From Prairie to Prison: The Life of Social Activist Kate Richards O'Hare* (Columbia: University of Missouri Press, 1993), 16.

53. Rosen, *Lost Sisterhood*, 14.

54. Asa E. Martin, *Our Negro Population: A Sociological Study of the Negroes of Kansas City, Missouri* (Kansas City: Franklin Hudson Publishing, 1913), 132.

Pierson head of the Parole Department of Delinquent Women in 1910. Pierson managed women's jails, industrial workhouses, and hospitals for prostitutes in Kansas City until 1912.[55] Board of Public Welfare investigators recommended new laws, made more arrests, and waged a "relentless warfare against the houses of prostitution."[56] As Board of Public Welfare investigator Fred Johnson stated in his 1910 study of Kansas City prostitutes:

> The unprejudiced observer is convinced that no system of suppression can totally eliminate prostitution. First there must be a radical change in the amusements we tolerate, in public opinion, in our treatment of sex problems, in our economic system, in the attitude of the church, and in the teaching and influence of the home itself. As we have before noted, this evil is deep rooted.[57]

In keeping with the ideas about morality and acceptable discourse in the turn of the century, police records are the primary source of information about activities in the red-light districts. However, Annie Chambers persisted in spite of the antiprostitution campaign and successfully operated her resort through 1924, at times with the backing of Kansas City boss Tom Pendergast. Progressive attacks against the resorts of the red-light district began in 1913. That year Annie Chambers was called to appear before the newly formed all-male Society for the Prevention of Commercialized Vice.[58] As the group reminded readers in 1944: "Previous to October, 1913, immoral conditions in Kansas City had reached an intolerable situation. The public became aroused and the Society for the Prevention of Commercialized Vice was organized."[59] Because of pressure from reform groups led by the society, Kansas City's mayor signed an injunction against "bawdy houses," under the explanation that prostitution was a public

55. Board of Public Welfare, *Third Annual Report of the Board of Public Welfare of Kansas City, Missouri, April 18, 1911–April 15, 1912* (Kansas City: Cline Printing, 1912), 295.

56. Johnson, "Social Evil," 137.

57. Ibid., 135.

58. Jane Fifield Flynn, *Kansas City Women of Independent Minds* (Kansas City: Fifield Publishing, 1992), 26.

59. "From Dark to Dawn: Condensed Information on a Great Moral Victory," *Social Improvement News* 2, no. 7 (January 1944): 28.

nuisance. The injunction briefly closed the Chambers resort in 1913, and Chambers herself was arrested and jailed.[60] The society secured injunctions against fifty brothels in 1913.[61] However, Annie Chambers refused to accept the ruling by city officials and reopened her house.

Kansas City's Society for the Prevention of Vice successfully pressured the state government for a nuisance law against brothels in 1921. The "Act of 1921" prohibited the maintenance of "all buildings, erections, room and places, and the ground itself in or upon such bawdyhouse, assignation house, or place of prostitution is conducted." According to the Act of 1921, any county prosecuting attorney could "abate and perpetually enjoin" houses of prostitution and temporarily close the brothels for whatever period of time city officials deemed appropriate.[62] Jackson County Prosecuting Attorney Cameron Orr initiated a raid at Chambers's house in June 1921, only three months after the law passed. Orr was encouraged to raid the Chambers home by another city prosecuting attorney, William B. C. Brown. Brown was a Harvard-educated lawyer and one of the founders of the Society for the Prevention of Vice. Kansas City police entered the Chambers house at 3 p.m. on June 29. According to police testimony, there were ten women and two men in the brothel. Police found one girl hiding under a bed and another standing on the roof attempting to escape capture.[63] One police witness testified:

Q: "When you got upstairs, what did you find up there?"
A: "Found several girls in the rooms with silk garments on and different colors."
Q: "Bright?"
A: "Bright colors, yes, and in one room we found a man and a woman. This man was on the bed in his B.V.D.'s and this girl didn't have anything on but a teddybear."[64]

60. "From Dark to Dawn: No. 3—The Case of Annie Chambers; Sinner, Saint," *Social Improvement News* 1 (September 1943): 12.
61. "From Dark to Dawn: Condensed Information," 28.
62. *The State ex. rel. Cameron L. Orr v. Leannah Kearns, alias Annie Chambers,* Supreme Court of Missouri case No. 24023 (264 S.W. 775), July 31, 1924.
63. *Political History of Jackson County: Biographical Sketches of Men Who Have Helped to Make It* (Kansas City: Marshall and Morrison Publishers, 1902; reprint, Boure, Md.: Heritage Books, 1997), 85.
64. Ibid.

Following the raid, Orr ordered the brothel closed for two months, and Annie Chambers was jailed until December. It was the first time in its history that Chambers's brothel had remained closed for more than a single day (Chambers's house had been closed one day upon her arrest in 1913). Orr successfully prosecuted Chambers in Jackson County Circuit Court and secured a permanent abatement for the infamous bawdy house. Throughout her incarceration and the abatement of her property, Chambers insisted that she simply ran a boardinghouse, and that she had not run a brothel in her home since the passage of Missouri's White Slave Act in 1913. Chambers was not prosecuted under her working name. Instead, Kansas City's prosecutors filed against Leannah Kearns, a name she had not used since 1869.

Chambers, however, did not give up easily. She reopened her home as a "boardinghouse" for railroad workers and homeless women in late 1921. She appealed her case to the Missouri Supreme Court in 1924, where she successfully argued that "keeping a bawdy house is not a public nuisance in any sense of the term."[65] Before the supreme court, Chambers's lawyer, J. Francis O'Sullivan, argued that the 1921 act violated his client's Fifth and Fourteenth Amendment rights. In response, the Jackson County prosecutors, Cameron Orr and Leslie Lyons, an officer from the Society for the Suppression of Commercialized Vice, maintained that the injunction was legal because the Chambers house caused immorality:

> Said defendant was, on said date, using said premises and property, furniture and equipment therein, for the purpose of keeping and harboring lewd, immoral, and lascivious women therein, and permitting and requiring said women so harbored therein, to receive and entertain men in rooms in said house and building for the purposes of unlawful sexual intercourse, assignation, and prostitution, and for immoral purposes and conduct. . . . [The brothels] are nuisances, and should be enjoined and abated, as prayed for in plaintiff's first amended petition.[66]

Along with the testimony of police officers and Prosecutor Orr himself, the testimony of Annie Chambers was read for supreme court

65. "From Dark to Dawn: No. 3," 12.
66. *State v. Kearns.*

justices. Chambers stated for the record that she paid Kansas City police protection payments for forty years. Chambers testified that she paid weekly fines at the court clerk's office, and occasionally a uniformed officer was sent to her home to collect the payments. One witness was Kansas City police captain Frank H. Anderson, who patrolled Chambers's neighborhood for thirty-five years. When asked if anyone ever told him the Chambers house was a brothel, Anderson replied that "they didn't need to tell me."[67]

The supreme court read Chambers's circuit court testimony into the record. Prosecutor Lyons questioned Chambers about her life as a madam during the Jackson County trial. When Annie Chambers was asked if she ran a bawdy house, she replied: "Not that I know of."[68] Chambers then told the court that her brothel closed at the date of her first arrest in 1913. According to Chambers, she closed due to a "kind of wave or something. . . that drove them all out." When asked if that wave was the Society for Prevention of Commercialized Vice, controlled by W. C. Brown, Chambers replied "yes."[69]

The Missouri Supreme Court found in favor of Chambers and remanded the decision of the Jackson County court. The supreme court decision did not find Chambers innocent of running a brothel, but the justices did agree that the Act of 1921 was not entirely legal. "So much of the judgement as constitutes a perpetual injunction upon the defendant against using the premises, in the maintenance of a bawdyhouse, should be affirmed," wrote Justice Lindsay, "and so much of it as closes the premises against any use whatsoever should be reversed."[70] Chambers returned to Kansas City and opened her house to working-class boarders and former prostitutes. She died that winter, months after her courtroom victory.

With the closure of its high-profile brothels, Kansas City's underground urban culture was driven further from public view. What happened to the crib girls of Kansas City's red-light district is unknown. However, the reporters and reformers of Kansas City carefully recorded the end of the three "queens of the red-light." Shortly after the

67. *State v. Kearns,* Appellant's Abstract of the Record and Bill of Exceptions, 137, 93.
68. *State v. Kearns.*
69. *State v. Kearns,* Appellant's Abstract, 139.
70. Ibid.

injunction law closed the resorts in 1921, Reverend David Bulkley moved to Kansas City to build a mission for the rehabilitation of drunkards and released criminals. Bulkley arranged for the purchase of the Madame Lovejoy house by coffee wholesaler Frank Ennis in the 1930s. "It had been vacant for years," wrote *Kansas City Star* reporter A. B. MacDonald, "ever since the moral revolution had wiped out the segregated district of this city." Ennis then rented the Lovejoy house to Reverend Bulkley as the first building of the City Union Mission. Bulkley, along with his wife and young daughter, moved into the Lovejoy house and opened its doors to reform "fallen men." As MacDonald wrote: "And in the room of Madame Lovejoy, on the first floor, with the trap door through which she used to draw up wine and other liquors from the iced troughs in the cellar, Dave [Bulkley] and his wife and daughter set up housekeeping."[71]

The resort next door to Madame Lovejoy's, the house of Eva Prince, was still in operation when Bulkley opened the City Union Mission. "Next door to the west was the old Eva Prince house," wrote Mac-Donald, "yet filled with women of the underworld, the very scum of it." According to MacDonald, the fall of the Prince house began with the death of a "baby of the underworld," an illegitimate child of one of Prince's prostitutes. The mother appealed to Bulkley and his wife for help, so the baby's funeral was held in the old parlor of the Lovejoy house. The crib girls of Prince's sat on the steps and in the windows of the Lovejoy house to listen to the service. At the back of the Lovejoy house, an elderly Annie Chambers opened her kitchen window to listen to the service. Shortly after the funeral, Eva Prince agreed to lease the Prince resort to Bulkley as an addition to the City Union Mission. Eventually, Eva Prince sold the house to the Bulkleys for two thousand dollars and a promise from Dave Bulkley that the house would be used as a home for wayward girls. Annie Chambers became friends with Mrs. Bulkley and even lent Mrs. Bulkley her famous Alaskan seal coat for a trip to lectures at the Moody Bible Institute in Chicago.[72] Chambers died in 1924 and willed her house to the Bulkley mission with the stipulation that it be used to assist women in need.[73] The red-

71. MacDonald, "Gift to Union Mission."
72. Ibid.
73. "From Dark to Dawn: No. 3," 12.

light district, which once helped women in need to earn a living, became a home for religious reform and urban missionary work.

Kansas City reformers and working-class residents struggled with the issues of commercial amusement and female sexuality throughout the early twentieth century. The battles took place in amusement parks, saloons, vaudevilles, and the red-light district. By the time the red-light district was closed, other working-class commercial amusements were either destroyed or appropriated by upper-class Kansas Citians. City reformers already created laws governing couples in dance halls, delineating sex-specific areas of parks, and closing traditional working-class saloons. The key to Kansas City's cultural struggle was the gendered definition of acceptable behavior, and how that definition was portrayed and enacted in popular culture. The gender roles that were considered fluid and blurred in working-class neighborhoods and in mass commercial amusements such as brothels in 1880 were strictly defined and policed by 1930. Victorian sexual divisions based on male and female spheres still existed in the 1930s. However, the experimentation with gender behavior and boundaries among working-class entertainment seekers created a new list of gender categories: homosexual men, prostitutes, lesbians, strippers, New Women, and independent single men and women. The power of sexual division remained, but new gender divisions altered the popular understanding of sexuality and acceptability.

There is no doubt that the success of working-class amusement spaces such as Kansas City's red-light district was largely due to the city's Wild West reputation. However, the end of the city's red lights was not the end of Kansas City's western distinction. Jazz flourished in Kansas City from the 1890s until the beginning of World War II, when city boss Tom Pendergast's patronage of jazz clubs ended with his incarceration for tax evasion. During the city's jazz scene years, amusements such as prostitution and cabarets were increasingly popular. Kansas City's working-class amusements were forgotten, but they were by no means gone. As the historian Kevin J. Mumford demonstrated, reform movements against vice districts only strengthened the working-class resolve of the city's marginalized people.[74] While it

---

74. Kevin J. Mumford, *Interzones: Black/White Sex Districts in Chicago and New York in the Early Twentieth Century* (New York: Columbia University Press, 1997), 178.

may appear that crib girls and madams left Kansas City for other western towns (such as Tulsa or Dallas), in fact other western cities were undergoing the same cultural shifts at the same time.

Working-class leisure spaces encompassed a variety of activities, from vaudeville theater to the red-light resorts of women such as Annie Chambers. These amusements experimented with gender definitions, class divisions, and middle-class morality during the years when the American psyche was beginning to shift. However, there was a "continuous flirtation with the impermissible" that caused some aspects of working-class ideas about gender to diffuse in the middle and upper classes.[75] Consequently, Kansas City's elite adopted and reshaped those ideas while strengthening the gender separation of the Victorian era. The famous stained-glass window of the Chambers resort became a central feature of a restaurant in the Country Club Plaza of Kansas City, which opened in 1924 as America's first shopping center. The famous Chambers brothel, transformed by Victorian morality and upper-class appropriation, became two symbols of modern Kansas City: a mission and a shopping mall. The history of women such as Annie Chambers fell away, leaving only cautionary local stories and police reports about the dangers of female sexuality and "fallen women."

75. Sinfield, *Out on Stage*, 73.

Contributors

Gregg Andrews is Professor of History at Texas State University (formerly Southwest Texas State University) in San Marcos. He grew up near Hannibal in Ilasco, Missouri. He is the author of *Shoulder to Shoulder? The American Federation of Labor, the United States, and the Mexican Revolution, 1910–1924* (Berkeley: University of California Press, 1991) as well as *City of Dust: A Cement Company Town in the Land of Tom Sawyer* (Columbia: University of Missouri Press, 1996) and *Insane Sisters: Or, the Price Paid for Challenging a Company Town* (Columbia: University of Missouri Press, 1999).

Janice Brandon-Falcone is Associate Professor of History at Northwest Missouri State University. She is the coeditor of *American Dreams, American Realities: An Introduction to the Uses of History* (Dubuque, Iowa: Kendall/Hunt, 1998).

Amber R. Clifford received her master's degree from Texas Tech University in Lubbock. She currently teaches at Central Missouri State University in Warrensburg.

Robert Faust recently completed his doctorate at the University of Missouri–Columbia. He currently teaches at the University of South Alabama in Mobile.

Daniel A. Graff recently completed his doctorate at the University of Wisconsin–Madison. He currently serves as Director of Undergraduate Studies in the Department of History at the University of Notre Dame.

Deborah J. Henry recently completed her doctorate at the University of Minnesota. She is the Director of Special Programs and an Affiliate Assistant Professor of History at the University of Missouri–St. Louis.

Thomas M. Spencer is Associate Professor of History at Northwest Missouri State University in Maryville. He is the author of *The St. Louis Veiled Prophet Celebration: Power on Parade, 1877–1995* (Columbia: University of Missouri Press, 2000). He currently serves as a member of the governing board of the Missouri Humanities Council.

Michael J. Steiner is Associate Professor of History and Social Science at Northwest Missouri State University. He is the author of *A Study of the Intellectual and Material Culture of Death in Nineteenth-Century America* (Lewiston, N.Y.: Mellen Press, 2003).

Bonnie Stepenoff is Professor of History at Southeast Missouri State University in Cape Girardeau. She is the author of *Their Fathers' Daughters: Silk Mill Workers in Northeastern Pennsylvania, 1880–1960* (Selinsgrove, Pa.: Susquehanna University Press, 1999) and *Thad Snow: A Life of Social Reform in the Missouri Bootheel* (Columbia: University of Missouri Press, 2003).

Index

Strikes: by journeymen tailors in St. Louis, 50–51, 55–58; 69–71
Sub-treasury system, 124–25

Taft-Hartley Labor Relations Act, 160
Tarkio Avalanche, 137
Test Oath, 9–12, 21, 27, 35
Thelen, David, 1, 137, 202–3
Tucker, Wade, 160–61
Twain, Mark, 1, 10

Urban League of St. Louis, 95, 96, 97, 100–101, 103
Urban Renewal, 81–82, 86–87

Vigilantism, 3, 36–37, 69

Welter, Barbara, 170
Whitfield, Owen, 147, 153–54, 156, 157

About the Editor

Thomas M. Spencer is Associate Professor of History at Northwest Missouri State University in Maryville. He is the author of *The St. Louis Veiled Prophet Celebration: Power on Parade, 1877–1995* (University of Missouri Press).